American Politics

After September 11

Third Edition

Editor
James M. Lindsay

BOOK ACTIVATION KEY

131

This key activates your online textbook.

- Scratch off gray area above to see your BOOK ACTIVATION KEY.
- If the key is already visible, then it has been used and is no longer valid. Contact us at www.atomicdog.com or 800-310-5661 x8 to purchase your Online Edition.
- Refer to the booklet, *How to Use Your Online Edition*, for further instructions.

ATOMICdogPUBLISHING

Cincinnati, Ohio
www.atomicdog.com

When ordering this title, use ISBN 1-59260-150-2.

To order only the online version (Online Study Guide Edition) of this title, use ISBN 1-59260-151-0.

Copyright © 2005 by Atomic Dog Publishing. All rights reserved.

Library of Congress Control Number: 2004108629

ISBN 1-59260-149-9

Printed in the United States of America by Atomic Dog Publishing, 1148 Main Street, Third Floor, Cincinnati, Ohio 45202-7236

10 9 8 7 6 5 4 3 2 1

Contents

Contributing Authors

Cary R. Covington

University of Iowa

Cary R. Covington is associate professor of political science at the University of Iowa. His research focuses on the presidency and presidential-congressional relations. He is co-author of *The Coalitional Presidency*, and he has published articles in such journals as *American Journal of Political Science, Journal of Politics*, and *Legislative Studies Quarterly.*

Ivo H. Daalder

Brookings Institution

Ivo H. Daalder is a senior fellow and Sydney Stein, Jr., Chair in the Foreign Policy Studies Program at the Brookings Institution in Washington, D.C. He has published widely on U.S. foreign policy, U.S.-European relations, and arms control. His many books include *America Unbound: The Bush Revolution in Foreign Policy* (with James M. Lindsay), which was awarded the 2004 Lionel S. Gelber Prize, named a finalist for the Arthur Ross Book Award, and recognized as a top book of 2003 by the *Economist*. His other books include *Protecting the American Homeland* (with other Brookings colleagues), *Winning Ugly: NATO's War to Save Kosovo* (with Michael E. O'Hanlon), and *Getting to Dayton: The Making of America's Bosnia Policy.*

Timothy M. Hagle

University of Iowa

Timothy M. Hagle is associate professor of political science at the University of Iowa. Holding a law degree as well as a doctorate, his expertise is in the field of judicial politics and behavior. He is the author of *Basic Math for Social Scientists*, and his research has appeared in such journals as *American Journal of Political Science, Journal of Politics*, and *Political Behavior*. In 2002, President George W. Bush appointed him to the Permanent Committee for the Oliver Wendell Holmes Devise.

James M. Lindsay

Council on Foreign Relations

James M. Lindsay is vice president, director of studies, and Maurice R. Greenberg Chair at the Council on Foreign Relations. He was previously deputy director and senior fellow in the Foreign Policy Studies Program at the Brookings Institution. His research focuses on American foreign policy. In addition to numerous articles in scholarly journals and major newspapers, his books include *America Unbound: The Bush Revolution in Foreign Policy* (with Ivo H. Daalder), which was awarded the 2004 Lionel S. Gelber Prize, named a finalist for the Arthur Ross Book Award, and recognized as a top book of 2003 by the *Economist*. His other books include *Defending America: The Case for Limited National Missile Defense* (with Michael E. O'Hanlon), *Congress and the Politics of U.S. Foreign Policy*, and *Congress and Nuclear Weapons.*

Eric R.A.N. Smith

University of California, Santa Barbara

Eric R.A.N. Smith is professor of political science and environmental studies at the University of California, Santa Barbara. His research focuses on public opinion, elections, and environmental politics. Professor Smith has authored or co-authored numerous articles and several books, including *The Unchanging American Voter* and the recently published *Energy, the Environment, and Public Opinion.*

Peverill Squire

University of Iowa

Peverill Squire is professor of political science at the University of Iowa and co-editor of *Legislative Studies Quarterly*. He is an expert on legislatures and elections at both the state and national levels. He has been a visiting professor at Meiji University in Tokyo, Japan, and a Fulbright Distinguished Lecturer, holding the John Marshall Chair in Political Science at the Budapest (Hungary) University of Economic Sciences. He is co-author of *Who Runs for the Legislature?* and co-editor of *Legislatures: Comparative Perspectives on Representative Assemblies*. His articles have appeared in such journals as *American Political Science Review, Journal of Politics*, and *Political Opinion Quarterly.*

The Song Remains the Same:

Is 2004 Just a Replay of 2000?

Peverill Squire

It is tempting to assume that the 2004 presidential election will be much like the one in 2000. After all, George W. Bush is again the Republican nominee. And as in 2000, Ralph Nader is running and threatening to siphon votes from the Democrats. Moreover, voter support for the two major parties continues to be split, and there is every reason to expect that almost every Republican will vote for Bush, while almost every Democrat will vote for Kerry. Thus, all the signs suggest that the 2004 election will be just as close as the race four years earlier.

But over four years, some things do change, and these changes may affect the results on Election Day. Three changes in particular might significantly affect the results of the 2004 presidential election: reapportionment in the Electoral College, shifts in who votes and where, and the adoption of new voting technologies.

1-1 Changes in the Electoral College

It is not news that the nation's population has grown over the past four years. But the timing of the 2000 and 2004 elections makes the population increase potentially significant for the presidential election. The U.S. Constitution requires a census to be conducted every decade. The population count is used to apportion seats in the U.S. House of Representatives among the states. The number of House seats each state has is used to calculate the number of Electoral College votes each state exercises. (Each state also gets a vote for each of its seats in the U.S. Senate, but, of course, that number—two—is constant.) Because the census was conducted in 2001 and House seats were apportioned before the 2002 election, eighteen states saw the number of Electoral College votes they cast change between the 2000 election and the 2004 election.

Table 1-1 shows which states gained or lost Electoral College votes and how many changed in each case. The states are divided into those that voted for Bush in 2000 and those that voted for Gore. The states that went for Bush added seven Electoral College votes after the 2000 election. That means, of course, that the states in the Democratic Party column lost seven votes. Thus, even if each party captures the same states in 2004 as it did in 2000, President Bush wins the Electoral College a second time by a slightly larger—and slightly more comfortable—margin.

1-2 Changes in Who Votes

Changes in the apportionment of votes in the Electoral College tell only part of the story. Another part of the story is changes in who votes in each state.

Population growth, by definition, changes the potential pool of voters. Some states have experienced very little, if any, population growth over the past few years. So, in states such as Iowa and West Virginia, virtually the same set of voters as in 2000 will be eligible to go to the polls in 2004.

The situation looks different in states that have experienced explosive population growth. According to the Census Bureau, Nevada, the state with the highest growth rate, added more than 223,000 residents between 2000 and 2003, or an increase of 12.2 percent. Bush carried Nevada by fewer than 22,000 votes in the 2000 election. If Nevada's new voters lean toward the Democrats, the president's margin of victory may be wiped out. If they lean toward the Republicans, Bush may win by a larger margin.

Table 1-1

The Political Implications of the Change in the Number of Electoral College Votes

States That Voted for Bush in 2000	Electoral College Votes, 2000	Electoral College Votes, 2004	Net Difference in Electoral College Votes
Arizona	8	10	+2
Colorado	8	9	+1
Florida	25	27	+2
Georgia	13	15	+2
Indiana	12	11	−1
Mississippi	7	6	−1
Nevada	4	5	+1
North Carolina	14	15	+1
Ohio	21	20	−1
Oklahoma	8	7	−1
Texas	32	34	+2
Net Change			**+7**
States That Voted for Gore in 2000			
California	54	55	+1
Connecticut	8	7	−1
Illinois	22	21	−1
Michigan	18	17	−1
New York	33	31	−2
Pennsylvania	23	21	−2
Wisconsin	11	10	−1
Net Change			**−7**

The possibility of such swings exists in a number of states that enjoyed rapid population growth, most notably Arizona, Florida, and Georgia, where increases exceeded 6 percent.

The composition of the voting age population also changes from election to election, and these changes can have important political consequences. Consider, for example, the growth in the Hispanic American population. Hispanics are now the largest minority group in the United States. Geographically, however, they are concentrated in the West and South. Thus, the growth in the Hispanic American population is likely to affect the politics of states in those regions to a far greater degree than elsewhere. In the 2000 election, Gore won 67 percent of Hispanic votes; Bush, 31 percent. If those percentages are replicated in the 2004 election—a big if—then the growth in the number of Hispanic voters would benefit the Democrats. States where the Hispanic population has grown significantly over the past four years and where the 2000 election results were tight could go the other way

this time. Such a swing could change the outcome in Nevada, or in Arizona, where Bush won by 80,000 votes. And, of course, the growth in Florida's non-Cuban Hispanic population could easily wipe out Bush's 537-vote margin in the 2000 election.

Both parties recognize the potential increased power of the Hispanic vote, and they have invested heavily both politically and financially to woo it. Should the Democrats take a greater share in 2004, or if President Bush improves his standing, the Electoral College map will change.

1-3 Changes in Voting Technology

In many ways, the outcome of the 2000 presidential election was determined by voting mishaps in Florida. After all the arguments over hanging chads and legal battles over how, if at all, the ballots should be recounted, Bush was determined to have won the state by 537 votes out of the 5,963,110 votes that were cast. The biggest problem with the vote in Florida may have been in Palm Beach County, where the punch card ballot design, known as a "butterfly ballot," apparently made it easy to cast an unintended vote and to double vote. Studies of the voting results in Palm Beach County and of the ballots themselves convincingly document that some 3,000 voters mistakenly voted for Reform Party candidate Pat Buchanan rather than for Gore, and that most of the more than 19,000 people who double voted on the ballot included Gore as one of the candidates they supported. It seems clear that had the voting mechanics in Palm Beach County worked better than they did, Gore would have easily picked up more than the 537 votes by which he lost the state. And, of course, had Florida's Electoral College votes gone to Gore rather than Bush, Gore would have been elected president.

The problems in Palm Beach County gained national prominence because of the incredibly tight contest in Florida. Other parts of the country experienced similar difficulties. These problems drew less attention because they appeared not to have influenced the outcome the way they had in Florida.

To avoid similar problems in future elections, Congress in 2002 passed and President Bush signed the Help America Vote Act, which provided federal money to help states upgrade their voting systems. The percentage of voters using punch card voting technologies in 2004 will be 21 percent, a sharp drop from the 31 percent using them four years earlier. The use of touch screen computer voting machines will increase from 12 percent of all voters to 25 percent. Setting aside the grave concerns about the use of touch screen voting systems—many computer experts worry about their security—the hope is that in 2004 fewer doubts will be expressed about the integrity of the vote. Although we can guess how the use of these new voting

Table 1-2	Tight Contests in the 2000 Presidential Election			
State	Total Votes Cast	Percent for Bush	Percent for Gore	Vote Difference
Florida	5,963,110	48.85%	48.84%	537
Iowa	1,315,563	48.22%	48.54%	4,144
New Mexico	598, 605	47.85%	47.91%	366
Oregon	1,533,968	46.31%	46.95%	6,765
Wisconsin	2,598,607	47.61%	47.83%	5,708

mechanics might have changed the outcome in the 2000 election, their partisan implications in the 2004 campaign are unclear.

1-4 Final Thoughts

Although in many respects the 2004 presidential election appears to be shaping up to be much like the race four years earlier, some things have changed. The number of Electoral College votes accorded to eighteen states has changed. The voting age population has changed in notable ways, at least in some states. And the mechanics of voting will change in many places, promising a better accounting of Americans' real preferences.

There is one final observation to offer that suggests the results of the current campaign may, in the end, look very different from the results from four years before,

even if only a few people change their minds about which candidate they support or whether to vote at all. In the 2000 election, Florida was not the only state where the vote was virtually even, as Table 1-2 documents. The election also was incredibly close in four other states, all of which went to Gore. The shift of just a few votes in each of those states would have changed the outcome, giving Bush a more comfortable margin in the Electoral College. Thus, the outcome in 2004 could differ from what it was in 2000 if just a few people change their preferences, just a few people choose to stay home this time, or just a few people opt to vote rather than abstain. Indeed, with an election as potentially tight as this one might be, the outcome could be altered by the vagaries of a power blackout, a flu epidemic, or bad weather.

Readings for Further Study

Jones, Randall J., Jr. 2002. *Who Will Be in the White House? Predicting Presidential Elections.* New York: Longman.

Longley, Lawrence D., and Neal R. Peirce. 1999. *The Electoral College Primer 2000.* New Haven, CT: Yale University Press.

Polsby, Nelson W., and Aaron B. Wildavsky. 2004. *Presidential Elections,* 11th ed. Lanham, MD: Rowman & Littlefield.

Websites to Check Out

Note: As we went to press, these sites were functional using the URLs provided. Check out the online text for the most up-to-date URLs.

Site name: The National Archives—U.S. Electoral College

URL: http://www.archives.gov/federal_register/electoral_college/

A wealth of information and statistics on presidential elections, past and present, compiled by the Office of the Federal Register, which coordinates the functions of the Electoral College.

Site name: U.S. Census Bureau—Hispanic Population of the United States

URL: http://www.census.gov/population/www/socdemo/hispanic.html

Detailed information about the Hispanic population in the United States, compiled by the U.S. Census Bureau.

Site name: Politics1.com

URL: http://www.politics1.com/p2004.htm

A comprehensive list of political information on the 2004 presidential election, including profiles of the major and minor party White House hopefuls.

And Then There Was One:

The 2004 Democratic Presidential Nomination Contest

Peverill Squire

At the beginning of January 2004, John Kerry's bid for the Democratic Party's presidential nomination looked dead. Political pundits pummeled him for running a lackluster campaign that gave voters no good reasons to vote for him. The Massachusetts senator's national poll numbers hovered in the single digits, badly trailing the two front-runners, former Vermont Governor Howard Dean and retired U.S. Army General Wesley Clark. And Kerry's prospects in Iowa and New Hampshire—the first two events of the nomination process—also looked bleak.

Despite this apparently dire situation, by the end of January 2004, Senator Kerry had vaulted to the front of the Democratic pack, taking a lead he never relinquished. What accounts for Kerry's political resurrection?

2-1 The Phases of the Nomination Process

Senator Kerry's long and winding road to the nomination started well before January 2004. Indeed,

his efforts began not long after the end of the ballot-counting battle in Florida that decided the 2000 presidential election. Kerry made his first appearance in Iowa in June 2001, more than two years before the first official nominating event, when he attended a campaign fund-raiser for Tom Vilsack, the state's Democratic governor. And in early August 2001, the senator went to New Hampshire to participate in campaign events for a state legislative candidate and the mayor of Manchester.

Kerry was not alone in beginning his nomination run early. Others contemplating presidential runs engaged in the same sorts of activities, and some started even before Kerry did. Senator John Edwards of North Carolina, for example, beat Kerry to Iowa by delivering the keynote address at a Drake University Law School dinner in March 2001. And Representative Richard Gephardt of Missouri began courting voters in New Hampshire in early June 2001 when he spoke at the Cheshire County Democratic dinner in Keene and put in appearances at the Rockingham/Strafford County continental breakfast, the Merrimack County

Democrats' Annual Pig Roast & Pot Luck Picnic, and the Manchester City Democrats' Flag Day Celebration the next day.

The travels of Kerry and his rivals point to a key lesson about presidential campaigning: The nomination process is a long, drawn-out affair that unfolds in several phases. The first phase is one of exploration, where potential candidates test the political waters to see whether they have sufficient support to plunge into the race. Those candidates who opt to run then participate in the second phase, referred to as the invisible primary, a period when they work hard to raise money to fund their campaigns and solicit party activists to work on their behalf. Much of this activity is designed to convince the national media that the candidate is serious about running and has good prospects for winning. During the latter part of this phase of the campaign, the candidates begin to actively appeal to voters, but most of their efforts are concentrated on people in the handful of states at the front of the election calendar. The final phase of the nomination process begins as the first votes are finally cast. This phase involves the whittling of the field of candidates, as candidacies fall by the wayside and ultimately one person emerges as the party's nominee. Unlike the other phases of the campaign, this one typically takes a relatively short period of time.

2-2 Dipping a Toe in the Water: The Exploration Phase

It seems reasonable to assume that most governors, members of Congress, and other major political figures entertain thoughts about running for president. Very few of them, however, ever get to the point of seriously exploring their chances. So no one can say with any certainty how many politicians or which ones contemplated running for the 2004 Democratic nomination. But we do know who among them appeared to be giving the idea enough thought to get to the point of taking some preliminary steps toward running.

Putting together a serious run for the nomination takes time. Democrats who thought about trying to win the nomination in 2004 had to begin preparing for their run in 2001, if not even earlier. At the beginning of 2001, most Democrats assessed their party's chances of recapturing the presidency as reasonably high, given that Al Gore had gotten 500,000 more votes in the 2000 election than had President Bush. So, for that reason, many Democrats probably gave some thought to the idea of running. But before they could take on the president, they had to secure the nomination. And for most potential Democratic candidates, winning that contest may have appeared to be more difficult than winning

the general election because the former vice president loomed as their potential competition. Many political observers reasoned that the Democrats would be hard pressed to deny Gore the nomination if he sought it.

During 2001, Gore sent mixed signals about his intentions. On the one hand, he adopted a low profile nationally, leaving the public stage to President Bush, suggesting he was not going to run in 2004. On the other hand, he made a few public appearances, notably giving keynote addresses at the Jefferson/Jackson dinners hosted by the state Democratic parties in Iowa and New Hampshire, and he took unpublicized drives around both states to meet informally with his supporters. Those actions led some observers to think Gore planned to run in 2004.

The possibility of a Gore candidacy did not, however, keep several other Democrats from testing the presidential waters. As noted earlier, Kerry, Edwards, and Gephardt all made public appearances in Iowa and New Hampshire in 2001. And they were not alone. Among the other potential candidates visiting one or both of those critical states were senators Joe Biden of Delaware, Tom Daschle of South Dakota, Russ Feingold of Wisconsin, and Joe Lieberman of Connecticut, along with Representative Marcy Kaptur of Ohio and former senator Bill Bradley of New Jersey. After assessing their chances, many of these potential candidates decided that the time was not right to run for the presidency, and their efforts never went beyond their exploratory visits. Of the early visitors to Iowa and New Hampshire, only Kerry, Edwards, Gephardt, and Lieberman eventually entered the race.

One factor that may have played into the decision calculus of the potential candidates who opted out of the race was the decreasing odds on their party's chances to take the White House in 2004. The tragic events of September 11, 2001, and President Bush's initial response to the crisis greatly enhanced his public standing. The prospect of running against the president in 2004 seemed less inviting after September 11 than it had before.

But 2002 did bring a few more Democrats into the nomination contest. None of them, however, was thought to be a major player in the party, and all were considered long shots to win. Controversial civil rights activist Al Sharpton emerged as a potential candidate after making the requisite appearances in Iowa and New Hampshire. Joining him in contemplating runs were Dennis Kucinich, a left-leaning House member from Ohio, and former Illinois senator Carol Moseley Braun. All these candidates understood that they were highly unlikely to win, but running gave them a platform to promote their issue agendas. Governor Dean of Vermont, who would leave office in early 2003, also indicated he was running, but although he was serious about contesting the nomination, most observers dismissed his chances.

The field of candidates for the nomination did not, however, take shape until mid-December 2002. In less than 24 hours during the weekend of December 14 and 15, the race changed dramatically. On that Sunday, following his well-reviewed performance on the previous evening's *Saturday Night Live*, former Vice President Gore appeared on *60 Minutes* to announce that he would not seek the Democratic Party's nomination. His decision created a wide-open race. Within a month, the field of candidates began to solidify. Senator Lieberman, Gore's vice presidential candidate, for example, was liberated from his pledge not to run if Gore did. He entered the race soon after Gore withdrew, and he was not alone. Others quickly followed with announcements that they, too, were running.

2-3 Taking the Plunge: The Invisible Primary Phase

The invisible primary phase of the nomination process is curious because it involves candidates declaring their candidacies several times in different ways. Initially, they enter the race informally, announcing their intentions and creating exploratory committees to allow them to begin collecting contributions to fund their races. Dean jumped in early by filing a statement of candidacy with the Federal Election Commission in May 2002. Kerry entered next by forming his exploratory committee in December 2002. In January 2003, Edwards, Gephardt, Lieberman, and Sharpton let it be known in one way or another that they too were running. The field expanded in February when Kucinich, Moseley Braun, and Florida Senator Bob Graham joined the race.

Several months later, all formally announced their candidacies. Senator Edwards, for example, declared he was running in an interview on the Comedy Channel's *The Daily Show* the night of September 15, 2003. The next day, he announced the start of his campaign again with a formal statement made in front of the textile mill in North Carolina where his father had worked. But these later announcements were made to generate publicity. By the time the candidates made them, everyone already knew they were running.

Although many Democrats announced that they were jumping into the race, several potential candidates announced that they would not be taking the plunge. In January 2003, Senator Daschle surprised supporters preparing campaign events in his home state of South Dakota and in Iowa by saying he would not run. Less surprisingly, in February, Senator Christopher Dodd, who had toyed with the idea of running, calculated that the field could support only one candidate from Connecticut, and he stepped aside in favor of his home state colleague, Joe Lieberman.

Thus, by March 2003, the field for the Democratic Party's presidential nomination appeared set with nine candidates. At this point in the campaign, the candidates were consumed with two activities. First, they had to begin to raise money because the media would use campaign cash to measure their chances for victory. Second, they had to assemble campaign organizations. At the national level, they needed staff to help them with scheduling, fund-raising, press relations, and the development of their campaign themes. They also needed campaign organizations in each state, but most immediately in Iowa. Because Iowa uses a caucus system, where voters have to be encouraged to attend precinct meetings in their neighborhoods on what would be, without a doubt, a cold winter's evening, every campaign strove to hire political operatives who were familiar with the state and had the necessary connections to find people to work on their candidate's behalf. The media tracked their hires and used them to gauge each candidate's chances to do well in the caucuses, and thereby, in the nomination contest.

Most of the candidates understood the likely dynamics of the nomination contest. With a large number of candidates running, Iowa and New Hampshire were apt to be even more important than in the recent past. Both events would whittle the field. Candidates who did well in one or both states would have the support they needed to continue their campaigns. Failure to do well in either state would likely force a candidate to the sidelines. Consequently, most of the candidates invested a great deal of time and effort in these two states, as Table 2-1 reveals. Between 2001 and the end of 2003—still three weeks before the Iowa caucuses in early 2004—Howard Dean had spent 176 days in the two states, while John Kerry and John Edwards had visited 138 days and 111 days, respectively.

During the invisible primary phase of the campaign, political observers grasp for any evidence that may indicate how the candidates are faring. The number of days spent campaigning is one such piece of data, but it is not necessarily very revealing. Arguably more useful are campaign fund-raising figures. Candidates are required to file quarterly reports on their fund-raising with the Federal Election Commission. The national media took the first-quarter 2003 figures released by the commission in April as the first hard evidence of the candidates' prospects. And the numbers provided a major surprise. The leading money

Table 2-1	Number of Days Spent Campaigning in the Early States by Leading Democratic Party Candidates, 2001–2003					
	Kerry	**Edwards**	**Dean**	**Clark**	**Lieberman**	**Gephardt**
Days in Iowa	66	63	96	3	19	58
Days in New Hampshire	72	48	80	32	57	34
Total Days in Early States	138	111	176	35	76	92

Source: Calculated by author from data collected by Eric M. Appleman, Democracy in Action (http://www.gwu.edu/~action/2004/).

raiser was John Edwards, who heavily mined his ties to his former trial lawyer colleagues to collect $7.4 million. Most observers had forecast that he would raise only between $4 and $5 million, and the higher figure his campaign reported was taken as a sign that he enjoyed much more support than anticipated. In second place was John Kerry with $7 million. The other candidates lagged well behind the two front-runners, leading the Edwards' campaign to claim that the race had already narrowed to their candidate and Kerry.

The picture of an Edwards-Kerry contest changed dramatically, however, with the release of the second-quarter figures three months later. In what was seen as another shocking development, former Governor Dean surged to the fund-raising lead by gathering more than $7.6 million, more than triple what his campaign had raised in the first quarter. Kerry again finished second, well behind with $5.9 million; the other candidates collected considerably less. But it was not simply the fact that Dean had raised much more money than any of the other candidates that turned the race upside down. It was also the way he had raised the money. In the second quarter, the Dean

campaign received contributions from 73,226 individuals. In contrast, Kerry's money was raised from only some 23,000 contributors. Dean tapped into a much larger supporter base by exploiting a relatively new technology—the Internet. Thus, while Kerry was raising large sums from relatively few people, Dean was raising smaller sums from far more people. The large number of people willing to contribute to the Dean campaign was interpreted as a powerful signal that the former governor was a stronger competitor than originally thought.

But Dean's success was also based on issues, not just a product of a technological innovation. Generally, the policy differences between the nine Democratic candidates on a wide range of issues were muted. They roughly agreed on most subjects and tended to draw distinctions between themselves and the Bush administration rather than among each other. But, by taking a politically aggressive stand against the U.S. military campaign in Iraq, Dean was able to distinguish himself from the rest of the field. He was not, of course, alone in his opposition to the president's Iraq policies—Kucinich and Sharpton were as well. But only Dean was

able to capitalize on the differences, and consequently, he became identified by anti-war Democrats as their champion.

Dean's success in raising money from large numbers of contributors helped generate considerable momentum for his candidacy. At the end of August 2003, he appeared on the covers of *Time* and *Newsweek*, and his campaign became the first to run television commercials in Iowa, New Hampshire, and several other states. Political observers began to consider Dean the front-runner. Support for Dean in the national polls, however, lagged a bit. As Table 2-2 shows, by late summer, national opinion was still unsettled. Lieberman led in August 2003, undoubtedly because of residual name identification from his vice presidential run three years before. A month later, Gephardt took the top spot, but just barely, as support was scattered across the leading candidates. In mid-September, the race was shaken up again, this time by the candidacy of retired Army General Wesley Clark. The general's military credentials and considerable foreign-policy experience made him a very attractive candidate in the eyes of many Democrats, and he immediately shot into the lead in national polls.

Although Clark proved to be adept at fund-raising, his efforts, like those of the rest of the Democratic field, paled in comparison to Dean's. In the third quarter, Dean raised more than $14 million, far more than the other candidates. And after the initial infatuation with the general began to fade, Dean emerged as the clear front-runner in the race. Dean's lead in the national polls built through the fall. And while he was thriving, other candidates began to struggle. In

Table 2-2	Candidate Preferences of Democrats Nationally, August 2003 to February 2004 (Leading Candidate in Bold Type)					
Date	Kerry	Edwards	Dean	Clark	Lieberman	Gephardt
Aug 3, 2003	10%	5%	12%	2%	**23%**	13%
Sep 9, 2003	12%	5%	14%	10%	13%	**16%**
Sep 21, 2003	11%	4%	13%	**22%**	10%	11%
Oct 8, 2003	13%	2%	16%	**21%**	13%	8%
Oct 26, 2003	10%	6%	**16%**	15%	12%	12%
Nov 12, 2003	10%	7%	**17%**	14%	15%	12%
Dec 7, 2003	7%	7%	**25%**	17%	10%	14%
Dec 14, 2003	10%	4%	**31%**	10%	13%	8%
Jan 5, 2004	11%	6%	**24%**	20%	10%	9%
Jan 11, 2004	9%	7%	**26%**	20%	9%	7%
Feb 1, 2004	**49%**	13%	14%	9%	5%	
Feb 8, 2004	**52%**	13%	14%	10%		
Feb 17, 2004	**65%**	19%	8%			

Source: CNN/*USA Today*/Gallup Poll for various dates.

October, not long after Clark's dramatic entrance into the race, Bob Graham calculated that his prospects were too dim to justify continuing his campaign, and he dropped out. And the efforts of many of the other candidates, notably those of Kerry and Edwards, were thought to be on life support.

2-4 The Voters Decide: The Final Phase

By Christmas 2003, national polls showed that almost a third of Democrats backed Dean, while the rest of his competitors strained to break into double digits. Political pundits were on the verge of conceding the nomination to the former Vermont governor. But then the wheels began to come off the Dean bandwagon.

The front-runner's problems were not caused by a lack of money. As Table 2-3 reveals, Dean raised more money than any of the other candidates through the end of February 2004, by which time the contest was effectively over. Dean raised more than $51 million, $10 million more than John Kerry, his closest competitor in the money-raising contest. Earlier in the campaign, both of them had opted out of the federal funding system for the primaries that provides matching funds for money raised by the candidates but forces them to abide by limits on overall spending and spending in each state. The other candidates, who participated in the federal system, raised far less money than Dean and Kerry, even with federal matching dollars swelling their coffers. And in addition to the large campaign war chest, Dean enjoyed the presumed benefit of having hundreds of thousands of contributors whose numbers should translate into votes.

If money was not the problem, what was? No single incident led to Dean's demise. Instead, a series of events conspired to damage the former governor's chances. When it became clear that Dean was in the lead, the other candidates trained their rhetorical fire on him. In candidate debates and other forums, Dean's opponents leveled charges against him. No single accusation was particularly damaging, but the cumulative effect took a toll. And some of Dean's wounds were self-inflicted. One of his qualities that supporters found attractive was a passion about current politics that bordered on outright anger. At times, however, this fury bubbled out in unappealing ways, as when the former governor yelled at an elderly Iowa heckler to "sit down, you've had your say." And even events that should have been positives for the Dean campaign appeared to rebound against them.

Table 2-3 Campaign Fund-raising Totals for Major Democratic Party Candidates (as of February 29, 2004)

Candidate	Total Receipts	Total Contributions from Individuals	Percent of Individual Contributions of $1,000 or More	Percent of Individual Contributions of $200–$999	Percent of Individual Contributions of Less Than $200
Kerry	$41,430,496	$31,535,751	66%	16%	18%
Edwards	$29,371,258	$21,612,672	71%	16%	14%
Dean	$51,618,737	$50,635,248	19%	22%	59%
Clark	$25,105,399	$17,278,020	49%	20%	31%
Lieberman	$18,355,741	$14,162,674	74%	17%	9%
Gephardt	$20,531,425	$14,309,785	72%	16%	13%

Source: Adapted by author from Campaign Finance Institute analysis of Federal Election Commission data.

Table 2-4 When the Voters Decided and the Vote Decision in the Iowa Caucuses

When Candidate Decision Made	Percent Supporting			
	Kerry	Edwards	Dean	Gephardt
Last Three Days (21% of caucus attenders)	37%	32%	18%	6%
Last Week (21%)	41%	38%	11%	6%
Last Month (27%)	39%	28%	18%	10%
Before Last Month (30%)	28%	12%	32%	20%

Source: Washington Post/National Election Pool Entrance Poll.

In December 2003, many Democrats were shocked when former Vice President Gore endorsed Dean. Up to that point, Dean had campaigned as a party outsider; Gore's seal of approval greatly diminished that claim. All of these problems gave credence to the biggest concern raised about Dean: that he could not beat President Bush in November. As many Democrats looked ahead to the fall campaign, they were united by a desire to defeat the president. The thought that Dean would be unable to do that caused many voters to shy away from backing him.

In the final weeks leading up to the Iowa caucuses, Dean's support began to wane. Democrats who decided that the former Vermont governor was not the answer scanned the rest of the Democratic field to assess the possibilities. Electability became the paramount consideration. Candidates such as Kerry and Edwards, who had been given little chance while the Dean juggernaut was building, were given a second look after it began to lose steam. And on second glance, both candidates had commendable qualities. Kerry was a much-decorated Vietnam War veteran

with considerable political experience, who became much less wooden as a candidate as the campaign wore on. Edwards was relatively young, attractive, and an excellent campaigner, whose decision to stay positive and not to criticize his opponents made him stand out from the rest of the field, particularly when Dean and Gephardt started leveling accusations at one another.

As Table 2-4 reveals, Iowans who decided on their preferred candidate early leaned toward Dean. But those who decided closer to caucus night opted for Kerry and Edwards. Both Dean and Gephardt failed to pick up many voters over the couple of weeks before the caucuses. Political analysts credited the drop in support for Dean and Gephardt as evidence that Democratic voters were punishing them for negative campaigning, whereas Edwards' rise in the polls was attributed to his positive message. This thinking colored the rest of the nomination campaign, which was remarkably tame in terms of personal attacks.

The results on caucus night were stunning, given where the race was thought to stand just a few weeks earlier. Kerry and Edwards did surprisingly well, as Table 2-5 shows. Dean finished a disappointing third. In his concession speech, the former governor became so worked up that he finished with what was characterized by the press as a primal scream. Subsequently dubbed his "I've got a scream" speech, the performance made him the butt of late-night comedians' jokes and caused many already skeptical Democrats to continue to back away from his candidacy. Gephardt, who had won the caucuses in 1988 and who was in a position of having to win again to keep his campaign alive, finished a devastating fourth. He was actually considered the evening's biggest loser, and he dropped out of the race the next day.

But there were two other big losers in Iowa, although the media generally failed to recognize their misfortune. During the late fall, both General Clark and Senator Lieberman had decided not to compete in Iowa, where both thought that they would not do well, and decided instead to concentrate their efforts on New Hampshire. This strategy backfired because it failed to calculate the impact Iowa would have on the campaign. During the weeks preceding the caucuses, national media attention was focused on the candidates competing in Iowa, and consequently, Clark and Lieberman's efforts in New Hampshire were given short shrift. And the surprising caucus performances by Kerry and Edwards made them the center of media attention the following week, leading to the voting in New Hampshire; Clark and Lieberman were virtually lost to public view.

The impact of Iowa can be seen in the New Hampshire re-sults. Up until the Iowa caucuses, Howard Dean led comfortably in the New Hampshire polls. But Kerry, to a much greater degree than Edwards, benefited from the media glow following his Iowa success, and he parlayed the increased attention into a big victory in New Hampshire. For the other candidates, the New Hampshire results staggered their campaigns. Dean's chances were greatly damaged by the failure to win his neighboring state. Edwards failed to get much bounce from his Iowa showing and lost the aura of momentum, and Clark did well enough only to keep his campaign alive. Perhaps the biggest loser, however, was Joe Lieberman, who had invested heavily in New Hampshire, but he failed to generate the "Joementum" he had predicted.

The results in Iowa and New Hampshire clearly separated Senator Kerry from the rest of the pack. Surprisingly, only Gephardt was knocked completely out of the race following the first two contests. But the rest of the candidates left in the field were forced to scramble to identify specific states where they might be able to stop Kerry's considerable momentum.

The pace of the campaign picked up the week following New Hampshire. Contests were held in six states on February 3. Senator Kerry handily won four of them. But Senator Edwards won easily in South Carolina—his birthplace—and General Clark eked out a narrow victory in Oklahoma. Thus, although Senator Kerry continued to command the field, both Edwards and Clark, his top two rivals, still had reason to hope that they might be able stop him by continuing to win in the South. Both

identified upcoming states where they intended to make last ditch efforts: Edwards in Virginia and Clark in Tennessee. But the campaign ended for Lieberman. He had pinned his hopes on a victory in Delaware, but Kerry demolished him, 51 percent to 11 percent, and he dropped out the next day.

The weekend before the voting in the two key southern states Kerry continued his march to the nomination by sweeping caucuses in Maine, Michigan, and Washington. He began to look invincible. And the results two days later in Virginia and Tennessee confirmed his dominance. He easily outdistanced Edwards in both states. Clark finished a disappointing third in each primary, causing him to leave the race the following day.

Edwards, however, decided to trudge on, although it was becoming increasingly clear that nothing short of a scandal of major proportions could stop Kerry from getting the nomination. And Dean hung in as well, even though he had yet to win a single state and had even failed to compete at all in several of them. But Dean staked his candidacy on doing well in the upcoming Wisconsin primary. When he finished third there behind Kerry and Edwards, Dean succumbed to the inevitable and left the race. His fall from grace was unprecedented. Just a few weeks before, he had been leading in the polls and had raised millions more than any of the others; by mid-February, he was out of the race, having lost all seventeen contests to that point.

After the Wisconsin primary, there was no doubt that Kerry would be the Democrats' nominee. The only question left to answer was when John Edwards

State	Date	Type of Election	Kerry	Edwards	Dean	Clark	Lieberman	Gephardt
IA	Jan 19, 2004	Caucus	**38%**	32%	18%	.1%	0%	11%
NH	Jan 27, 2004	Primary	**38%**	12%	26%	12%	9%	*
AZ	Feb 3, 2004	Primary	**43%**	7%	14%	27%	7%	
DE	Feb 3, 2004	Primary	**51%**	11%	10%	10%	11%	
MO	Feb 3, 2004	Primary	**51%**	25%	9%	4%	4%	
NM	Feb 3, 2004	Caucus	**43%**	11%	16%	20%	3%	
ND	Feb 3, 2004	Caucus	**51%**	10%	12%	24%	1%	
OK	Feb 3, 2004	Primary	27%	30%	4%	**30%**	7%	
SC	Feb 3, 2004	Primary	30%	**45%**	5%	7%	2%	
MI	Feb 7, 2004	Caucus	**52%**	14%	17%	7%	*	
WA	Feb 7, 2004	Caucus	**48%**	7%	30%	3%		
ME	Feb 8, 2004	Caucus	**45%**	8%	27%	4%		
TN	Feb 10, 2004	Primary	**41%**	27%	4%	23%		
VA	Feb 10, 2004	Primary	**52%**	27%	7%	9%		
NV	Feb 14, 2004	Caucus	**63%**	10%	17%	*		
DC	Feb 14, 2004	Caucus	**47%**	10%	18%			
WI	Feb 17, 2004	Primary	**40%**	34%	18%			
HI	Feb 24, 2004	Caucus	**49%**	13%	*			
ID	Feb 24, 2004	Caucus	**54%**	22%				
UT	Feb 24, 2004	Primary	**55%**	30%				
CA	Mar 2, 2004	Primary	**65%**	20%				
CT	Mar 2, 2004	Primary	**58%**	24%				
GA	Mar 2, 2004	Primary	**47%**	41%				
MD	Mar 2, 2004	Primary	**60%**	26%				
MA	Mar 2, 2004	Primary	**72%**	18%				
MN	Mar 2, 2004	Caucus	**51%**	27%				
NY	Mar 2, 2004	Primary	**61%**	20%				
OH	Mar 2, 2004	Primary	**52%**	34%				
RI	Mar 2, 2004	Primary	**71%**	19%				
VT	Mar 2, 2004	Primary	34%		**58%**			
Caucus Wins			11%	0%	0%	0%		
Primary Wins			16%	1%	1%	1%		
Total Wins			27%	1%	1%	1%		

Table 2-5 Election Results during Contested Phase of the Nomination Process (Winner in Bold)

*Gephardt dropped out of the race on January 20, Lieberman on February 3, Clark on February 11, Dean on February 18, and Edwards on March 3.

would concede. He stayed in the race for two more weeks and thirteen more contests. He finally departed in early March with the results of so-called Super Tuesday, when nine states—among them California, New York, and Ohio—voted. Kerry won eight of the contests that day, losing only in Vermont, where Dean's former constituents loyally supported his already terminated candidacy.

2-5 Why Kerry?

Why did John Kerry win the nomination? In large part, his rise reflected Dean's collapse. As Democrats canvassed the field to find another candidate after the Dean bubble burst, their efforts were largely motivated by a strong desire to identify a candidate who was electable. Kerry, more than the other candidates, fit the bill. He had a compelling military record at a time when national security issues were important to Democratic voters, and he had political and electoral experience. In essence, many Democrats thought that Kerry had the stature necessary to be a competitive candidate in a race against an incumbent president.

The Democrats arrived at their decision remarkably quickly. Only 44 days elapsed between January 19, when Kerry won the Iowa caucuses, and March 3, when John Edwards ended his campaign. But arguably, Kerry won the race long before Super Tuesday. Some might point to February 10, when he defeated his closest challengers in Tennessee and Virginia, as the point when he sewed up the race. But really, from the moment he won in New Hampshire, Kerry was the Democrats' nominee. From this perspective, Iowa and New Hampshire decided the race to an even greater degree than ever before.

The quick ending to the Democratic nomination fight had one important political consequence. It set the stage for the longest general election battle on record. Early on, Bush campaign officials knew Kerry would be their opponent, and they were able to prepare to run against him. And, because of the president's prodigious campaign fund-raising efforts, the Bush campaign was able to finance a large and aggressive television advertising campaign early in the spring. But because Kerry had opted out of the primary campaign finance system, he was able to raise the money needed to counter the president's advertising campaign. Thus, the general election campaign commenced months before the party conventions, and well before most Americans were probably ready.

Readings for Further Study

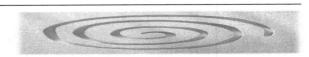

Cook, Rhodes. 2004. *The Presidential Nominating Process.* Lanham, MD: Rowman & Littlefield.

Kranish, Rhodes, Brian C. Mooney, and Nina J. Easton. 2004. *John F. Kerry: The Complete Biography: By the Boston Globe Reporters Who Know Him Best.* New York: PublicAffairs.

Mayer, William G., ed. 2004. *The Making of the Presidential Candidates 2004.* Lanham, MD: Rowman & Littlefield.

Websites to Check Out

Note: As we went to press, these sites were functional using the URLs provided. Check out the online text for the most up-to-date URLs.

Site name: Online NewsHour Democratic Primaries 2004
URL: http://www.pbs.org/newshour/vote2004/primaries/
PBS's compilation of information on the 2004 race for the Democratic Party's nomination.

Site name: Federal Election Commission
URL: http://www.fec.gov/
The Federal Election Commission collects and reports campaign finance data.

Site name: Project VoteSmart
URL: http://www.vote-smart.org/election_president.php
Project VoteSmart provides a wealth of information about the 2004 presidential election and the Electoral College.

The 2002 Election Surprise

Peverill Squire

The news media hailed the 2002 elections as a dramatic victory for the Republicans and a devastating defeat for the Democrats. Headlines in the *Wall Street Journal* two days after the election typified the sentiment. One trumpeted, "GOP Sweep Gives a Boost to Bush." Another lamented the Democrats' performance, calling it a "Dismal Election."

These characterizations held a good deal of truth. The Republicans gained control of both houses of Congress, maintained a majority of governorships, and for the first time in forty years came out of an election holding more state legislative seats than the Democrats. That the Republicans' accomplishments came during a midterm election—historically contests in which the president's party loses seats—made their achievements even more impressive. Indeed, the 2002 elections gave the GOP greater control over government than at any time in the past half century.

The impression many people took from the 2002 election results, then, was that the country had shifted sharply to the right. After all, these results stood in stark contrast with those in the 2000 elections. Then the country divided right down the middle. George W. Bush barely eked out a victory, winning narrowly (and controversially) in the Electoral College while actually getting fewer popular votes than Al Gore. The Senate split 50–50, and the Republicans held the House by only a few seats. Two years later, the voters clearly put the GOP in charge.

But are the 2000 and 2002 elections really that dissimilar? On close inspection, probably not. When we look beyond who won and who lost and examine the margins of victory and where the victories occurred, we get a much more textured picture of the 2002 elections. The Republican triumph was not as decisive as it appeared at first glance, and the voters were still as politically divided as they were in 2000. This suggests that the conventional wisdom to the contrary, the 2004 elections are apt to be tightly contested.

3-1 Electoral Prospects

Most observers expected that the 2002 elections would produce a close contest in the struggle between Democrats and Republicans for political supremacy. How close and who had the advantage depended on whether the subject of discussion was the Senate, the House of Representatives, or the state capitols.

3-1a The Senate

Heading into the 2002 elections both parties had good reason to think they could win control of the Senate. The Democrats had wrested control of the Senate away from the Republicans in June 2001 when Senator Jim Jeffords of Vermont formally defected from GOP ranks and became a political independent. That gave Senate Democrats a 50–49 advantage over Republicans and the right to run the chamber. If the Democrats held their one-seat edge after the 2002 elections, they would continue to be in control.

Democrats believed their prospects for holding their slim majority were reasonably good. Of the one-third of the Senate seats to be contested, the Republicans had more to defend and therefore potentially more to lose. Moreover, most Democratic incumbents looked reasonably strong.

Republicans had reasons of their own to be optimistic about their chances for regaining control of the Senate. If they picked up only a single Democratic seat, they would hold the 50–49 advantage and with it control of the Senate. They saw several Democratic Senate incumbents as vulnerable. They also anticipated that several open seats where neither party had an incumbent running would go their way.

3-1b The House of Representatives

At first glance, the contest for control of the House appeared to mirror the very competitive situation in the Senate. The Republicans held just a slight numerical advantage in the House heading into the campaign; the Democrats needed only seven seats to become the majority party. Moreover, Democrats looked to have history on their side. Since 1946, the president's party had lost, on average, twenty-five House seats in midterm elections.

In fact, however, the electoral outlook in the House was markedly different than in the Senate. Few analysts gave the Democrats much chance of picking up seven House seats, regardless of history. The dominant view was that, barring a miracle, the GOP would maintain its House majority.

Why would the Democrats find it so hard to pick up just seven seats when all 435 House seats were being contested? Two factors gave the Republicans an edge. First, in accordance with the Constitution, which requires congressional districts to be redrawn every ten years to reflect population shifts, House seats were redistricted before the 2002 elections. State legislatures drew the district lines in most states. In states where the GOP controlled both houses of the legislature and the governor-

ship, notably Michigan and Pennsylvania, they gerrymandered the lines with an eye toward increasing the number of seats their party might win. The Democrats did the same in a few other states. In the end, the net effect of the two parties' gerrymandering efforts was close to a wash.

More important, in states where control of the redistricting process was split between Republicans and Democrats, the two parties essentially colluded to protect the status quo. They drew district lines to protect incumbents. Thus, nationwide, redistricting made most House seats uncompetitive, with one or the other party holding a clear advantage. Indeed, in the 2002 election, at most only forty House seats were thought to be at all competitive.

The outcome of the 2002 House races in Iowa illustrates the power of redistricting to dampen electoral competition. Iowa is the only state where a nonpartisan legislative staff draws the district lines without regard to political calculations. Four of its five House races, each involving an incumbent, were strongly contested. That means that Iowa, with 1 percent of the seats in the House, accounted for 10 percent of the competitive House elections. With so few seats up for grabs nationally, the Democrats would have to win a disproportionately large percentage of them to take control of the House.

Ironically, the second factor working against the Democrats was the very closeness of the 2000 elections. A victorious presidential candidate normally has electoral coattails—he sweeps into office some of his party's House candidates who otherwise would have lost. But President Bush's

coattails were very short in 2000. Republicans actually lost House seats. The silver lining in this dark cloud—one that was little noticed at the time—was that the GOP had few vulnerable seats to defend in 2002. The Democrats also had few seats where Republicans stood a good shot at defeating the incumbent.

The net effect of redistricting and the narrowness of the 2000 election was that only a few House races in 2002 were in doubt. This electoral reality made the Democrats' task far more daunting than it appeared. After all, they were the ones who needed to pick up seats to fulfill their goal of retaking control of the House.

3-1c State Houses

Gubernatorial elections were the one place where the Democrats' chances for victory looked to be excellent. Most states elect their governor during midterm elections; thirty-six governorships were up for grabs in 2002. Only seventeen of those contests involved incumbents. Most of the ten Republican incumbents seeking reelection were thought to be safe. But Democratic incumbents were thought to be in strong shape, and their party was expected to pick up a majority of the nineteen open seat races.

3-1d The Issues

Factors such as redistricting and whose incumbents are up for reelection affect elections, but so do issues. How issues might affect the 2002 elections triggered considerable disagreement. On the one hand, the national economy had performed poorly, especially in contrast to the boom of the 1990s, ever since President Bush came to office. Many believed this economic weakness would help the chances of Democratic candidates because voters tend to blame the party in control of the White House when things go badly.

On the other hand, lingering concerns about homeland security and an anticipated military conflict with Iraq favored Republican candidates. Polls repeatedly show that the American public has far greater confidence in the ability of the Republican Party to handle foreign and defense policy than the Democratic Party. During the campaign, Republicans emphasized national and homeland security issues, while playing up their support for a wartime president.

In the end, neither party appeared to have an edge with the voters on the issues. But although the issues proved to be a wash, the Republicans did enjoy one huge campaign advantage over the Democrats: a popular president. President Bush helped recruit GOP candidates, raised more than $140 million for their campaigns, and traveled extensively to rally voters on their behalf. Indeed, during the week before the election, his efforts were almost nonstop. He made seventeen stops in fifteen states, urging voters to cast their ballots for Republicans. He clearly put his personal popularity on the line. The Democrats had no one to counter the president's fundraising prowess or his ability to generate news coverage.

3-2 Election Results

What the 2002 elections revealed about the American electorate depends on what evidence you examine. In terms of races won and lost, 2002 was a big year for the GOP. But when you examine how votes were distributed between the two parties, it is clear that voters remain deeply divided.

3-2a An Overview

On one level, the 2002 election results were unsurprising. Incumbents almost always win reelection, and 2002 proved no different. Incumbents won more than 96 percent of the House races they contested, 86 percent of Senate races, and 71 percent of gubernatorial races.

On another level, the results were surprising. Republicans picked up two seats in the Senate, raising their total to 51 and regaining control of the chamber. The GOP actually extended its lead in the House by several seats, coming out of the elections holding 229 seats, or 52.6 percent. To see how unusual this was, one needs to know that the president's party gained House seats in only two midterm elections in the entire twentieth century.

Perhaps the biggest election surprise came not in Congress but at the state level. The GOP retained a majority of governorships, though again, only by a hair, with 26 Republican governors to 24 Democratic governors. The more historic accomplishment for the GOP was that it took the lead in the number of state legislators for the first time since 1952. But this too was by a razor-thin edge: 49.6 percent of state legislative seats for the Republicans to 49.4 percent of state legislative seats for the Democrats.

3-2b Digging Deeper

Although the Republicans came out ahead at each level in the elections, overall, the results were very close. Digging a bit deeper reveals how remarkably tight they were. Table 3-1 tabulates the votes cast by party in contested Senate races. The Republicans received slightly less than 51 percent of all the votes cast in Senate races; the Democrats received a bit more than 49 percent. Some individual races were incredibly close. In South Dakota, for example, Democratic Senator Tim Johnson won reelection by just 524 votes out of 337,508 cast. Had that race gone the GOP's way,

Table 3-1 Vote Totals and Percentages in the 2002 Senatorial and Gubernatorial Elections

Contest	Number of Contests[a]	Total Number of Votes for Republicans	Total Number of Votes for Democrats	Vote Percentage for Republicans	Vote Percentage for Democrats
Senate	30	18,840,799	18,204,157	50.8%	49.1%
Governor	36	30,171,360	27,073,046	52.7%	47.3%

Source: Calculated by author from preliminary election returns.

[a]Only races contested by candidates from both major parties.

pundits would have been hailing an even larger Republican victory nationally.

Although the South Dakota race broke against Republicans, events elsewhere worked in their favor. In Minnesota, the Democratic incumbent, Paul Wellstone, whom polls showed was leading the race, died in a plane crash just days before the election. Former Vice President Walter Mondale took his place on the ballot. But Mondale's chances of returning to the Senate, where he had served in the 1970s, were severely damaged by the widespread public perception that Wellstone's supporters had inappropriately turned his memorial service into a campaign rally. On election night, the Republican candidate, Norm Coleman, a former Democrat and mayor of St. Paul, won by a comfortable margin.

In Missouri, the Republicans defeated Democratic incumbent Jean Carnahan. She had been appointed to her late husband's seat after he died in a plane crash just before Election Day in 2000. She proved unable to secure her seat and lost the election by a relatively close margin to a veteran politician.

Perhaps the most surprising GOP victory came in Georgia where Democratic incumbent Max Cleland lost to his Republican challenger, Representative Saxby Chambliss. The Republicans hammered Cleland for failing to support President Bush's version of a plan to create a Department of Homeland Security, implicitly questioning Cleland's patriotism. The charges stuck with many Georgia voters, even though Cleland lost three limbs fighting for the United States in Vietnam. Cleland's political fate was sealed when rural voters in Georgia turned out at an unusually high rate, possibly drawn to the polls by the controversy over the new state flag in the gubernatorial race. In the end, Chambliss won comfortably.

The GOP's victories in Minnesota and Georgia, coupled with its success in holding open seats in states such as New Hampshire, North Carolina, and Tennessee, earned it control of the Senate. But this big Republican triumph almost didn't happen. Had 41,000 of the more than 77 million votes cast gone differently, Democrats would have retained control of the Senate. By the same token, however, had a few thousand votes shifted in several races the Democrats won, the GOP's margin in the Senate would have been even greater. Small vote changes in close contests can easily distort the overall impression of the outcome.

Republicans actually did a bit better in gubernatorial races than they did in the Senate contests. As Table 3-1 shows, the GOP received almost 53 percent of the votes in elections for governor. Their vote percentages benefited from impressive victories in big states such as Florida, New York, and Texas, while the Democrats' vote totals were reduced by a surprisingly tight contest in California. The Republicans also posted a number of impressive victories nationally. Republican candidates won the governorships in Hawaii, Maryland, Massachusetts, New York, and Rhode Island, all of which are heavily Democratic states.

Looking at the outcome of those races in isolation would confirm the impression that the nation is moving the GOP's way. But one of the most curious aspects of the 2002 elections was that even as Republicans were winning in places no one might have anticipated, they were losing in places they traditionally won. Democrats won the governorships in the predominantly Republican states of Arizona, Kansas, Oklahoma, and Wyoming. The net effect was that the GOP's unexpected pickups were largely offset by its unanticipated losses.

Perhaps the most telling Republican advances came in state legislative elections. Unlike higher profile contests for Congress and governor, in which voters usually have considerable information about the candidates, state legislative races occur in relative obscurity. Thus, voters usually vote their party preferences in state legislative elections, unaffected by candidates or issues. After the 2002 elections, the Republicans controlled three more lower house chambers and three more upper house chambers than they did before the elections. Overall, the GOP increased the number of seats it held in fifty-two state legislative chambers, while the Democrats improved their seat totals in only twenty-two state legislative chambers.

But just how big is the Republican advantage in state legislative seats? Following the 2002 elections, the GOP held 34 more seats than the Democrats. Given that there are 7,382 state legislative seats nationally, a 34-seat edge does not amount to much. Indeed, in the 400-seat New Hampshire House of Representatives, where each representative represents only 3,000 people, there are 162 more Republicans than Democrats, more than accounting for the GOP's lead nationally.

3-3 Explanations

If the president's party typically loses seats in midterm elections and voters generally punish the president's party when the economy is performing poorly, why did Republicans gain seats in the 2002 elections rather than lose them?

The answer lies in who turned out to vote. Before Election Day, Gallup surveys showed that Americans were evenly divided in terms of party identification. But Republicans turned out to vote at a much higher rate. In the election, Republican and Democratic identifiers both voted for their parties' candidates in the same proportion. But the overall House vote went to the GOP by roughly 51 percent to 45 percent. The GOP's advantage in turnout stemmed in part from the fact that middle-aged and older Americans, the age cohorts most likely to vote, lean Republican. In contrast, younger Americans tilt toward the Democrats' way, but they are much less likely to cast their ballots. Similarly, college-educated Americans are more supportive of Republicans and more likely to vote than less well-educated, Democratic-leaning Americans.

Thus, the Republicans benefited from the fact that their supporters were more inclined to go to the polls than the Democrats' supporters. The GOP also enjoyed a mobilization advantage. Republican candidates raised and spent more money than did Democratic candidates in both House and Senate races. This helped them get out their message. More important, perhaps, President Bush's nonstop campaigning during the last week of the campaign rallied GOP voters. Gallup found that during the weekend before Election Day, Republican voters became much more energized about the campaign than were Democrats. This suggests that the president's efforts paid off.

Just how big an impact did President Bush have on the elections? Table 3-2 compares the total number of visits he and Vice President Cheney made to battleground states in 2002 with the eventual outcome in each state's senatorial and gubernatorial elections. This comparison suggests that President Bush's efforts were, at best, marginal. For example, the president and vice president visited Iowa eleven times during 2002. Nonetheless, Iowans reelected the incumbent Democratic governor and senator. Overall, Democrats actually won five Senate races in the heavily visited states, whereas Republicans won four races. In gubernatorial races, the GOP won six elections to the Democrats' five.

Even a marginal effect, however, can be critical in a closely divided election. Given how closely

Table 3-2 Election Outcomes in Selected States Visited Six or More Times in 2002 by President Bush and Vice President Cheney

State	Number of Visits by Bush	Number of Visits by Cheney	Total Number of White House Visits	Party Winning Senatorial Race	Party Winning Gubernatorial Race
Pennsylvania	17	5	22		D
Iowa	10	1	11	D	D
Minnesota	5	4	9	R	R
Missouri	7	2	9	R	R
Arkansas	4	4	8	D	R
South Dakota	5	2	7	D	R
North Carolina	5	2	7	R	R
California	5	1	6		D
Colorado	3	3	6	R	R
Michigan	3	3	6	D	D
Louisiana	4	2	6	D	
New Mexico	4	2	6		D

Source: Visit data calculated by author from "White House 2004: Candidate State Visit Tallies," *National Journal*, December 30, 2002.

divided the country was going into the election, changing the outcome in only a state or two made a huge difference in the final numbers.

3-4 Did Voters Shift Right?

The 2002 elections placed control over the federal government in Republican hands. Does that mean the American people shifted significantly to the right? The very closeness of the election suggested the answer was no. Additional evidence came from post-election polls. They showed that Americans expressed confidence that Republicans in Congress would do a good job on issues as diverse as the war on terrorism and education. The same polls, however, also showed that Americans still preferred the Democrats' positions on issues such as the environment, Social Security, and Medicare. So voters continued to express mixed preferences.

The 2002 elections offered one final insight on Americans' political preferences. In a number of states, voters had the chance to take positions on ballot measures. A look at the votes on tax measures confirms the muddled nature of public opinion. In some states, voters approved tax increases. In other states, they said no. Arkansas voters rejected a proposed cut in the sales tax on food and medicine. Meanwhile, Massachusetts voters turned down a proposal to eliminate the state income tax. In Arizona, voters raised taxes on tobacco products, but Missouri voters defeated such an increase. A plan to increase income tax rates to finance a comprehensive health care system lost in Oregon.

Voters sent equally mixed messages on other issues. Voters generally backed measures to support education. But efforts to ease marijuana laws failed in Arizona, Nevada, and Ohio. Overall, on some ballot measures, voters expressed liberal preferences; on others, they took more conservative positions. There is no discernable policy shift one way or the other.

3-5 Looking Ahead to 2004

What, if anything, do the 2002 elections tell us about the next campaign? Heading into the 2004 election, the Republicans held clear electoral advantages. The power of incumbency worked in their favor in congressional races, making it easier for them to keep their majorities. And President Bush's own incumbency and fund-raising prowess made him a difficult (but not impossible) candidate to defeat.

But there were some positive signs for the Democrats. In December 2002, they won run-off elections for a Senate seat and a House seat in Louisiana, a state that had been trending toward the Republicans. More generally, voters continued to prefer the Democrats' positions on the critical issues of Social Security and Medicare. And attacks on U.S. troops in Iraq had diminished President Bush's once lofty public approval ratings. Given how tight the last two elections have been, unless something extraordinary happens to unsettle current partisan leanings, expect the 2004 elections to be tight as well.

Readings for Further Study

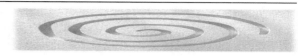

Drehle, David Von. 2002. "Bush Bets His Popularity and Scores a Big Victory." *Washington Post.* November 6.

National Conference of State Legislatures. 2002. "Voters Act on 200-plus Ballot Measures." November 6. Available at http://www.ncsl.org/programs/press/2002/pr021106.htm

Pew Research Center. 2002. "Big GOP Gain in Popular Vote Not Reflected in Modest House Seat Shift." November 11. Available at http://people-press.org/commentary/display.php3?AnalysisID=58

Websites to Check Out

Note: As we went to press, these sites were functional using the URLs provided. Check out the online text for the most up-to-date URLs.

Site name: Politics
URL: http://www.washingtonpost.com/wp-dyn/politics/
The *Washington Post* website devoted to all aspects of American politics, including detailed information about the 2002 elections.

Site name: *New York Times* Campaigns 2004
URL: http://www.nytimes.com/pages/politics/campaign/index.html
This site presents the most recent articles on elections in the *New York Times,* along with biographies of the 2004 Democratic presidential candidates.

Site name: The League of Women Voters
URL: http://www.lwv.org/voter/
The nation's premier grassroots citizen organization presents information likely to be of interest to voters.

What Is Treason?

John Walker Lindh and the U.S. Constitution

James M. Lindsay

The news from Mazar-e-Sharif, Afghanistan, shocked America. For days, a bloody revolt by Al Qaeda and Taliban prisoners had raged inside Qala Jangi prison. Hundreds of prisoners and dozens of Northern Alliance guards were killed in the fighting. Also dead was CIA agent Johnny "Mike" Spann, the first American to die in Afghanistan. As the fighting died down on the sixth day, the last group of Taliban and Al Qaeda fighters emerged from their basement hiding spot when it was flooded with ice-cold water. Among the heavily bearded and dirt-caked prisoners, one stood out. He was John Walker Lindh, a twenty-year-old American.

Many of Lindh's fellow citizens immediately denounced him as a traitor. Some demanded that he be executed. Former President George H.W. Bush weighed in with an alternative punishment: "Make him leave his hair the way it is and his face as dirty as it is, and let him go wandering around this country and see what kind of sympathy he would get." As the debate over what to do with Lindh picked up momentum, two issues quickly emerged. Had he

committed treason? If not, what laws, if any, had he broken?

4-1 From Marin County to Mazar-e-Sharif

The facts surrounding Lindh's case are clear. In 1997, the then-sixteen-year-old Lindh converted from Catholicism to Islam. He began attending a local mosque in Marin County, California, a wealthy area just north of San Francisco. In late 1998, he traveled to Yemen to learn Arabic, the language of the Koran. He came back home to Marin in early 1999 for a few months before returning to Yemen.

By this time, Lindh was openly hostile toward the United States. In October 2000, Al Qaeda operatives bombed the *USS Cole* when it made a refueling stop in Aden, Yemen. In an email to his father, Lindh said that the attack was justified because by sending a warship into an Islamic port the United States had committed an "act of war." Several months later, he sent his mother an email urging her to move to England. "I really don't know what your big attachement [sic] to America is all about. What has America ever done for anybody?"

In November 2000, Lindh moved to Bannu, a village in northwestern Pakistan, to study at an Islamic school. In May 2001, he left Bannu, and eventually fought with Pakistani militants in Kashmir, a predominantly Muslim region that both India and Pakistan claim as theirs. After the September 11 attacks, Lindh traveled to the Afghani city of Kunduz, to fight for the Taliban. His fighting days were short. His commanding officer switched sides soon after he arrived, and before long, he and his fellow soldiers surrendered and were shipped to Qala Jangi. There, Lindh was interrogated by Mike Spann, but he refused to answer Spann's questions. When the prison revolt erupted, Lindh was shot in the leg.

The key question, though, was what Lindh did while he was in Kashmir and Afghanistan. The federal government initially alleged that when he left Bannu in May 2001 he went to Al Farooq, an Al Qaeda training camp. There he eventually met Osama bin Laden. Lindh completed his training at Al Farooq, even though he had learned early on that bin Laden had sent several dozen terrorists to attack U.S. and Israeli targets. The government later backed off this claim, asserting only that he received military training in Afghanistan that he subsequently used to aid terrorist groups.

4-2 The Constitution's Treason Clause

Did Lindh commit treason? Answering that question requires reading the Constitution. Treason is one of only three crimes mentioned in the Constitution—piracy and counterfeiting are the other two—and it is the only one defined at any length. Article 3, Section 3 is devoted entirely to the question of treason. The first paragraph reads:

Treason against the United States, shall consist only in levying War against them, or in adhering to their Enemies, giving them Aid and Comfort. No Person shall be convicted of Treason unless on the Testimony of two Witnesses to the same overt Act, or on Confession in open Court.

The requirement that the government produce either a confession or two eyewitnesses raises a very high bar for the prosecution. In most trials, prosecutors have no eyewitness testimony. They often rely instead on circumstantial evidence, that is, facts that don't prove guilt directly, as eyewitness testimony and DNA testing might, but from which guilt can be inferred.

The second paragraph of Article 3, Section 3 limits the punishment for treason:

The Congress shall have Power to declare the Punishment of Treason, but no Attainder of Treason shall work Corruption of Blood, or Forfeiture except during the Life of the Person attainted.

Congress long ago made treason a capital offense. And while talk of an "attainder" sounds odd to our ears today, the basic idea is simple: Only a person convicted of treason in a court of law can be punished for the crime. Eighteenth century England frequently punished both the convicted person and his family, typically by barring them from politics ("Corruption of Blood") and seizing their property ("Forfeiture").

The Constitution singles out treason for discussion for a reason. The framers wanted to avoid what had been common practice in England—using treason charges to silence, if not outright kill, political opponents. James Madison explained in Federalist #43 why it was important to have a high standard for proving treason:

As treason may be committed against the United States, the authority of the United States ought to be enabled to punish it. But as new-fangled and artificial treasons, have been the great engines, by which violent factions, the natural offspring of free Governments, have usually wrecked their alternate malignity on each other, the [Constitutional] Convention have with great judgment opposed a barrier to this peculiar danger, by inserting a constitutional definition of the crime, fixing the proof necessary for conviction of it, and restraining the Congress, even in punishing it, from extending the consequences of guilt beyond the person of its author.

Madison's view was widely accepted by his contemporaries. The Constitution's high standard helps explain why treason prosecutions have been rare in American history. (The fact that exceedingly few Americans desire to commit treason matters as well.) There have been only about thirty treason trials since 1789, and none since 1952. In that case, Tomoya Kawakita, a Japanese American, was sentenced to death for mistreating American prisoners of war during World War II. Even America's most notorious spies—such as Ethel and Julius Rosenberg during the early years of the Cold War and Aldrich Ames in the 1990s—were not charged with treason. Instead, prosecutors charged them with—and won convictions for—espionage.

The government's track record in winning convictions when it does press treason charges is spotty. Many treason trials have ended with acquittals. The most famous came in 1807 when a jury acquitted Aaron Burr, Thomas Jefferson's first vice president and the man who killed Alexander Hamilton in a duel, of charges that he had tried to establish a rival country. Even those who are convicted seldom are put to death. No American was executed during the twentieth century for committing treason. (President Dwight D. Eisenhower commuted Tomoya Kawakita's sentence to life in prison.)

4-3 Did Lindh Commit Treason?

These legal realities forced the Bush administration to grapple with two questions in deciding what crimes to charge Lindh with: Did his behavior meet the constitutional definition of treason? Could the government prove it in court?

Government prosecutors quickly realized they did not have an open-and-shut case. One problem is that much of Lindh's behavior was reprehensible but not treasonous, or even criminal. Many Americans were understandably outraged by Lindh's emails to his parents and by his comment to a *Newsweek* reporter that he "supported" the September 11 attacks. But the First

Amendment's protections apply to even the most vile views.

So what, then, might qualify as the "overt Act" that Lindh committed against the United States? His presence in Afghanistan by itself does not qualify. The United States did not go to war against the Taliban until October 7, 2001. So any fighting he engaged in before that date would not qualify as treasonous. Between the time that the United States first attacked Afghanistan and his capture several weeks later, his efforts were mostly devoted to avoiding U.S. bombs. He never engaged any U.S. troops in combat. He refused to speak to Spann, but silence is not a crime. Nor did the federal government claim that Lindh participated in the prison revolt or contributed to Spann's death. Finally, the government itself contended that Lindh refused a request by Al Qaeda officials to train for a martyrdom mission against the United States. A jury could read this to mean that he had no intent to "levy war" against the United States or provide "aid and comfort" to its enemies. And without a specific "overt Act" to point to, the whole question of finding two eyewitnesses becomes moot.

Besides charging Lindh with treason, which would have meant a trial in an ordinary federal court, federal prosecutors had the possible option of trying him in a military tribunal. President Bush had created these tribunals to prosecute Taliban leaders and Al Qaeda operatives. (See Reading 15, "Trying Terrorists: Military Commissions and the American Legal System," for more details on these tribunals.) They operate under much less restrictive rules than those governing standard criminal trials. A military tribunal could not try Lindh for treason, but it would have great leeway to sentence him to death if it convicted him on any number of other charges.

But proposals to prosecute Lindh in military tribunal were stillborn. President Bush's order creating the tribunals specifically gave them jurisdiction only over noncitizens. (This is why a military tribunal could not try Lindh for treason. Only an American citizen or resident can be tried for treason.) The government could have tried to strip Walker of his citizenship, thereby making him eligible for the tribunals. One federal law says that an American automatically loses his or her citizenship by "serving in the armed forces of a foreign state if such armed forces are engaged in hostilities against the United States." But the law adds that this is true only if the person joins the foreign army "with the intention of relinquishing United States" citizenship.

This wording created problems for the prosecutors that are similar to those they faced in trying to prove treason. Did Lindh intend to renounce his citizenship by fighting with the Taliban and Al Qaeda? Did he join Al Qaeda and the Taliban with the intent of fighting in a war against the United States? In trying to make the case that the answer to both questions is yes, prosecutors knew they would have to overcome the federal courts' historical reluctance to strip people of their citizenship. The courts generally regard citizenship as a right that can be relinquished and not something that can be taken away.

4-4 Lindh's Indictment

These legal obstacles ultimately persuaded the Bush administration not to press treason charges or seek to prosecute Lindh in a military tribunal. Instead, in January 2002, the Justice Department indicted him for violating several federal laws. The main charges were conspiracy to kill Americans outside the United States, which carries a penalty of up to life in prison; providing material support to foreign terrorist organizations, which also carries a penalty of up to life in prison; and providing aid to the Taliban, which carries a penalty of up to ten years. The conspiracy charge was crucial. The standards for proving participation in a conspiracy are relatively lax. No eyewitness testimony is needed. Circumstantial evidence can be enough. And it is not necessary to show that the defendant had complete knowledge of a plan to commit a crime. Partial knowledge can be sufficient to convict.

To give itself the best chance of winning, the Justice Department filed its charges against Lindh in the District Court for the Eastern District of Virginia rather than in the District Court for the Southern District of New York. (Federal law gives prosecutors some say over where to file criminal charges.) Justice Department officials calculated that a jury composed of Virginians, who tend to be conservative, would be more inclined to convict than a jury composed of New Yorkers, who tend to be more liberal. The District Court for the Eastern District of Virginia also has a record for trying cases quickly, so much so it is nicknamed the "rocket docket." Finally, the District Court for the Eastern District of Virginia is part of the Fourth Court of Appeals, which is regarded as the most conservative appeals court in the United States. Federal prosecutors calculated that if Lindh ever filed an appeal, the Fourth Court of Appeals would be the place where they would get the most sympathetic hearing.

4-5 Striking a Plea Bargain

The case against John Walker Lindh never went to trial. In a surprise move in July 2002, prosecutors announced they had struck a deal that would send the American Taliban to prison for up to twenty years. The government agreed to drop nine of the ten charges it had filed, including the charge of conspiracy to murder Americans abroad and assisting terrorists. Lindh, in turn, agreed to plead guilty to the remaining charge—knowingly supplying his services to the Taliban—as well as to a new charge of carrying an explosive device while committing a felony. (He had carried a rifle and two grenades while fighting in Afghanistan.) Lindh also agreed to help the government in other terrorist prosecutions and to tell investigators everything he knew about Al Qaeda.

Prosecutors described the plea bargain, which President George W. Bush personally approved, as a victory. They had secured a stiff punishment for Lindh, while avoiding a public trial that might have forced them to reveal sensitive intelligence information in open court. They also avoided the embarrassing possibility that they might fail to convict Lindh on the most serious charge—that he had conspired to kill Americans overseas.

Lindh's defenders noted that the plea deal spared him a possible life sentence. A trial would have been a risky proposition even though the government's case was not airtight. Public opinion was solidly against Lindh, and the trial judge had dismissed several defense motions to suppress statements he had made to his military captors. Lindh's defenders also saw the plea agreement as a partial vindication. Prosecutors admitted he had never fired on Americans, and he was convicted of helping the Taliban and not Al Qaeda.

In early October 2002, a clean-shaven John Walker Lindh appeared before U.S. District Judge T. S. Ellis III. In a twenty-minute address to the court, Lindh apologized for his actions. "I went to Afghanistan because I believed it was my religious duty to assist my fellow Muslims militarily in their jihad against the Northern Alliance," he said. "I did not go to fight against America, and I never did. . . I have never supported terrorism in any form and I never will. . . . I made a mistake by joining the Taliban." Judge Ellis accepted the government's request that Lindh be sentenced to twenty years in prison. Under federal guidelines, he can receive up to a 15 percent reduction in his sentence for good behavior. That would mean the earliest John Walker Lindh can become a free man is 2019.

Readings for Further Study

"A Long, Strange Trip to the Taliban." 2001. *Newsweek.* (December 17): 30–35.

Archer, Jules. 1971. *Treason in America: Disloyalty Versus Dissent.* New York: E. P. Dutton.

Mayer, Jane. 2003. "Lost in the Jihad." *New Yorker.* (March 10): 50–59.

Websites to Check Out

Note: As we went to press, these sites were functional using the URLs provided. Check out the online text for the most up-to-date URLs.

Site name: Crimelynx: Criminal Justice Center

URL: http://www.crimelynx.com/terrtrials1.html

This site provides a compendium of links to news stories and commentary on the John Walker Lindh case, as well as other current and past terrorism trials.

Site name: Jurist: Legal Intelligence

URL: http://jurist.law.pitt.edu/issues/issue_walker.htm

This site contains a wealth of resources on the John Walker Lindh case, including links to news stories, copies of the legal motions filed in the case, and expert commentary on the legal issues that the case raises.

Site name: TalibanJohn.Info

URL: http://www.henrymarkholzer.com/talibanjohn.info/

A professor emeritus at Brooklyn Law who believes that the federal government should have charged John Walker Lindh with treason offers his personal commentary on developments in the case.

The Middle East Is Us:

Middle Easterners, Arabs, and Muslims in American Life

James M. Lindsay

Herman Melville, the author of *Moby Dick,* once wrote, "You cannot spill a drop of American blood without spilling the blood of the whole world." September 11 attested to the truth of his observation. While the nineteen terrorists who carried out the attacks claimed to be striking a blow for Islam, their victims included not just the descendants of European immigrants and African slaves but also fellow Arabs and Muslims. Indeed, while the United States is seen to be the leader of the Western world, it is home to millions of people whose ethnic roots lie in the Middle East and whose prayers are to Allah.

In the wake of September 11, Middle Eastern, Arab, and Muslim Americans suddenly found themselves thrust into the spotlight. Journalists with notebooks and reporters with camera crews ventured into mosques, visited stores selling halal meat, and queried women wearing headscarves. Yet, despite this media coverage, it is safe to say that most Americans probably know little about their fellow citizens whose ancestors came from the Middle East or who go to mosque rather than church or temple. Simplistic stereotypes that lump all people from the Middle East or all Muslims into a single category abound. But when looked at closely, these communities turn out to be as diverse and complex as the America in which they live.

5-1 Middle Eastern, Arab, or Muslim?

The terms *Middle Eastern, Arab,* and *Muslim* are often used as if they were just different labels for the same group of people. Although membership in these groups overlaps, and some people belong to all three, they are not identical. Many Americans of Middle Eastern descent are not Arab. Most Arab Americans go to church, not a mosque. Most American Muslims have no ethnic ties to the Middle East. So it is useful to explore how these three groups differ.

5-1a Middle Easterners

The Middle East's exact boundaries are debated. In the most expansive definition, it extends from Morocco in the west to Afghanistan in the east and includes all of the Arab world plus countries such as Iran, Somalia, and Turkey. The Census Bureau calculates that 2 million of the 281 million people living in the United States in 2000 were either immigrants from this region or were the children of these immigrants. Although the absolute number of Middle Easterners is relatively small—less than 1 percent of the total U.S. population—it is growing rapidly. By some counts, it increased more than 50 percent in the 1990s.

What accounts for the rapid growth in the Middle Eastern community in the United States? Births are one answer. According to Census Bureau data analyzed by the *Washington Post,* Middle Eastern households are more likely to have children than the typical American household. But immigration plays a major role as well. More than 450,000 people emigrated to the United States from the Middle East in the 1990s. As Figure 5-1 shows, Iran provided the most legal immigrants, but sizable numbers came from

Egypt, Lebanon, and Jordan, among other countries. On top of this influx, an estimated 150,000 Middle Eastern immigrants entered the country illegally. The fact that Middle Easterners come from a range of countries with different historical experiences complicates their efforts to act as a cohesive group in American politics. The problems troubling the Afghani community often differ from those bothering the Iranian community, which in turn differ from those of people from Egypt or Lebanon.

Middle Easterners can be found in all fifty states, but more than half can be found in five states: California, New York, Michigan, New Jersey, and Illinois. Different national groups tend to cluster around specific cities, as new immigrants locate where older immigrants have already settled. (Such clustering has always characterized American immigration. That is why so many Italian Americans live in the New York City area and so many Irish Americans live in Boston.) Most Iranians live around Los Angeles and Washington, D.C. America's largest Arab-American community is centered in Dearborn, Michigan. Fremont, California, hosts America's largest Afghan community.

5-1b Arab Americans

The Census Bureau estimates that 1.25 million people in the United States trace their ancestry to the Arab world, although other estimates put the number as high as 3.5 million. California, New York, and Michigan have the greatest number of residents of Arab descent. On the whole, Arab Americans are better educated than the national average, which explains why they earn higher than average incomes.

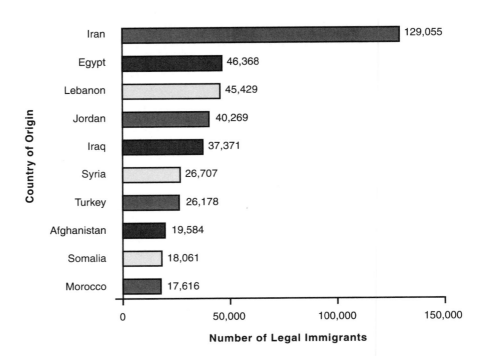

Figure 5-1 Top ten sources of Middle Eastern immigration into the United States, 1990–1999.

Source: U.S. Census Bureau.

Many Arab Americans trace their roots in the United States back more than 100 years. Lebanese Christians emigrated to the United States in sizable numbers at the end of the nineteenth century. Many eventually settled in southeastern Michigan because Detroit's automobile factories were looking for workers and paid high wages. A second wave of Arab immigration began in the late 1960s when the United States made it easier for non-Europeans to immigrate. As Figure 5-1 shows, this more recent wave of immigrants has brought people from a wider array of Arab countries than just Lebanon. Some of these immigrants have been well-educated professionals looking to pursue their careers. Others have been simply fleeing turmoil and poverty in their homelands. Many of these more recent immigrants have yet to become U.S.

citizens, and as a result, do not have the right to vote. This obviously limits their ability to influence American politics.

One characteristic of the Arab-American community will surprise most Americans: According to the Arab-American Institute, three out of every four Arab Americans is Christian, not Muslim. To put that number in perspective, Christians constitute fewer than one out of ten people in the Arab world. Arab Americans are predominantly Christian because the first Arab immigrants were. Muslims, however, dominate the more recent wave of Arab immigration. As a result, they will constitute an increasing share of the Arab-American community in the years to come. Religious differences, as well as those based on national origin, have at times impeded Arab-American efforts to act in a unified political fashion.

Muslim Arabs complained after September 11 that Christian Arabs sought to protect themselves against discrimination by wearing crosses prominently around their necks.

5-1c Muslims

The number of Muslims living in the United States is hotly debated. The federal census would be the best source of such information, but federal law prohibits the Census Bureau from asking questions about religious faith. Muslim advocacy groups put the number at 6 to 7 million. This is the figure that most of the news media use, and it would make America's Muslim community roughly the size of its Jewish population. But the methods used to generate this number reflect guesswork more than anything else. (One study produced its 6 million figure by estimating the membership of American mosques and multiplying that number by three to account for Muslims who did not belong to a mosque. The study's author admitted that this reflected an "educated guess." Critics say there was nothing educated about it.) More systematic studies using survey techniques place the number of Muslims at around 2 million, or even less. Whether one accepts the higher number of 7 million or the lower number of 2 million, the basic lesson remains the same: Muslims are a distinct minority in the United States, at less than 2.5 percent of the total U.S. population.

Although the exact number of Muslims living in the United States is disputed, no one disagrees that their number is growing rapidly. The American Religious Identification Survey—which surveyed 50,000 U.S. residents and concluded that 2.8 million Muslims lived in the United States in 2001—found that the number of adults in the United States who described themselves as Muslims more than doubled between 1990 and 2001. The sharp growth in the Muslim community results from two trends. The perhaps more obvious one is immigration to the United States from Islamic countries. The other is conversion, as Americans who were not raised in the Islamic faith choose to join it.

The exact ethnic and racial composition of the Muslim community in the United States is as uncertain as its total number. But if you think—as most Americans apparently do—that Arab Americans constitute the bulk of the Muslim community in the United States, you would be wrong. The largest single identifiable ethnic or racial group of American Muslims is actually African Americans. They constitute somewhere between 25 and 40 percent of the American Muslim community. Another sizable segment of the American Muslim community traces its ethnic roots to South Asia (particularly India and Pakistan) and Southeast Asia (especially Indonesia and Malaysia). Thus, even though Arab Americans were featured prominently in news shows and governmental prayer services in the weeks and months following September 11, they in fact constitute a minority of the Muslims in the United States. (This caused some resentment among African-American Muslims, who understandably complained after the attacks that the news media and government officials treated them as if they were invisible.)

Like Christians and Jews, American Muslims differ in how they interpret their religious obligations and how strictly they observe the tenets of their faith.

Some prefer the austere version of Islam associated with Saudi Arabia. Far more—no one knows for sure—are more comfortable with the less austere versions of Islam found in much of the rest of the Islamic world. Likewise, while many American Muslims attend mosque prayers regularly, others are more secular than religious.

5-2 Arab- and Muslim-American Opinion

September 11 immediately raised concerns about how Middle Eastern, Arab, and Muslim Americans would be treated. Many political leaders—led by New York Mayor Rudy Guiliani—moved quickly to warn their fellow Americans against anti-Arab and anti-Muslim bigotry. Yet, instances of discrimination, some of which involved violence, occurred. So how do Arabs and Muslims living in the United States view the way they have been treated since September 11? And do they view the war on terrorism in the same way that the broader American public does?

These questions are easier to ask than to answer. Few pollsters have sought to survey Arab and Muslim opinion over the years. This makes it impossible to determine trends. Moreover, the uncertainty surrounding the size of these communities hinders efforts to generate representative samples. So the polls that have been done should be viewed cautiously.

So what do we know? A poll commissioned by the Arab-American Institute in fall 2001 found that one in five Arab Americans said he or she had experienced discrimination because of his or her ethnicity in the wake of September 11. Nearly half (45 percent) said they knew someone who had been discriminated against for being of Arab descent. Yet, a majority of Arab Americans (54 percent) said that law enforcement officials were justified in extra questioning and inspections of people who looked Middle Eastern or spoke with a Middle Eastern accent.

Another fall 2001 poll commissioned by Muslims in American Public Square found that roughly half (52 percent) of the American Muslims it surveyed reported that they knew of individuals, businesses, or religious organizations that had experienced anti-Muslim discrimination. A sizable minority (41 percent) said they were not aware of any discrimination. When asked to assess American attitudes toward Muslims in the wake of September 11, 41 percent said that "Americans have been respectful and tolerant of Muslims," while another 33 percent said that "Americans have been respectful and tolerant of Muslims, but American society overall is disrespectful and intolerant of Muslims."

What about attitudes toward the war on terrorism? The poll by the Arab-American Institute, which was done before U.S. warplanes began bombing Afghanistan, found that 88 percent of Arab Americans gave President Bush positive marks for his handling of the U.S. response to the terrorist attacks. Seven out of ten (69 percent) also endorsed an all-out war against countries that harbor or aid the terrorists responsible for September 11. That level of support was slightly lower than the roughly 85 percent support that polls of the entire American public were typically finding at that time.

The poll by Muslims in American Public Square found decidedly less support for the war on terrorism among Muslims—51 percent. At the time this poll was conducted—November and December 2001—polls typically showed that nine out of every ten Americans supported the war. Those in the Muslim community most likely to support the war on terrorism were South Asians (61 percent), those 65 and older (63 percent), and those born abroad (58 percent). Opposition to the war was strongest among African Americans and those between the ages of 18 and 29 (56 percent). When it came to deciding whom the United States was fighting, two out of three Muslims said terrorism. Only 18 percent said Islam.

One point that Arab Americans and Muslim Americans agree on is that U.S. policy toward the Middle East was a major reason behind the September 11 attacks. Nearly two out of three Muslims (63 percent) said that U.S. Middle East policy had a "strong impact" on the attacks, and a nearly identical number (67 percent) said that if they could do only one thing to wage the war on terrorism, they would change U.S. policy toward the Middle East. Three in four Arab Americans (78 percent) believed that a U.S. commitment to settle the Israel-Palestine dispute would help win the war on terrorism.

5-3 Looking Ahead

One question that only time can answer is how September 11 will affect the incorporation of Middle Easterners, Arabs, and Muslims into American society. This question is the most relevant for America's Muslim community given its relative newness in American society and its considerable immigrant roots. It is less relevant to the Arab-American community given that its much longer history in the United States means it has become more deeply woven into the fabric of American society. Indeed, Arab Americans vote at slightly higher rates than the national average. And Americans of Arab descent who have played prominent roles in American politics include consumer activist and 2000 presidential candidate Ralph Nader, former U.S. Senate Majority Leader George Mitchell, former Michigan senator and current Secretary of Energy Spencer Abraham, and former Director of the Office of Management and Budget Mitchell Daniels.

Nevertheless, the possibility exists that September 11 may disrupt the integration of Arabs and Muslims—especially those who are immigrants—into American society. Americans might perpetually discriminate against Arab and Muslim Americans, or they themselves could reject the idea of becoming part of the American family. Pessimists frequently point out that Federal Bureau of Investigation (FBI) crime statistics show that the number of hate crimes against Muslims jumped seventeen-fold in 2001 compared with 2000. The Equal Employment Opportunity Commission (EEOC) reports that between September 11, 2001, and May 7, 2002, the number of complaints it received from Muslims alleging discrimination on the basis of their religion rose 157 percent over the comparable period one year earlier. Many Arabs and Muslims bristled when the Immigration and Naturalization Service for a time required male nonimmigrant aliens over the age of sixteen from most Middle Eastern countries to be photographed, fingerprinted, and interviewed under oath as a condition of remaining in the United States.

But there is good reason to doubt that a permanent schism is developing between Arabs and Muslims and the rest of American society. As displeased as Arab and Muslim Americans have been to witness or experience discrimination, there is scant evidence that they are giving up on America and what it represents. Indeed, 41 percent of Muslims reported being more patriotic in the wake of September 11; only 5 percent said they felt less patriotic. Nor do Americans appear to blame Arab or Muslim Americans for September 11. Roughly eight out of ten (77 percent) believe that Arab Americans and immigrants from the Middle East are no more sympathetic to the terrorists' acts than other Americans. Seven in ten (68 percent) say it would be wrong to put Arab Americans under special surveillance. Six in ten (62 percent) believe they are loyal to the United States. Fewer than one in five Americans (17 percent) looks unfavorably upon Muslim Americans.

These latter sentiments appear to be more than empty rhetoric. In the 2002 elections, 40 Arab Americans ran for political office. Roughly 70 percent won. The winners included a U.S. senator from New Hampshire (John Sununu, son of the former governor), the governor of Maine (John Baldacci), and the mayor of Lexington, Kentucky (Teresa Isaac). Moreover, focusing on the percentage increases in the FBI and EEOC data on hate crimes and allegations of religious discrimination is misleading. Although the percentage increases are dramatic, the actual numbers are quite low. The FBI recorded 481 hate crimes against Muslims in 2001 (up from 28 in 2000), and the EEOC recorded only 497 anti-Muslim bias claims (up from 193). This in a country of more than 285 million people.

In short, the central tenet of America's civic religion—the embrace of fellow citizens who hail from different cultural traditions—appears to extend to people whose ancestral roots lie in the Middle East. And that bodes well for America's future.

Readings for Further Study

Bagby, Ishan, Paul M. Perl, and Bryan T. Froehle. 2001. *The Mosque in America: A National Portrait*. Washington, D.C.: Council on American-Islamic Relations. Available at http://www.cair-net.org/mosquereport/

Human Rights Watch. 2002. "'We Are Not the Enemy': Hate Crimes Against Arabs, Muslims, and Those Perceived to Be Arab and Muslim after September 11." Vol. 14, no. 6. November. Available at http://www.hrw.org/reports/2002/usahate/usa1102.pdf

Smith, Tom W. 2002. "The Muslim Population of the United States: The Methodology of Estimates." *Public Opinion Quarterly* 66 (Fall): 404–17.

Websites to Check Out

Note: As we went to press, these sites were functional using the URLs provided. Check out the online text for the most up-to-date URLs.

Site name: American Muslim Alliance
URL: http://www.amaweb.org/
Analysis of issues relevant to Muslim Americans, articles about the Muslim community in the United States, and detailed information about Muslim political participation.

Site name: Arab-American Institute
URL: http://www.aaiusa.org/index.htm
Information about the demographics of the Arab-American community, analyses of issues relevant to Arab Americans, and detailed data on Arab-American political attitudes and behavior.

Site name: Council on American-Islamic Relations
URL: http://www.cair-net.org/default.asp
News briefs, advocacy pieces, background information about Islam, and reports in Arabic and English on issues relevant to Muslim life in the United States.

The Pendulum Continues to Swing:

Civil Liberties Three Years after September 11

Peverill Squire

The United States is remarkably blessed as countries go—it has historically faced relatively few threats to its security. But at times Americans have felt their existence threatened. Some of these fears proved justifiable, others turned out to be greatly exaggerated. Yet in each instance the federal government responded in a similar way: It acted to curtail individual civil liberties at home so as to reduce the danger to society as a whole. Washington's response to the September 11 terrorist attacks was no exception.

That crises invariably force us to rethink our approach to civil liberties is not surprising. Civil liberties always represent a delicate balancing act between the rights of the individual and the interests of society as a whole. The proper place to strike that balance is always a question over which reasonable people can disagree. And when people fear their security is threatened, they are often willing to give up some of their civil liberties if they believe doing so will bring them greater security. Conversely, when people feel safe, they are likely to bridle at constraints on their personal liberties.

But American history also teaches another lesson when it comes to civil liberties. How far the government can go in curtailing individual freedoms depends on the extent of the threat. So while all crises tend to move the pendulum in the direction of protecting society, they don't all move the pendulum to the same extent. At some points in U.S. history, Washington enacted laws that sharply curtailed the civil liberties of all Americans. At other times, it took steps that severely curtailed the civil liberties of specific groups of Americans. And at still other points, its actions meant only minor restrictions on individual freedoms. With this range of historical possibilities in mind, the steps that Washington took after the September 11 terrorist attacks to restrict civil liberties, while certainly not trivial, fall toward the less drastic end of the continuum. Its more recent actions, however, raise more serious questions.

6-1 Civil Liberties in Times of Crisis

The first example of government sharply curtailing civil liberties came early in the history of the United States. In 1798, many Americans feared war with the French (which never amounted to anything more than a few minor naval skirmishes). Congress passed two laws, known jointly as the Alien and Sedition Acts. One law targeted the 25,000 noncitizens ("aliens") living in the United States. It raised the number of years foreigners had to live in the United States from five to fourteen before they would be eligible for citizenship, and it gave President John Adams the authority (which he never used) to deport any alien he deemed subversive. The sedition law aimed to silence critics of the Adams administration. This law made it illegal for anyone to write, speak, or publish defamatory statements about the federal government. Ten people were convicted under the sedition law. One of them was Matthew Lyon, a member of the U.S. House of Representatives from Vermont who was found guilty of accusing Adams of "ridiculous pomp, foolish adulation, and selfish avarice." (The conviction didn't faze Lyon's constituents; they promptly reelected him to Congress.)

Such harsh restrictions on civil liberties were not confined to the eighteenth century. History

35

repeated itself 120 years later when, amidst the highly charged political atmosphere of World War I and the communist revolution in Russia, Congress passed the Espionage Act. This law made it illegal to interfere with any military activity, including recruitment and induction, or to advocate insubordination or mutiny. The even more sweeping Sedition Act passed a few months later. This law made it illegal to "say, print, write, or publish anything intended to cause contempt or scorn for the federal government, the Constitution, the flag, or the uniform of the armed forces, or to say or write anything that interfered with defense production." Almost 1,000 people were convicted under the Espionage and Sedition Acts. Among them was Eugene V. Debs, the five-time presidential nominee of the Socialist Party. He was found guilty of inciting insubordination in the military by giving a speech in which he declared that it is the "working class who fight all the battles, the working class who make the supreme sacrifices, the working class who freely shed their blood and furnish the corpses, have never yet had a voice in either declaring war or making peace." (Like Matthew Lyon, Debs's political career was not hurt by the conviction. Campaigning from his jail cell, he received 919,000 votes in the 1920 election, the most of any of his five campaigns.)

A few decades later, during World War II, President Franklin Roosevelt ordered the relocation of all people of Japanese ancestry living on the West Coast—more than 100,000 people—to detention camps. (Much smaller numbers of people of German and Italian ancestry were detained as well.) Here, the issue was not that some

residents posed a threat to the United States because they were Japanese citizens—70 percent of the internees were American citizens. Simply being of Japanese descent was enough to lose the rights that all other Americans enjoyed. The internment policy lasted for four years, and most internees lost virtually all of their property and possessions. And they received no relief from the courts. The Supreme Court upheld the legality of the relocation order as well as several other directives that restricted the rights of people of Japanese ancestry. (In 1988, Congress passed a law formally apologizing for the internment and providing financial compensation to the survivors.)

While Washington substantially curtailed people's rights in each of these instances, arguably the most comprehensive dismantling of civil liberties occurred during the Civil War. The Lincoln administration, placing a higher value on saving the Union than on maintaining civil liberties, sanctioned widespread abuses of established rights and procedures. On several occasions, the president or those working on his authority suspended the writ of habeas corpus, or the requirement to bring a prisoner before a judge to determine whether he or she should continue to be held in custody. (The Constitution explicitly allows for suspending the writ of habeas corpus but does not give that power to the president. In fact, the Constitution addresses habeas corpus in Article I, which is devoted to the organization, procedures, and powers of Congress.) During the course of the Civil War, more than 13,000 dissidents and Southern sympathizers were imprisoned. Some were held for long periods without being brought before a judge

and told of the charges or evidence against them. When the chief justice of the Supreme Court declared the president's suspension of the writ of habeas corpus to be unconstitutional, Lincoln simply ignored the ruling.

Other examples of the Lincoln administration trampling on civil liberties abound. Union troops arrested a number of Maryland state legislators to prevent them from voting to allow Maryland to secede from the Union. A member of the U.S. House of Representatives from Ohio was arrested, imprisoned, and ultimately expelled forcibly from Union territory because of his disloyal beliefs and statements. Lincoln's civil liberties record did not go unnoticed. His opponents tried to make an issue of it in the 1864 campaign. But the voters still reelected him.

6-2 Civil Liberties after September 11

President George Bush moved within days of the attacks on the World Trade Center and the Pentagon to push the pendulum away from protecting individual rights and back toward protecting the interests of society as a whole. His administration unveiled draft legislation that proposed changing the laws regarding how the government investigates suspected criminal activity, particularly potential terrorist threats. Most of the ideas in these proposals had been percolating in Washington for years, but a few were entirely new. The administration initially expected that Congress would move rapidly, perhaps in no more than a week, and enact its proposals into law with little or no change.

The bill's passage was not as smooth, however, as the administration had anticipated. In keeping with the old saying that "politics makes for strange bedfellows," an odd coalition of very liberal and very conservative members of Congress formed to criticize the administration's proposals. Although these members disagreed on issues such as tax cuts and health care, they shared a mutual skepticism about giving the federal government more law enforcement powers. They worried that such powers might easily be abused.

These objections slowed down the bill's passage. For several weeks, administration officials and members of Congress conducted intense negotiations over how to revise the bill to address the critics' complaints. These revisions eventually produced a compromise bill that few members were willing to oppose, though many could still point to provisions they did not like. The chair of the Senate Judiciary Committee, Patrick Leahy (D-Vt.), for example, predicted that, "Some of these provisions [in the bill] will face difficult tests in the courts." But he nonetheless pushed for the legislation's passage because he wanted "to preserve national unity in this time of crisis." Ultimately, both houses passed the bill by overwhelming margins: the House by 356 to 66, and the Senate by 98 to 1. President Bush signed the bill into law on October 26, 2001, only five weeks after it was initially proposed.

Formally titled the Uniting and Strengthening America by Providing Appropriate Tools Required to Intercept and Obstruct Terrorism Act but better known by its acronym as the USA Patriot Act, the bill ran 342 pages. It made far-reaching changes and complex additions to existing law. Among its many provisions, it created a new crime, "domestic terrorism." The definition of domestic terrorism was largely borrowed from the existing definition of international terrorism, and it applies to behaviors that "involve acts dangerous to human life that are a violation of the criminal laws of the United States or of any State; appear to be intended to intimidate or coerce a civilian population; to influence the policy of a government by intimidation or coercion; or to affect the conduct of a government by mass destruction, assassination, or kidnapping; and occur primarily within the territorial jurisdiction of the United States." Those found guilty of harboring domestic terrorists are subject to criminal penalties.

This definition of domestic terrorism may sound reasonable and even unobjectionable. Civil libertarians worry, however, that the definition is too broad and vague. They argue that it can be used to indict not only groups that attempt to blow up buildings, which everyone would agree constitutes terrorism, but also groups that are vigorously opposing government policy, which most people would say isn't terrorism. For instance, the pro-life group Operation Rescue and the environmental groups Greenpeace and the Environmental Liberation Front often aggressively protest abortion clinics, missile defense tests, and logging activities by blocking access to buildings and disrupting normal business. These protests could be construed as appearing "to be intended to intimidate or coerce a civilian population" or "to influence the policy of a government by intimidation or coercion." Indeed, concerns about the vagueness of the domestic terrorism language proved so great that many state legislatures declined to include it in the anti-terrorism legislation they passed after September 11.

Another set of provisions in the USA Patriot Act allows the government to more easily engage in "sneak and peek" searches where federal agents with a warrant can enter (either physically or electronically) and examine and take note of various kinds of evidence. With the court's permission, federal agents may delay for days or weeks notifying the subject of the search that his or her effects had been examined. The act also makes it much easier for various government police and intelligence agencies to share information. Information sharing of this sort makes civil libertarians nervous because it raises the possibility that the Central Intelligence Agency will be able to do indirectly what it is now barred by law from doing directly—engaging in domestic spying operations.

Other provisions of the USA Patriot Act make it much easier for federal law enforcement agents to gather various kinds of electronic information, to intercept cell phone conversations, email, and Internet traffic. (Many law enforcement agencies had lobbied for these changes for years because surveillance laws had not kept up with rapid advances in communications technology.) Most of the legal changes making it easier for government to collect electronic information, however, contain a sunset clause, which means these expanded governmental powers will expire at the end of 2005 unless Congress acts to extend them. (President Bush used his 2004 State of the Union Address to try to persuade Congress to renew the expiring provisions a year early.) Finally, noncitizens can be detained for up to seven days without being brought before a judge if the Attorney General certifies that he or she has "reasonable grounds to believe" that the person is a threat to national security.

In addition to the USA Patriot Act, the Bush administration took several other steps after September 11 that worry civil libertarians. Some are high-profile actions, such as the detention of more than 5,000 people, almost all noncitizens, for extended periods following September 11. In most cases, no charges were brought against the detainees linking them to the terrorist acts, or even to any other criminal activity. Nor was the federal government forthcoming about who was being held on what charges.

Another high-profile administration step that caused consternation was the decision to have the Federal Bureau of Investigation and local law enforcement officials interview young Arab and Muslim men about their potential ties to terrorist groups. The Justice Department culled the names of nearly 5,000 potential interviewees from lists of foreigners who had recently entered the United States on temporary visas. In March 2002, the Justice Department announced that it would interview an additional 3,000 young Arab and Muslim men. Attorney General John Ashcroft argued that the effort was needed to generate information about terrorists who might be hiding in immigrant communities. Critics responded that the interviews were not truly voluntary, that they amounted to impermissible "racial profiling" (that is, investigating people based on who they are rather than what they do), and that they would work mostly to intimidate immigrants.

Some of the other measures the Bush administration took at-tracted less attention in the press, but civil libertarians worry that they might constitute possible "slippery slopes." In one instance, public opposition was sufficient to force the federal government to abandon a planned surveillance program. In January 2002, the Bush administration proposed the Terrorism Information and Prevention System (TIPS), a program the Department of Justice would develop in cooperation with several other federal government agencies. TIPS was to be a hotline and web-based reporting system using "those who work in the trucking, maritime, shipping, and mass transit industries" to report "suspicious, publicly observable activity that could be related to terrorism." The idea was that a single national system would collect tips about possible terrorist activities from people such as UPS drivers (Big Brown!) and disseminate that information to federal, state, and local law enforcement agencies.

Although TIPS initially enjoyed the support of the White House, it encountered considerable resistance from Democrats and Republicans on Capitol Hill. Senator Leahy failed in his bid to persuade the Senate to stop TIPS from going into effect. Opponents had more success in the House. Representative Dick Armey (R-Texas), the House majority leader, opposed TIPS because he believed it would encourage "Americans to spy on one another." He used his clout to pass a legislative provision prohibiting the federal government from implementing TIPS.

Civil libertarians expressed even greater worries about another government project, the Total Information Awareness (TIA) program. TIA was the brainchild of the Defense Advanced Research Projects Agency, a unit of the Department of Defense. The idea was to pull together into one giant database all the information the government can gather from existing government and private sector data banks. Then the government would use sophisticated "data mining" software programs that would scour the compiled records looking for patterns that might indicate someone is involved in terrorist activities. Critics opposed letting the government rummage through people's student transcripts, loan applications, criminal and civil judicial records, credit card purchases, web-surfing records, telephone bills, travel records, medical histories, and the like. They said it would constitute a massive invasion of personal privacy that could easily lead to abuse—and that it would be far more likely to finger innocent people than hardened terrorists.

TIA generated vehement opposition from both liberal Democrats and conservative Republicans. Notable among the latter group was William Safire, a *New York Times* columnist and veteran of the Nixon White House. He characterized TIA as "a supersnoop's dream" on par with George Orwell's nightmare scenario in *1984*. As part of the final deal on the 2003 federal budget, the House and Senate agreed to a proposal advanced by Senators Grassley (R-Iowa) and Wyden (D-Ore.) prohibiting TIA from being used against American citizens and cutting off funding for the program completely unless the Defense Department could justify its cost, goals, impact on civil liberties, and likely success in fighting terrorists. Then, in September 2003, Congress tightened the funding restriction further. It barred almost all spending on the program, which by that time had been renamed the Terrorists Information Awareness program. In May 2004, a federal advisory committee established by the Defense Department recommended that Congress pass laws requiring federal agencies to safeguard the privacy of American citizens when they used data mining to identify terrorists.

6-3 What the Public Thinks about the Threat to Civil Liberties

Although civil libertarians have warned about the dangers they see in the USA Patriot Act and other governmental actions since September 11, most Americans support the steps that the Bush administration has taken. As Table 6-1 shows, as the first anniversary of the September 11 attacks approached, almost 50 percent of Americans surveyed thought that the war on terrorism justified new government limitations on civil liberties. Only 38 percent expressed concern that the government would go too far in its efforts. Other surveys showed that Americans were consciously willing to sacrifice some of their civil liberties to gain greater security against terrorist threats.

But that is not to say that Americans are willing to sacrifice all of their liberties to support the fight against terrorism. One proposal being floated is to require Americans to carry a national identity card, something required of citizens in many other democracies. The idea, which Congress rejected in the late 1970s, has never been popular in the United States. Civil libertarians object to national identity cards for several reasons. One is that this system won't work. Criminals and terrorists would be able to obtain such cards illegally, just as they obtain

Table 6-1	Public Opinion on Restricting Civil Liberties in the Fight against Terrorism

"Do you think it is necessary to give up some civil liberties in order to make the country safe from terrorism, or do you think some of the government's proposals will go too far in restricting the public's civil liberties?"

	Percent Agreeing
Necessary to give up some civil liberties	49%
Government will go too far	38%
Don't know	13%

Source: Los Angeles Times Poll, conducted August 22–25, 2002. N = 1,372 adults nationwide.

Table 6-2	Public Opinion on National Identity Cards

"Would you favor or oppose the following measures to curb terrorism: Requiring that all citizens carry a national identity card at all times to show to a police officer on request?"

	Percent Who		
	Favor	Oppose	Don't Know
Mid-August 2002	58%	38%	3%
Mid-September 2001	70%	26%	4%

Source: Pew Research Center for the People and the Press, poll conducted August 14–25, 2002. N = 500 adults nationwide.

fake driver's licenses and birth certificates today. More important, national identity cards would allow the government to create a central database on Americans, potentially raising concerns about surveillance of ordinary citizens by "big brother." Such concerns may explain the reservations many Americans have about a national identity card. As Table 6-2 shows, support for such a card has declined to 58 percent of Americans, down substantially from the 70 percent in favor just after the attacks.

The Defense Department's Total Information Awareness program also disturbed many people, as Table 6-3 reveals. About one third of Americans knew too little about the program to express an opinion. But among

those who were aware of it, more than half were uncomfortable with the idea of government collecting extensive records on their personal behavior. Democrats and Independents, however, expressed greater reservations than did Republicans, most of whom were inclined to support the program.

6-4 Civil Liberties in Historical Perspective

American history is replete with examples of government acting, sometimes none too wisely, to curtail civil liberties when national security is thought to be threatened. Many people worry that Washington's response to the September 11 terrorist attacks foreshadows a similar shift. Most Americans see little change in

| Table 6-3 | Public Opinion on the Total Information Awareness Program |

"The Department of Defense is developing a program which could compile information from sources such as phone calls, emails, web searches, financial records, purchases, school records, medical records and travel histories to provide a database of information about individuals in the United States. Supporters of the system say that it will provide a powerful tool for hunting terrorists. Opponents say it is an invasion of individual privacy by the government. Based on what you just heard, are you inclined to support this program, or inclined to oppose it, or haven't you heard enough about it to say?"

	All	Democrats	Independents	Republicans
Inclined to support	31%	18%	30%	50%
Inclined to oppose	36%	42%	40%	22%
Haven't heard enough	28%	34%	26%	25%
Don't know	5%	6%	4%	3%

Source: Los Angeles Times Poll, conducted December 12–15, 2002. N = 1,305 adults nationwide.

their own lives. This is not surprising because many of the changes on the civil liberties front affect primarily foreigners living in the United States. They clearly enjoy fewer protections today than they did before September 11.

But the USA Patriot Act and other government measures do have some potential to affect the lives of American citizens as well. Like any law, the USA Patriot Act may produce unintended consequences. Whether it does will depend on how aggressive law enforcement officials are in interpreting the law, as well as how threatened Americans feel by terrorists.

But what is perhaps more striking about America's civil liberties since September 11 is how little they have changed. Unlike many previous episodes in U.S. history, we have not experienced a sharp restriction in civil liberties. Our First Amendment free speech rights have not been threatened, and the debates about how far Washington can go in curtailing civil liberties have been robust. So although we may be on a slippery slope as some civil libertarians warn, three years after the attacks on the World Trade Center and the Pentagon, that slope appears to be gentle. But recent threats to civil liberties, particularly the TIA, raise serious questions about how the relationship between Americans and their government might change in the future.

Readings for Further Study

Doyle, Charles. 2001. "Terrorism: Section by Section Analysis of the USA Patriot Act." *CRS Report for Congress.* Congressional Research Service. December 10. Available at http://fpc.state.gov/documents/organization/7952.pdf

McClintock, Michael, and others. 2002. *A Year of Loss: Reexamining Civil Liberties Since September 11.* New York: Lawyers Committee for Human Rights. Available at http://www.lchr.org/us_law/loss/loss_report.pdf

Posner, Richard A. 2001. "Security Versus Civil Liberties." *Atlantic Monthly* 288 (December): 46–48. Available at http://www.theatlantic.com/issues/2001/12/posner.htm

Weich, Ronald. 2001. *Upsetting Checks and Balances: Congressional Hostility toward the Courts in Times of Crisis.* Washington, D.C.: American Civil Liberties Union.

Site name: IWS—The Information Warfare Site

URL: http://www.iwar.org.uk/news-archive/tia/total-information-awareness.htm

This online resource on the subject of information security provides a variety of primary documents on the Total (Terrorist) Information Awareness Program.

Site name: Cato Institute

URL: http://www.cato.org

This conservative think tank with a libertarian orientation offers arguments against the Total (Terrorist) Information Awareness Program.

Site name: Wikipedia—The Free Encyclopedia

URL: http://en.wikipedia.org/wiki/Total_Information_Awareness

This free Internet encyclopedia offers information about and links to websites about the Total (Terrorist) Information Awareness Program.

Websites to Check Out

Note: As we went to press, these sites were functional using the URLs provided. Check out the online text for the most up-to-date URLs.

Racial Profiling Meets the War on Terrorism

James M. Lindsay

Should a frail seventy-year-old woman be given the same scrutiny at an airport security gate as a strapping twenty-five-year-old Middle Eastern–looking man? Or should law enforcement officials look more closely at passengers who resemble the perpetrators of the September 11 attacks, all of whom were Arabs and Muslims? These questions raise the volatile issue of racial profiling—using considerations of race, ethnicity, and national origin to help law enforcement officers decide which people to investigate.

The argument for racial profiling at airport security gates begins with three simple observations. First, metal detectors, bomb "sniffers," and other electronic screening devices that can survey all passengers miss far too often. Second, subjecting every passenger to a personal search is impractical. Third, anything that increases the odds of catching a terrorist means saving hundreds, and perhaps even thousands, of lives. So if potential terrorists have a distinct race, ethnicity, or national origin, taking these criteria into account is only sensible. Doing so enables law enforcement to target its efforts where they are most likely to pay off. All law-abiding citizens benefit, even those who belong to the groups singled out by the profiles.

Although the argument for racial profiling is easy to state, it is not irrefutable. Critics see two flaws. First, racial profiling does not work. It casts its net far too widely, making it more likely to point the finger of suspicion at someone who has done no wrong than at someone who is plotting evil. It also encourages law enforcement "to fight the last war." Police focus on the nationalities of the last set of terrorists and miss the activities of individuals whose race, ethnicity, or national origin does not fit the profile. Second, even if racial profiling worked, many critics argue it violates any sense of fairness. It targets who people are, not what they are doing.

The legal and political status of racial profiling is complicated. The courts have made clear that relying solely on race, ethnicity, or national origin to catch terrorists—or any criminal for that matter—is unconstitutional. But if profiling uses these criteria in a longer list of factors for identifying suspects, it may be legal under some circumstances. The political debate follows the same line of division. Virtually everyone in American political life opposes racial profiling if it means relying solely on race, ethnicity, or national origin. But considerable difference of opinion exists on the question of whether it is permissible to use these factors along with other criteria. And there are no signs that this difference of opinion will be settled anytime soon.

7-1 "Driving While Black"

Questions about the propriety of racial profiling predate September 11. Profiling emerged as a hot political issue in the late 1990s when a lawsuit against the New Jersey State Police drew attention to the fact that Blacks constituted 13 percent of the drivers on the New Jersey turnpike but 53 percent of the consensual drug searches conducted during traffic stops on the turnpike. Nor was New Jersey alone. The state of Maryland lost a lawsuit in which its state police were accused of stopping Black motorists disproportionately. These and other incidents popularized talk in the African-American community of being charged with DWB—"Driving While Black."

Critics attack racial profiling—whether it targets Blacks or other minority groups—for both

43

practical and principled reasons. With regard to the former, critics argue that it is an ineffective law enforcement tool at best and counterproductive at worst. They note that no systematic studies have been done that show it works. At the same time, because most members of the targeted group are not criminals, ethnic and racial profiling inevitably focuses too much attention on people who have done nothing wrong. Such treatment imposes an emotional cost on those individuals. It also drives a wedge between police and part of the community they are pledged to protect because these groups come to see law enforcement officers not as protectors but as harassers. That can frustrate police efforts to stop and solve crimes.

But many opponents would not endorse ethnic and racial profiling even if it were shown to reduce crime. For them, it is fundamentally illegitimate because it targets people based on who they are rather than what they do. The Fourteenth Amendment to the U.S. Constitution guarantees all Americans equal treatment under the law. It is grossly unfair, therefore, say the critics, to single out any group of people for greater government law enforcement scrutiny based on their race and ethnicity. Unlike an individual's conduct, race and ethnicity are immutable characteristics that people cannot alter to avoid attracting government attention.

These two criticisms—and especially the criticism based on fairness—have won considerable political support. President Bill Clinton condemned racial and ethnic profiling as a "morally indefensible, deeply corrosive practice." Vice President Al Gore pledged during the 2000 presidential campaign that he would see to it that the first civil rights law of the twenty-first century banned racial profiling. George W. Bush also joined the cause. He used his first State of the Union address to say that "racial profiling is wrong and we will end it in America." Bush reportedly became a convert to the anti-profiling cause during a campaign visit to a small Iowa town. Local Hispanics told him that they were repeatedly stopped simply for being Hispanic. Their point was driven home when the town's police stopped one of Bush's advance men, who was a Latino.

7-2 The Argument for Racial Profiling

The practice of singling out people for investigation solely on the basis of their race and ethnicity has no respectable support. The practice of using race or ethnicity as one factor among many in law enforcement operations, however, does have many supporters. They defend the practice on several grounds. First, they argue that it is common sense. They point out that statistics show that members of some groups are more likely to commit certain types of crimes than members of other groups. For instance, young Black males commit a disproportionate share of the street crime in the United States. So taking race into account in crime fighting is merely a matter of playing the percentages. (Defenders of profiling usually note in this regard that the Rev. Dr. Jesse Jackson admitted engaging in his own racial profiling. In 1993 he said, "There is nothing more painful to me at this stage in my life than to walk down the street and hear footsteps and start to think robbery and then look around and see somebody white and feel relieved.")

Second, defenders argue that although racial profiling takes race (or ethnicity and national origin) into account, it is not motivated by bigotry. They note that the race or ethnicity relevant to an investigation will vary with the circumstances. If the issue is cocaine, police might focus on Mexicans or Colombians because Mexican and Colombian gangs are heavily involved in cocaine trafficking. If it is a question of heroin trafficking, profiles might target Asians because much of America's heroin comes from East Asia. And if the concern is neo-Nazi violence, being White would become a factor in a profile.

Third, defenders say that when used properly—that is, in conjunction with other factors that might indicate criminal intent—racial profiling works. This assessment is not based on scientific study; again, no definitive research has been done. Rather, it is based on personal experience. Defenders acknowledge that even when used properly, racial profiling imposes a cost on innocent people who otherwise fit the profiling criteria. They argue, however, that the price these individuals pay pales in comparison to the benefits that society reaps by having an effective crime-fighting tool.

7-3 "Flying While Arab"

Law enforcement operations that singled out African Americans for special scrutiny dominated the racial profiling debate before September 11. After the terrorist attacks, however, talk quickly switched to whether profiles that took into account whether people boarding planes were Arabs and Muslims would help catch terrorists. The news media reported numerous instances of airline personnel suddenly asking Middle Eastern–looking passengers to leave their planes or to submit to extra questioning. None of these episodes led to the apprehension of a terrorist. All the individuals targeted were law-abiding people seeking what all airline passengers want—to get to their destination safely and with minimum hassle. Because these actions stopped no terrorist plots, talk began that the airlines were singling out people for FWA—"Flying While Arab."

These incidents were annoying, and possibly even traumatic, for the individuals who found themselves singled out. At the same time, however, these incidents all involved uncoordinated and impromptu decisions by individual airline personnel to scrutinize specific passengers. The broader question is whether such ad hoc considerations of ethnicity and race should be done systematically. Specifically, should the federal government make race and ethnic origin part of a little-known profiling process in place at all U.S. airports?

The profiling process in question is the Computer-Assisted Passenger Prescreening System (CAPPS). It was created in the aftermath of the midair explosion of TWA Flight 800 off Long Island in July 1996. Although a mechanical problem caused the plane to explode, terrorism was suspected initially. So President Bill Clinton put Vice President Al Gore in charge of a special White House commission to write new rules for airline safety. One of its recommendations was the creation of CAPPS. The idea was to use known information about each passenger—such as their names, addresses, where and how they bought their tickets—to discern a pattern that might suggest someone is a terrorist. The underlying assumption is that terrorists tend to act in distinctive ways—such as paying cash at the last moment for one-way tickets.

When word leaked out that the Gore Commission was debating whether to recommend a profiling system, civil liberties groups and Arab and Muslim organizations immediately protested. These protests may not have had any effect on the commission's recommendations; many of the commission members opposed racial profiling to begin with. In any event, the final Gore Commission recommendation said explicitly, "No profile should contain or be based on . . . race, religion, or national origin." And before the Federal Aviation System put CAPPS into operation, the Justice Department's Civil Rights Division certified that the CAPPS criteria "do not consider passengers' race, color, national or ethnic origin, religion or gender," or even "names or modes of dress." (The criteria that CAPPS uses are kept secret for a reason; if terrorists knew what was in the profile, they would change their behavior to avoid detection.)

CAPPS was operating on September 11. It reportedly flagged six of the nineteen hijackers for extra scrutiny. This information turned up no evidence of the terrorist plot, however, because of the way airport security officials used the CAPPS conclusions. Civil liberties groups and Arab and Muslim organizations had worried that even if ethnicity and national origin were not used as criteria, CAPPS might disproportionately single out Arab and Muslim passengers. (This could happen if, say, one of the criteria in the profile was recent travel to the Middle East, which Arab and Muslim passengers might be more likely to do.) So they persuaded the federal government not to use CAPPS to decide which passengers should be singled out for intrusive searches of their clothing or carry-on bags. Instead, passengers that CAPPS flagged would have their checked luggage quietly subjected to special screening.

The decision not to use CAPPS to decide which individuals to interview reflected two judgments. First, the system would produce a high number of "false positives," that is, people who were law-abiding travelers. Second, no one would try to destroy a plane that he or she was traveling on. September 11 showed that this latter judgment was disastrously wrong. However, even if CAPPS had been used to decide whom to subject to intensive personal searches, the September 11 attacks still might not have been prevented. At the time, FAA rules did not prohibit airline passengers from carrying small knives in their carry-on baggage.

Calls for rethinking the reluctance to include race, national or ethnic origin, and religion in the CAPPS criteria became popular after September 11. Nonetheless, the Bush administration showed no interest in adding any of these factors to the system. Secretary of Transportation Norman Mineta repeatedly criticized racial profiling and told one interviewer that he believed that a seventy-year-old White woman should be scrutinized just as closely as a young Muslim man. And the FAA's rules for airport security screeners still forbid them from using a passenger's outward characteristics—skin color, dress, accent, and the like—in deciding whom to search. Indeed, to avoid claims of discrimination, U.S. airport screeners continue to select passengers for thorough searches on a random basis. Defenders of racial profiling argue that random searches waste scarce law enforcement resources because screeners must check people who are obviously not terrorists—for example, the young mother traveling with two small children. Critics of racial profiling argue that random searches are in keeping with America's egalitarian principles.

7-4 Profiling and the Courts

What is the legality of racial profiling? As President Bush's pledge to end the practice suggests, it is legal under at least some circumstances. What those circumstances are and whether they should matter are issues of contention.

Ever since the civil rights revolution, the U.S. Supreme Court has subjected laws and practices that differentiate among people on the basis of race, ethnicity, or national origin to so-called strict scrutiny. This is the most demanding standard for judicial review. It holds that the classification scheme is unconstitutional unless the government can show it serves a "compelling" government objective and is "narrowly tailored" to achieve that end. Government profiling that considers only race or ethnicity flunks the strict scrutiny test almost by definition because it is not narrowly tailored.

But classification schemes that look only at race or national origin are the easy cases. The tougher question is whether racial profiling is constitutional if race, ethnicity, or national origin is only one among many factors in the profile. This is precisely the situation raised by proposals to inject racial and ethnic considerations into deciding whom to subject to intrusive searches at airports. The argument is not that all people of Arab descent should be frisked. Instead, it is that Arabs (and Muslims) who also meet certain other criteria, such as paying cash for a ticket or traveling recently to a Middle Eastern country, should be scrutinized more closely.

When the question has been phrased in this fashion, the courts have tended not to see a constitutional violation as long as the profiling serves a legitimate law enforcement purpose. In the 1992 case *United States v. Weaver*, for example, the Eighth Circuit Court of Appeals ruled that a Drug Enforcement Agency (DEA) officer in Kansas City committed no constitutional violation when he stopped a suspected drug courier in part because he was Black. The DEA agent said he considered several other factors as well: The suspect had just gotten off a plane from Los Angeles (LA gangs were known to be trying to set up drug operations in Kansas City); he was young (as most drug runners are); he paid for his ticket in cash (which criminals often do to avoid leaving a paper trail of their activities); and he carried no checked baggage, only two carry-ons (which held cocaine). The court concluded that although law enforcement officers should not regard entire groups of Americans "as presumptively criminal based on race," the facts of disproportionate Black involvement in drug crime "are not to be ignored simply because they are unpleasant." The U.S. Supreme Court has not endorsed this decision, but neither has the Court rejected it.

7-5 Public Assessments

What does the American public think about using racial profiling in the war on terrorism? The answer depends on when the question was asked. Polls taken in the days immediately following September 11 show the greatest support. A Gallup poll taken on September 14–15, 2001, found that 58 percent of those surveyed supported "requiring Arabs, including those who are U.S. citizens, to undergo special, more intensive security checks before boarding airplanes in the United States"; 41 percent were opposed. A *Los Angeles Times* poll taken at the same time found that 68 percent agreed (41 percent strongly) that "law enforcement should be allowed to randomly stop people who may fit the profile of suspected terrorists."

Polls taken only a few weeks later, however, found Americans essentially split on the merits of racial profiling. A series of polls that Zogby International conducted in late September and early October 2001 consistently found that 50–55 percent of those surveyed opposed "any policy that singles out Arab Americans for special scrutiny at airport check-ins"; only 40–45 percent supported the idea. Conversely, an ABC News poll in early October found that 51 percent supported and 45 percent opposed making "being Arab or Muslim" a "part of the profile of a suspected terrorist." A November *Los Angeles Times* poll found that 49 percent disapproved of allowing law enforcement "to stop people whose ethnicity resembles that of the terrorists," and 47 percent approved. And when another November 2001 poll asked (without any reference to terrorism) about the merits of racial profiling, 43 percent said it was "un-American, unconstitutional and plain wrong," while 45 percent said "law enforcement officials must use whatever actions necessary to stop crime and protect American citizens."

Analysis of the poll results shows that Republicans look more favorably on racial profiling, whereas Democrats and Independents look less favorably on it. Whites also tend to be more supportive than Blacks. These differences contain a considerable irony. As the legal scholar Randall Kennedy points out, these groups swap viewpoints on the merits of discriminating on the basis of race and ethnicity when it comes to affirmative action. On that issue, Democrats and African Americans generally believe that taking race and ethnicity into account is permissible and even laudable. Conversely, Republicans and Whites tend to oppose efforts to make race or ethnicity a factor in hiring or college admissions. This is not to say that these groups are hypocritical. Rather, their assessments about the extent to which the government should take racial and ethnic consideration vary with the results they think are being achieved.

7-6 A Continuing Debate

Like affirmative action, the debate over ethnic and racial profiling will not be easily settled. Opponents insist that it harms the public good by unfairly stigmatizing entire groups of people for the acts of a few individuals. Supporters counter that it serves the public good by potentially saving thousands, perhaps even tens of thousands, of lives. Different people will come to different judgments on how to weigh these competing impulses—the right of individuals not to be singled out for government attention by virtue of who they are versus the right of society to be safe from attack.

The debate might be settled if the effectiveness of racial profiling in preventing terrorist attacks—as well as its collateral costs to law-abiding travelers mistakenly singled out for scrutiny—could be established with some confidence. If it could be shown that profiling substantially improved the chances of catching terrorists, and its costs to the members of groups included in the profile were low, some critics might drop their opposition. (Of course, this would not change the minds of those who oppose profiling on principle.) By the same token, if it could be shown that racial profiling does not work, the case for using it evaporates.

But a definitive test that establishes the effectiveness of racial profiling probably cannot be done. One obstacle is that profiling cannot be assessed until it is instituted, and opponents vehemently oppose trying it. Another problem is that terrorist hijackings are rare events. As a result, the fact that racial profiling fails to identify a terrorist may not mean the tool is ineffective; there may not have been an attack to stop. A third problem is establishing an appropriate level of cost. How many false positives are an acceptable price to pay to stop a terrorist attack? Is a ratio of 1,000-to-1 acceptable? What about 100,000-to-1? Or 1,000,000-to-1?

Of course, defenders say that the minor inconvenience of an intrusive search at an airport security gate is a small price to pay for a safe flight. But some travelers—say, Arab Americans whose jobs require them to travel around the country—could find themselves repeatedly singled out for inspection. They probably would see the inconvenience as substantial.

So the debate over racial profiling is likely to continue. It is worth noting, however, that profiling is not a magic bullet. Profiles are designed to identify people who might be more likely than the average person to be a terrorist. No one claims profiles can identify who is a terrorist. At the same time, profiles may have short shelf lives. Over time, terrorists learn which criteria are included in the profile and then change their operations so that they don't match the profile.

Terrorists can even change such immutable traits as race and ethnicity by changing who they send on a mission. In the 1970s, for instance, Palestinian terrorist groups increasingly found themselves stymied by law enforcement officials on the lookout for suspicious Palestinians. So they turned to Western terrorists such as the Venezuelan Illich Ramirez Sanchez—better known as Carlos the Jackal—to carry out their operations. Al Qaeda and affiliated organizations could easily employ the same tactic. Indeed, they appear to have done so already. Richard Reid, the so-called shoe bomber who tried to blow up a transatlantic flight bound for Miami, reportedly was acting at the behest of Al Qaeda. He was not Arab. Rather, he was a British citizen of Jamaican parentage.

Readings for Further Study

Kennedy, Randall. 1999. "Suspect Policy." *New Republic*. September 13–20: 30–35.

MacDonald, Heather. 2003. *Are Cops Racist?* Chicago: Ivan R. Dee.

Taylor, Stuart, Jr. 2003. "Right, Liberties, and Security." In *Agenda for the Nation*, Ed. Henry J. Aaron, James M. Lindsay, and Pietro S. Nivola. Washington, D.C.: Brookings Institution Press.

Websites to Check Out

Note: As we went to press, these sites were functional using the URLs provided. Check out the online text for the most up-to-date URLs.

Site name: American Civil Liberties Union
URL: http://www.aclu.org
The American Civil Liberties Union, America's foremost civil liberties organization, provides a wealth of material on civil liberties issues, including racial profiling and immigrants' rights.

Site name: EthnicMajority.com—Racial Profiling
URL: http://www.ethnicmajority.com/racial_profiling.htm
A list of news stories on racial profiling, plus links to several organizations active on the issue.

Site name: Yahoo! News—Racial Profiling
URL: http://news.yahoo.com/fc?tmpl=fc&cid=34&in=us&cat=racial_profiling
A list of recent news stories on racial profiling, plus links to websites that discuss racial profiling issues.

Apathy and Interest:

The American Public Rediscovers Foreign Policy after September 11

James M. Lindsay

How did September 11 change the politics of foreign policy in the United States? To answer this question, we obviously need to know how public attitudes changed in the wake of the attacks on the World Trade Center and the Pentagon. Even more important, we need to understand the relationship between what Americans think about the world abroad and what their elected representatives do.

Politicians seldom look to the public for guidance on what to do abroad. The average citizen lacks the detailed knowledge needed to recommend specific policy choices. This does not mean, however, that the public is irrelevant. Rather, its impact on foreign policy is both more subtle and profound. Much as climate shapes the buildings that architects design or terrain shapes how generals fight battles, public opinion shapes the environment in which politicians operate. That is, public opinion influences how politicians address foreign-policy issues or whether they address them at all.

This lesson is crucial to grasp because the public's foreign-policy attitudes have changed over the past two decades, and foreign-policy making has changed as a result. When the Soviet Union collapsed and the Cold War ended in 1991, Americans did not embrace isolationism as many expected. They instead remained internationalist in outlook. What changed was that foreign policy tumbled down their list of priorities. At the very moment that the United States had more influence than ever on world affairs, Americans saw little in the world abroad that concerned them. The result was the rise of apathetic internationalism—a general belief that the United States should play a leading role in world affairs combined with a lack of interest with whether, or how, it did.

Apathetic internationalism reshaped the politics of American foreign policy in the 1990s. It encouraged politicians to neglect foreign affairs, distorted policy choices to favor the noisy few over the quiet many, and made American foreign policy more capricious and inconsistent. But September 11 made foreign policy a priority once again for the American public and for politicians as well. In doing so, it greatly strengthened the White House's say in foreign policy. The question that remains is how long America's newfound interest in events abroad will last.

8-1 Public Opinion before September 11

How much influence does public opinion have on American foreign policy? The answer depends on answering two other questions. First, what do the American people want their government to accomplish abroad? Second, how much do Americans actually care about foreign policy?

8-1a Isolationism or Internationalism?

With the end of the Cold War, many pundits warned that Americans would return to their isolationist past. Americans supposedly wanted to focus their energies on problems at home and turn their backs on the outside world. Some commentators went so far as to argue that there is a deep strain in American political life that is suspicious of the outside world and committed to an anti-internationalist, unilateralist approach to foreign policy. With a looming foreign threat no longer forcing Americans to engage abroad, the argument went, suspicion of foreign do-gooding would reemerge and intensify.

Predictions of the death of internationalism were greatly exaggerated, however. Polls showed that Americans overwhelmingly continued to support an internationalist foreign policy. Figure 8-1 shows the public's responses over a half century to a standard polling question: "Do you think it will be best for the future of this country if we take an active part in world affairs or if we stay out of world affairs?" Throughout the 1990s, a majority of Americans favored taking an active role in world affairs. And although the percentage of Americans saying "take an active part" was slightly lower in the 1990s than in the 1950s, they still outnumbered those saying "stay out" by nearly two to one.

The public's broad internationalist inclinations in the 1990s carried over to questions about activism to specific issues. Gallup found that public support for "U.S. participation in NATO air strikes in Yugoslavia" in 1999 reached as high as 61 percent and never fell below 50 percent. Despite fears that the American public had turned against free trade, a February 2000 poll by the Pew Research Center found that 64 percent of Americans believed that free trade is good for the country and 62 percent said the same about U.S. membership in the World Trade Organization (WTO), the multilateral body that sets and administers the rules for international trade. These numbers were virtually unchanged from what Pew and other polling organizations found before an alliance of environmental, human rights, and labor groups grabbed headlines by disrupting a WTO

summit meeting in Seattle in December 1999.

Americans also remained believers in multilateralism, that is, working with other countries to solve common problems. A 1998 poll conducted for the Chicago Council on Foreign Relations found that 72 percent of Americans believed that the United States should not act in international crises if it did not have the support of its allies. This multilateralist preference included support for international organizations. Public opinion polls done in the 1990s repeatedly showed that substantial majorities of Americans preferred to strengthen international institutions such as the United Nations and the WTO. Indeed, one poll by the Program on International Policy Attitudes found that two-thirds of those surveyed supported creating an International Criminal Court, even after they were told the reasons the U.S. government opposed it.

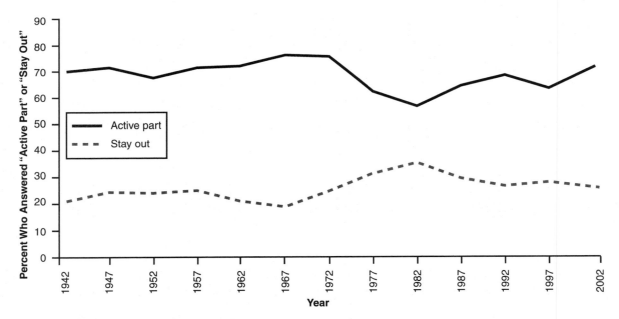

Figure 8-1 Public opinion on U.S. activity in world affairs. *Polling question:* "Do you think it will be best for the future of this country if we take an active part in world affairs or if we stay out of world affairs?"

Source: Data provided by the Program on International Policy Attitudes and based on responses to questions asked by various polling organizations.

The results at the ballot box substantiated the poll results. George W. Bush and Al Gore both staked out mainstream internationalist positions on foreign policy during the 2000 presidential campaign. The two leading third-party candidates, Pat Buchanan and Ralph Nader, staked out policy positions that were decidedly more isolationist and protectionist. Yet Bush and Gore took 96 percent of the votes cast in 2000, and Buchanan and Nader only 3 percent. And although being major party candidates gave Bush and Gore an advantage in winning votes, both men had every reason to adopt positions popular with the voters. The fact that they shunned isolationism and protectionism suggests they understood what the public did and didn't want.

8-1b Apathy or Interest?

Knowing what the public thinks about foreign policy tells only part of the story. Just as important is how intensely it holds its preferences. And here public attitudes changed substantially in the 1990s.

As Figure 8-2 shows, during the first two decades of the Cold War, foreign policy topped the public's list of concerns. Upward of 50 percent of respondents regularly named foreign-policy issues as the most important problem facing the country. Foreign-policy concerns ebbed after the Vietnam War as international tensions declined and the Cold War consensus over American foreign policy broke down. Still, in the 1970s and 1980s, 20 to 30 percent of respondents regularly told polling organizations that a foreign-policy issue was the most important problem facing the country.

With the end of the Cold War, public interest in foreign policy dropped nearly to zero. As

Figure 8-2 shows, when pollsters asked people in the 1990s what was the most important problem facing the United States, only about 5 percent named a foreign-policy issue. Simply put, with the Soviet threat gone, Americans were much more worried about what was happening at home than what was happening abroad.

The conclusion that in the 1990s Americans lost interest in events overseas held up even when pollsters focused specifically on foreign policy. Many Americans had trouble identifying any foreign-policy issues that worried them. The 1998 Chicago Council on Foreign Relations poll asked people to name "two or three of the biggest foreign-policy problems facing the United States today." The most common response by far, at 21 percent, was "don't know." No doubt swayed by unprecedented peace abroad and prosperity at home, Americans were similarly skeptical that much of what happened overseas would affect their lives. When asked to assess how much impact

the rest of the world had on the United States, solid majorities of Americans answered "very little." In one Pew poll, for example, 60 percent said that western Europe—home to most of America's major allies and a market for many U.S. firms—had little or no impact on their lives.

So in the 1990s, Americans became apathetic internationalists. They understood in the abstract that the United States had important interests abroad and should be engaged in the world, but they didn't see much to worry about. After all, the United States was an unchallenged superpower, it had a vibrant economy, and far more than any other country could shape its own destiny. Why worry when things were going so well?

8-2 Consequences of Apathetic Internationalism

By itself, the public's apathetic internationalism was nothing to

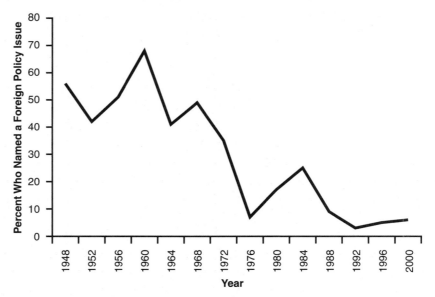

Figure 8-2 Public perception of the most important problem facing the United States, presidential election years.

Source: The Gallup Organization, various years.

decry. If politicians in Washington agreed on America's role in the world, public apathy might even have been a good thing. They could have enacted their agenda confident the public would follow their lead.

The problem in the 1990s was there was no such consensus. Republicans and Democrats, realists and neo-conservatives, isolationists and internationalists continually bickered over what should replace containment as the cornerstone of American foreign policy. Just as important, foreign policy ranked relatively low with American political leaders. Bill Clinton arrived at the White House committed to concentrating on domestic issues, and during his presidency, he addressed foreign-policy issues episodically and reactively. Interest in foreign affairs was even lower on Capitol Hill. As a result, political leadership that might have overcome the public's apathy was not to be found.

The political elite's diminished interest in foreign affairs was itself no accident. Public opinion shapes which politicians are elected as well as what they pay attention to and what they do. Politicians naturally gravitate toward issues that voters care about. The reason lies in a basic rule of politics: How many people line up on each side of an issues matters less than how intensely each side holds its opinions. Politicians know that opposing impassioned voters may mean looking for a new job. So silent majorities are ignored. In politics, as in the rest of life, squeaky wheels get the grease.

Thus, the rise of apathetic internationalism encouraged American politicians to neglect foreign affairs. Most foreign-policy issues offered no political payoff from

the average voter. That was clear during the 2000 presidential campaign. Although Vice President Al Gore presumably had an edge in foreign affairs given his vastly greater experience, both candidates largely avoided the topic. Their pollsters saw the unmistakable message in Figure 8-2—foreign policy was not on the minds of the voters. And they were right. During the town-hall style format of the third Bush-Gore debate, not one of the citizen-questioners asked about foreign policy.

When politicians did address foreign-policy issues, they often did so to satisfy interest group demands. Ethnic, commercial, and ideological groups were willing to reward or punish politicians when the broader public wasn't. The result was what one former U.S. ambassador called "the franchising of foreign policy." Groups came to dominate specific issues and drive the agenda. Indian-Americans used their growing political clout to block efforts to persuade Congress to condemn Pakistani "aggression" in Kashmir. Human rights activists, labor unions, and environmentalists kept President Clinton from winning authority to negotiate new trade deals that would receive privileged consideration on Capitol Hill. Conservative groups turned U.S. participation in UN peacekeeping missions into political poison.

Of course, interest groups have always sought to influence U.S. foreign policy. What changed in the 1990s was that the political fear of being seen as pandering to narrow interests declined. The broad public cannot punish behavior it does not notice. And if no one opposes narrow interests, politicians may come to equate them with the broad public inter-

est. As former Representative Lee H. Hamilton (D-Ind.) described his former colleagues: "Too many people place constituent interests above national interests. They don't see much difference between lobbying for highway funds and slanting foreign policy toward a particular interest group." The not-too-surprising result was that American foreign policy in the 1990s was often inconsistent and shortsighted.

8-3 September 11

September 11 shattered the basic premise of apathetic internationalism—that what happens outside America's borders matters little for our lives. Foreign policy suddenly became a top priority. Not surprisingly, many interest groups found themselves pushed toward the sidelines, and power swung sharply back toward the White House.

Shortly after the attacks, Gallup found that two out of every three Americans named terrorism, national security, or war as the most important problem facing the United States. Foreign policy reached this level of political salience only twice before since the advent of scientific polling—during the early stages of both the Korean and Vietnam wars. Equally important, Americans did not react to the attacks by seeking to withdraw from the world, as Figure 8-1 shows. In November 2001, 81 percent of those polled agreed that it would be "best for the future of the country if we take an active part in world affairs." This marked the highest percentage favoring active engagement ever recorded. Seven months later, this figure had fallen only slightly, to 71 percent. Nor was the public's reaction to September 11 particularly unilateralist or militaristic. Nearly three in four told Pew "it would be better if more countries would join with" the U.S. military operations in Afghanistan. And 86 percent favored—57 percent strongly—"building goodwill toward the U.S. by providing food and medical assistance to people in poor countries."

The dramatic change in public attitudes profoundly changed the politics of U.S. foreign policy. On numerous issues, powerful interest groups suddenly found themselves swept aside. The coalition of conservative groups that for several years had frustrated a plan to pay much of the outstanding U.S. dues to the United Nations saw Congress suddenly appropriate the money. Human rights groups and democracy activists watched the Bush administration do two things that would have been unthinkable before September 11— lift the sanctions that the United States had imposed on Pakistan after General Musharraf seized power in 1999 and begin to side rhetorically with Russia in its brutal fight in Chechnya. With the public now watching, politicians who wanted to resist interest group pressure understood that they had the freedom to do so. Those who preferred to protect the status quo backed off. They understood that they risked being seen as courting special interests at the expense of the national interest.

The main beneficiary of the dramatic change in the politics of U.S. foreign policy was the White House, not Congress. The reasons were two-fold. First, the public was not split on what the government should do in response to the terrorist attacks—as was the case, for example, in the latter half of

the Vietnam era—but remarkably unified. President Bush's public approval ratings soared to 90 percent—a figure seen only once before, and even then only fleetingly, when his father successfully waged the Persian Gulf War. Second, congressional Democrats, who would normally have the greatest political incentive to criticize a Republican president, lacked the credibility to do so. Polls have shown for years that the American public has much greater confidence in the ability of Republicans to handle national security issues than Democrats. Worried that their criticisms might sound unpatriotic, many Democratic lawmakers opted for silence.

With the public firmly behind the president, members of Congress who might have preferred to be elsewhere on policy grounds quickly decided they had to be there as well. Three days after the attack, a near-unanimous Congress gave the president a blank check to retaliate against the terrorists, authorizing him "to use all necessary and appropriate force against those nations, organizations, or persons he determines planned, authorized, committed, or aided the terrorist attacks that occurred on September 11, 2001, or harbored such organizations or persons." Congress surrendered on other issues as well. Before September 11, Senate Democrats planned to attack the administration's plans for missile defense. After September 11, they abandoned the idea. And President Bush's December 2001 announcement that he was withdrawing the United States from the 1972 Anti-Ballistic Missile (ABM) Treaty caused barely a ripple on Capitol Hill.

President Bush continued to wield the upper hand on foreign policy throughout 2002. Members of Congress, and especially Democrats, were reluctant to challenge the White House. Those who did found themselves subject to withering criticism. In the fall of 2002, the president asked Congress to give him authority to use U.S. troops to oust Saddam Hussein from power. Many lawmakers grumbled privately that invading Iraq would divert attention from the war against Al Qaeda and potentially destabilize the Middle East. Few were willing to make that case publicly though. The House and Senate passed the authorizing legislation by overwhelming margins—even though President Bush said he had not made up his mind to use force and none of the lawmakers knew what circumstances might lead him to opt for war.

As the ABM Treaty withdrawal and Iraq resolution both attested, President Bush made the most of his newfound power after September 11. But in making these and other decisions, he was carrying out his agenda, not the public's. Although the public knew it wanted to win the war on terrorism, it had few well-formed opinions on how to achieve that end. Indeed, the results of the multitude of polls taken in the weeks following September 11 could be read to support a broad array of different strategies for dealing with terrorism, ranging from those that emphasized military force to those that gave long-term economic and political aid an equal priority. What mattered in political terms was that the public was willing to support President Bush in whatever he did, as long as his strategy appeared to be working, or at least not clearly failing.

8-4 Lasting Change or Temporary Deviation?

The new, White-House–dominated politics of U.S. foreign policy proved to be fleeting. Although the Iraq War resulted in a decisive U.S military victory, American efforts to win the peace soon faltered. By fall 2003, U.S. troops in Iraq faced a rising insurgency. More U.S. soldiers died occupying Iraq in April 2004 than had died in April 2003 while trying to liberate the country. The not-too-surprising result was that public enthusiasm for the U.S. presence in Iraq, and for President Bush's handling of the issue, plunged. By May 2004, polls showed that more than one out of four Americans favored withdrawing U.S. troops from Iraq. And in a finding that no one predicted only a few months earlier, the American public was split roughly down the middle in terms of whether they believed President Bush or likely Democratic presidential nominee John Kerry would do the best job of handling the situation in Iraq.

Flagging public support for President Bush's policy toward Iraq translated into greater congressional activism on foreign policy. Congressional questioning of administration officials in late spring 2004 was notably more critical than it had been a year earlier. This more skeptical attitude could be found among many congressional Republicans, as well as among almost all congressional Democrats. President Bush's fellow party members not only worried that the administration had no clear strategy for winning the peace in Iraq; they also feared that the administration's mishandling of the occupation could damage the GOP's chances of winning big in the November 2004 elections.

Congress's renewed willingness to challenge the White House does not mean, however, that foreign-policy making is reverting to its pre-September 11 form. It won't, at least not any time soon. Fighting terrorism and the states that might aid terrorists will likely remain a focal point of American foreign policy for years to come. Potential congressional opponents will operate with the residual fear that another terrorist attack could change public attitudes overnight and that their criticisms, if not properly phrased, could be portrayed as unpatriotic. In a country newly sensitized to the importance of patriotism, that is an advantage that the White House will put to use, regardless of which party controls it.

Readings for Further Study

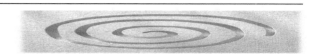

Holsti, Ole. 1996. *Public Opinion and American Foreign Policy.* Ann Arbor: University of Michigan Press.

Kull, Steven, and I. M. Destler. 1999. *Misreading the Public: The Myth of a New Isolationism.* Washington, D.C.: Brookings Institution Press.

Reilly, John E. 1999. "Americans and the World: A Survey at Century's End." *Foreign Policy* 114 (Spring): 97–114.

Site name: Americans and the World

URL: http://www.americans-world.org

Maintained by the Program on International Policy Attitudes at the University of Maryland, the site offers a source of comprehensive information on U.S. public opinion on international issues.

Site name: Pew Research Center for the People and the Press

URL: http://www.people-press.org/

A comprehensive source on polling data about a wide variety of issues.

Site name: America after 9/11: Public Opinion on the War on Terrorism and the War with Iraq

URL: http://www.aei.org/docLib/20030425_Terrorism3.pdf

A collection of polling results on a wide range of questions about the war on terrorism and the war with Iraq.

Websites to Check Out

Note: As we went to press, these sites were functional using the URLs provided. Check out the online text for the most up-to-date URLs.

The Unloved Trumpet:

The News Media Report on the War on Terrorism

James M. Lindsay

What most Americans know about September 11 and the war on terrorism they know from watching television, listening to the radio, and reading newspapers and magazines. Indeed, the terrorist attacks drove home how reliant we all are on the news media for information about the world we live in. Which stories the media cover and how they cover them shape how we view issues and what we expect government to do.

Yet, as important as the news media are to a healthy democracy, Americans are often critical of the news media. Polls show that the public often doubts whether journalists share their values, believes they too often get the facts wrong, and worries that they are too negative and sensational. The news media may be the trumpet that brings us information we need to know, but it is frequently an unloved trumpet.

So in this context, it is important to examine how the news media covered the story of September 11 and the war on terrorism. That, in turn, requires asking three questions: How did news coverage change in the wake of the attacks? What kind of access did the news media have

to the stories they covered? And how well did the news media cover the biggest story of the last half-century? It turns out that Americans gave the news media reasonably high marks for covering September 11 and its aftermath. But they didn't share the media's conviction that the Bush administration hid information that they needed to know.

9-1 Coverage

For nearly a quarter century, critics have complained that television, radio, and newspapers have all drifted away from covering what was once their staple—hard news, that is, stories about domestic politics and international affairs. The data back them up. According to the Project for Excellence in Journalism, in 1977 hard news constituted roughly 70 percent of the stories that appeared on the network evening newscasts. About 15 percent of airtime was devoted to "soft news" stories about celebrities and lifestyle matters, with the remainder devoted to stories about crime, business, and technology. In contrast, in June 2001, hard news constituted less than half (46 percent) of the stories on the nightly newscasts; celebrity news and lifestyle features constituted

a quarter of the stories (25 percent); and crime, business, and technology stories made up the remainder. Studies of radio and newspaper coverage over the past quarter century have shown a similar trend toward soft news, which, given its emphasis on improving the listener's or reader's personal skills (e.g., cooking, home improvement, personal finance), is often advertised as "news you can use."

September 11 changed the news mix dramatically. When the Project for Excellence in Journalism studied the network evening newscasts in October 2001, it found that hard news constituted 80 percent of the stories. With the greater emphasis on hard news, coverage of celebrities and lifestyle matters virtually disappeared from the evening news— such reports constituted only 1 percent of all news stories. And although the trend toward hard news was most dramatic on the nightly newscasts, it carried over to radio and newspapers as well. This is not to say that the news media abandoned their standard daily features about food, technology, and real estate. They didn't. But most expanded the number and length of their hard news stories, which not surprisingly focused on the war on terrorism.

And the print press had one advantage over its electronic competitors—whereas radio and television generally could not expand the amount of time they devoted to the news, newspapers had the option of printing additional pages to better cover the news.

In shifting decidedly toward hard news stories, the news media found a willing audience in the American public. CNN's audience quadrupled in the first week after the September 11 attacks, and the audience for the nightly news shows on the three broadcast networks rose by 40 percent or more. And polls showed that Americans were also paying closer attention to the news. The Pew Research Center for the People and the Press found that two out of three Americans said they were more interested in the news after September 11 than they had been before it. Newspapers, which can cover more stories in more depth than either television or radio, may have been the biggest beneficiaries of the public's new appetite for hard news. The percentage of the public that told Pew that they relied primarily on newspapers for their news tripled after September 11. Moreover, roughly half of the people surveyed said they were reading more newspapers than they had been before the terrorist attacks and that they were reading news stories more closely.

The public's intensified interest in hard news stories should not be surprising. People are most likely to pay close attention to a news story if it directly affects their lives. That's why local news media often discuss a faraway tragedy (e.g., the crash of a jumbo jet in Germany that kills 300 people) in terms of how it affects their audience (e.g., "Iowa Man Dies in German Plane Crash" might read the headline in a Des Moines paper). September 11 affected the lives of most Americans in a very deep and personal way.

The news media's rededication to hard news and the public's intense interest in it had an ironic side, though. Although the news media drew larger audiences, this did not necessarily mean bigger profits. (Remember, with the exception of public television and radio, all news organizations are in the business of making money, and they make money by delivering large audiences to potential advertisers.) Indeed, this change may have cost many of them money. Why? One problem is that during a crisis, the story itself—plus a sense of good taste—crowds out advertisements. For several days after September 11, the three broadcast networks dropped all advertising and stuck with round-the-clock news coverage. Even when the networks began accepting advertising again, many companies did not want their products associated with the terrorist attack. The other problem is that, during a crisis, the news media typically devote more resources to covering the story. Permanent staff work overtime, temporary workers are hired, and camera crews have to be flown around the world. All this costs money. During the first month after September 11, for example, the *New York Times* went $4 million over budget paying the cost of extra newsprint, temporary staff, and communications.

9-2 Access

The news media may have paid more attention to hard news after September 11, but how good was their access to the story? According to many journalists, the answer was "not very." They complained that the U.S. government hampered their efforts to cover the war on terrorism. On this point, they received little sympathy from the American public.

The terrorist attacks on September 11 were an easy story to cover. Anyone with a camera or reporter's notebook could describe what was happening in New York City and in Washington, D.C. But the aftermath was a far harder story to cover because the news media had to rely heavily on the government for information. The terrorists who plotted the attacks were either dead or not talking—at least to American news organizations. Most news organizations also had either no or very little presence in, or experience covering, the Middle East and Central Asia. And after the U.S. military began attacking Taliban and Al Qaeda forces in Afghanistan, news organizations found it difficult (though not impossible) to get to the war zone, and as a result, they were hard pressed to report accurately on what was happening there. So journalists had to depend on Bush administration officials to keep them informed about what was happening.

All these factors gave the Bush administration considerable—but by no means complete—ability to determine what kinds of information reached journalists and, in turn, the American public. This was especially the case with coverage of the war in Afghanistan. Because the battlefields were distant and remote, the Pentagon could restrict reporters' access to American troops in the field to an extent far greater than any previous war.

And because the U.S. military's strategy relied so heavily on special commando forces rather than on regular combat troops, the Pentagon could argue that restricted access was justified for reasons of operational security. But journalists complained that even when operational security was not an issue, the Pentagon refused to grant them access to American troops. "Imagine this," said Sandy Johnson, the Associated Press's Washington bureau chief. "There is a war being fought by Americans, and we are not there to chronicle it. We have access to the Northern Alliance, we have access to the Taliban, we have practically zero access to American forces in the theater."

Journalists complained that the Pentagon's briefings back home were not much better. Throughout President Bush's first year in office, his administration had frustrated many journalists because, unlike previous administrations, it had kept a tight lid on what it told the press. Many journalists believed the Pentagon's war briefings elevated this selective release of information into an art form. Secretary of Defense Donald Rumsfeld apparently directed senior military officers not to speak with reporters, thereby denying journalists one of their major sources of information. Rumsfeld also led many of the Pentagon's briefings himself, seemingly taking it as a point of personal pride to answer reporters' questions without conveying any important information. When one reporter asked him if he could describe what was being done to capture senior Taliban officials, he replied, "I certainly can, and I'm not inclined to."

Did any of this bother the American public? According to public opinion polls, no. To be sure, Americans remained firm believers that the news media have an important role to play as a watchdog on government behavior. Pew found in its post-September 11 polls that a majority of Americans said that media scrutiny of the military serves the public interest and that they did not expect the news media to tout the White House's positions on issues. Pew also found that a majority of the public favored neutral rather than pro-American news coverage, and nearly three out of four said that news stories should include the views of countries hostile to the United States.

But despite this sympathy for the news media's job, most Americans believed that the Bush administration was acting in good faith. More than eight of ten people surveyed told Pew that they did not believe the Pentagon was hiding bad news. Eighty percent said they had confidence that the Bush administration was giving them an accurate picture of the war. And 70 percent said that to the extent that the government engaged in censorship, it was seeking to protect the lives of American soldiers, not to keep stories from the press. The overall message from the public opinion surveys is clear: When it comes to the war on terrorism, the American public is giving the government the benefit of any doubts.

9-3 Did the News Media Do a Good Job?

How well did the news media cover September 11 and its aftermath? Much like beauty, assessments of the news media's performance lie in the eye of the beholder. A story that strikes one person as balanced and comprehensive might strike someone else as simplistic or unpatriotic. But although definitive assessments about the news media's performance are elusive, we can note some of their successes and failures, as well as track how the American public rated their coverage.

Even the most die-hard press aficionados admit that journalists make mistakes. Coverage of September 11 and the war on terrorism was no exception. In the first few hours after the attacks on the World Trade Center and the Pentagon, many news agencies erroneously reported that a car bomb had detonated outside the State Department. During the anthrax crisis of October 2001, newspapers often contradicted each other, as well as themselves, over the potency and origins of the anthrax spores. As for coverage of the war in Afghanistan, news reports grew increasingly pessimistic about the utility of the bombing campaign and the prospects for victory during the first two weeks of November 2001—at precisely the moment the Taliban began collapsing as a military force.

Yet, there may be less to these failures than meets the eyes. The news media may have reported bad information, but in many instances, they did so in good faith. It is not surprising that in the first few hours after the terrorists' attacks, the news media reported parts of the story wrong. Accuracy almost always suffers in the early hours of a crisis because so much confusion reigns. Even when the immediate crisis passed, there is little evidence that journalists were inventing stories or consciously trying to make the government look bad. Rather, in most instances, they were reflecting what government officials and policy experts were telling them. In the case of the anthrax crisis, much of the information that federal health officials released turned out to be wrong. And although news reports from Afghanistan were pessimistic in early November 2001, so too were the Pentagon's own briefings. The military had initially hailed the U.S. air campaign as a great success, saying that the Taliban's forces had been "eviscerated" in the first days of bombing. When those upbeat assessments proved premature, military briefers began describing the war in far more cautious terms. To judge by their public statements, the U.S. military was as surprised by the sudden collapse of the Taliban in mid-November 2001 as the press.

By the same token, much of the news media's coverage of September 11 and its aftermath was stunning. Millions of Americans watched live as a hijacked airplane struck the south tower of the World Trade Center and then later as both towers collapsed. The country was treated to extensive cultural and geography lessons about Islam, the Arab world, and Central Asia. And when Kabul fell, journalists were there broadcasting live as joyous Afghanis celebrated the downfall of the Taliban.

As for the American public, it gave the news media high marks for its coverage of the war on terrorism, especially early on. According to Pew surveys, the news media rose substantially in the public's estimation after September 11. A late September 2001 poll found that 89 percent of Americans rated the news coverage as either excellent or good. The number fell to 77 percent in a November poll, but this number was still much higher than the 50 to 60 percent that Pew typically found before the attacks. The

September poll also found that 46 percent of Americans thought that news stories were usually accurate. This may not sound like much, but it is the highest response Pew had recorded since it first began asking the question in 1992. And the public saw the press as patriotic. The November survey found that 69 percent believed that news organizations "stand up for America," a sizable increase over the 43 percent who had said so in September. So, although the news media may have misfired on occasion, the American public appeared to have their miscues in stride.

9-4 The Future

Did September 11 permanently change the way the news media operate or how the public consumes news? No. The news media's shift to hard news turned out to be only temporary. The war on terrorism proceeded without major setbacks for the United States in 2002, and fear of another attack receded. Hard news coverage shrank as a result. The public's consumption of news also reverted to traditional levels. Pew found by May 2002 that only 49 percent of those surveyed said they followed international news occasionally—about the same percentage as before September 11. Overall, Pew researchers found that "reported levels of reading, watching, and listening to the news are not markedly different than in the spring of 2000."

Some things did change, however. In response to the complaints that it denied reporters access to U.S. troops in the field in Afghanistan, the Defense Department decided to give journalists "long-term, minimally restrictive access" to U.S. soldiers during the Iraq War. The Pentagon "embed-

ded" more than 500 individual reporters in existing military units. The reporters lived with the soldiers in their assigned unit, traveled with them, and in a few tragic instances, died with them. In many cases, journalists were embedded in military units from their local area. Newspapers, because of their sheer number, had the most reporters traveling with U.S. troops. The embedding program also included foreign reporters. *Al Jazeera*, an Arab-language cable news channel known for its often-hostile coverage of U.S. foreign policy, had a reporter traveling with U.S. soldiers.

The Defense Department's embedding plan did not win unanimous applause from the news media before the war. Many journalists argued that the Pentagon's offer came with prominent strings attached. Journalists had to agree to operate under specific rules, rules so detailed they filled nine single-spaced pages. Nine paragraphs alone were devoted to what reporters could write about battlefield casualties. The rules also required journalists to conduct all interviews with U.S. troops on the record. Reporters argued that this would effectively discourage troops from saying anything negative and thereby help guarantee positive coverage of the U.S. military. Moreover, even if reporters observed all the rules, the Pentagon insisted that unit commanders would have the right to restrict a journalist's access as they saw fit.

In practice, however, most journalists appeared pleased with the way the embedding program worked. They got a ground-view picture of the Iraq War, and the U.S. military seldom made overt attempts to influence their reporting. Moreover, journalists discovered that U.S. commanders were not shy at identifying what they saw as shortcomings in the American military strategy. Indeed, when news reports from the field showed that the U.S. advance on Baghdad had bogged down during the second week of fighting, some of the war's strongest supporters back home argued that the Pentagon had made a mistake in giving the news media access to the battlefield.

The Defense Department also had reason to be pleased with the embedding program. The mere fact that reporters were on the battlefield spared the Pentagon from criticisms that it was hiding information. Journalists also proved useful in corroborating administration claims that the Iraqi military and Saddam loyalists were deliberately putting Iraqi civilians in harm's way. Contrary to the fears of some senior military leaders, the embedding program did not endanger the operational security of military operations. Only one reporter was removed from the field for divulging sensitive information. The news coverage also highlighted the bravery of U.S. troops and no doubt cemented the public's already high opinion of the military. Finally, many Pentagon officials concluded that the embedding program would have a long-term pay-off for the Defense Department. With so many journalists exposed for the first time to the reality of what the military does for a living, the Pentagon could expect greater understanding and sympathy from the news media in the future.

Will the Pentagon's new openness in dealing with the news media continue? Perhaps. However, officials in the White House and the Defense Department follow the polls as closely as anyone, and they know that they are under no pressure from the American public to accommodate the press. One ABC News poll taken in January 2003 found that six of ten Americans believed that the government's ability to keep secrets during wartime was more important than the right to a free press. So if reporters complain about a lack of access without producing evidence that the administration is hiding something, the public is more likely to fault them than the government. But that may be inevitable. Although Americans cherish the idea of a free press, they are often dissatisfied with how it actually operates.

Readings for Further Study

Gup, Ted. 2002. "Working in a Wartime Capital." *Columbia Journalism Review* 40 (September/October): 21–27. Available at http://www.cjr.org/year/02/5/gup.asp

Hess, Stephen, and Marvin Kalb, eds. 2003. *The Media and the War on Terrorism*. Washington, D.C.: Brookings Institution Press.

Hickey, Neil. 2002. "Access Denied: The Pentagon's War Reporting Rules Are the Toughest Ever." *Columbia Journalism Review* 40 (January/February): 26–31. Available at http://www.cjr.org/year/02/1/hickey.asp

"Special Report: Covering the War in Real Time." 2003. *Columbia Journalism Review* 41 (May/June): 15–43. Available at http://www.cjr.org/issues/2003/3/

Websites to Check Out

Note: As we went to press, these sites were functional using the URLs provided. Check out the online text for the most up-to-date URLs.

Site name: Pew Research Center for the People and the Press
URL: http://people-press.org/
Extensive polling data on how Americans view the press, as well as on their viewing and reading habits.

Site name: Journalism.org
URL: http://www.journalism.org/
Extensive sets of analysis, commentary, and data on the practice of journalism, including coverage of the war on terrorism.

Site name: The Role of the Press in the Anti-Terrorism Campaign
URL: http://www.brookings.edu/dybdocroot/GS/Projects/Press/Press.htm
Transcripts of a weekly discussion series, co-sponsored by the Brookings Institution and Washington office of Harvard University's Joan Shorenstein Center on the Press, Politics and Public Policy, on news media issues growing out of the anti-terrorism campaign. Each transcript contains a short list of readings relevant to the week's topic.

Rallying 'Round the Flag after September 11 and the Iraq War

Eric R.A.N. Smith

September 11 changed many things, not least of all the landscape of American politics. As Labor Day brought the summer of 2001 to a close, Democrats were increasingly confident that momentum was on their side. President George W. Bush's public approval ratings were slowly eroding, and polls showed that the public favored the Democrat's political agenda. But the moment that jetliners crashed into the Pentagon and the twin towers at the World Trade Center, the center of gravity in American politics shifted. George Bush suddenly found himself the most popular politician in America. Democrats found themselves scrambling to say that they too supported the man from Crawford, Texas.

President Bush's stratospheric public popularity after September 11 spawned a new conventional wisdom—the Republicans now had the upper hand in American politics. Many political commentators penciled Bush in for a second term and began to hold a wake for the Democratic Party. But how convincing is the conventional wisdom? A close examination of public opinion suggests not very. The public's newfound enthusiasm for Wash-ington was not limited to George Bush. It extended to both parties in Congress as well. Moreover, the Bush rally faded away.

George Bush's commanding lead in the polls after September 11 stemmed from a public rally in response to the attacks. His standing in the polls on Election Day 2004 will depend most of all on two things: the state of the economy and whether the public judges the Iraq War to have been a wise decision.

10-1 The Rally-'Round-the-Flag Effect

Political scientists have discovered a recurrent pattern in public opinion when the United States is threatened or its troops enter potentially deadly hostilities—support for the president surges. This phenomenon is called the *rally-'round-the-flag* effect. The events that trigger this rally need to be sudden and attention grabbing, such as a terrorist attack on an American military base or a foreign nation seizing a U.S. embassy. Routine reports of battles during a war or other widely expected events do not produce rallies, even if American soldiers are wounded or killed.

Pollsters measure these rallies by looking for surges in the presi-dent's Gallup poll approval ratings. Since 1938, Gallup has been asking samples of American adults, "Do you approve or disapprove of the way [president's name] is handling his job as president?" Some of the foreign-policy crises that have triggered surges of support for the president include:

- **The Cuban Missile Crisis.** In October 1962, U.S. spy planes discovered that the Soviet Union was building a missile base on Cuba, an island 90 miles off the coast of Florida. Even worse, missiles with nuclear warheads were on Soviet ships bound for Cuba. President Kennedy ordered a naval blockade of Cuba and demanded the Soviets withdraw the missiles. The world came to the brink of World War III. The Soviets turned their ships around, and nuclear holocaust was avoided. President Kennedy's popularity jumped 12 percentage points.

- **The *Mayaguez* Incident.** In May 1975, Khmer Rouge troops captured a U.S. merchant ship, the *Mayaguez*, as it sailed along the Cambodian coast in the Gulf of Siam. President Ford responded by ordering the U.S. military to rescue the *Mayaguez* and its crew. A combined Marine/Navy/Air Force operation recovered the *Mayaguez,* though 41 Americans died during the mission when a helicopter crashed. Unbeknownst to the United States at the time, the Cambodians had already released the 39 merchant marines. President Ford's popularity jumped 11 percentage points.

- **The Seizure of the American Embassy in Teheran.** In November 1979, shortly after the Iranian revolution overthrew the Shah and put Ayatollah Khomeini in power, Iranian militants attacked and captured the U.S. embassy and its staff in Teheran. President Carter did not respond immediately with military force. Instead, he hoped to win the captives' release by diplomatic means. Nevertheless, immediately following the capture of the U.S. embassy, President Carter's popularity jumped 13 percentage points.

- **The Bombing of the Marine Battalion Headquarters in Beirut.** In October 1983, slightly more than a year after President Reagan sent U.S. marines to Lebanon to help secure the peace there, terrorists drove a truck bomb into a barracks of marine peacekeepers at the Beirut airport. The attack killed 241 marines. President Reagan's popularity jumped 8 percentage points.

As these examples demonstrate, the rally-'round-the-flag effect typically increases the president's popularity by 8 to 15 per-

centage points. Even the attack on Pearl Harbor boosted President Franklin Roosevelt's popularity by only 12 percentage points. So the pattern is that disaster strikes, and the public rewards the president with a boost in popularity. Whether the president helped or hurt the situation or, indeed, had anything to do with the disaster is irrelevant. Americans rally around their leader.

The only exception to this pattern of moderate jumps in approval—at least until the September 11 attacks—was the public's reaction to the liberation of Kuwait in 1991. In August 1990, Iraq invaded its southern neighbor, Kuwait. President George H. W. Bush responded by sending U.S. troops to Saudi Arabia. Over the next few months, he persuaded U.S. allies to join an American-led force under the United Nations banner to liberate Kuwait. When the war began in January, Bush's popularity surged from 58 percent to 82 percent. It eventually reached 89 percent in March when the war ended. This was the highest approval rating Gallup had recorded. Most observers credited Bush's stunning surge in popularity to the fact that the Gulf War was short, caused very few American casualties, and was carried live on television as no war before had been. At the time, most observers also expected that Bush's stellar popularity would translate into an easy reelection victory in 1992. They were wrong.

10-2 George W. Bush's Rally

The American public rallied around the elder President Bush during the Gulf War. Did they

rally in similar fashion behind his son, George W. Bush, after September 11?

In a word, yes. Figure 10-1 presents Gallup's approval ratings for the younger Bush from his inauguration in January 2001 through early May 2004. After Bush entered office with an approval rating of 57 percent, his approval ratings improved to 63 percent in an early March poll. Following this early peak, his approval ratings bounced around a bit but generally declined until he hit 51 percent approval—the low mark of the first half of his presidency—in a poll conducted between September 7 and 10, 2001. By historical standards, Bush's ratings were low for a newly elected president during his "honeymoon" period. Every one of the ten presidents since World War II received greater public support in the opening months of their presidencies than did Bush. (A partial exception is President Ford, who saw his initial 66 percent public approval plummet after he pardoned former President Nixon.)

September 11, however, changed everything. The rally-'round-the-flag effect took hold, and Bush's popularity soared. In a Gallup poll conducted just three days after the attacks, Bush's approval rating stood at 86 percent. In the next poll, conducted September 21 and 22, he broke his father's record and notched the highest level of support ever recorded by Gallup—90 percent approval. Just as important, although Bush's approval ratings fell throughout the remainder of 2001 and into 2002, they remained relatively high. By the end of 2002, 61 percent of the public still approved of the way he was handling his job.

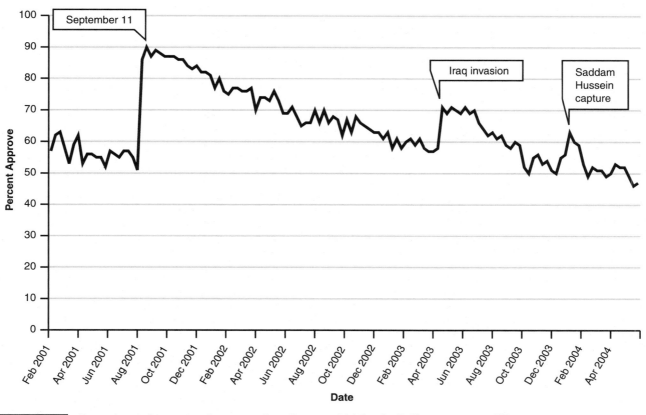

Figure 10-1 Presidential approval ratings for George W. Bush. *Polling question:* "Do you approve or disapprove of the way George W. Bush is handling his job?"

Source: Gallup Poll and CNN/*USA Today*/Gallup Poll, reported at PollingReport.com, http://www.pollingreport.com/BushJob.htm

At the time, these strato-spheric public approval ratings suggested that the prospects were good that Bush would do what his father did not—win reelection. The peculiar nature of the younger Bush's election—losing the popular vote to Al Gore but winning the presidency—and his low and declining popularity had prompted considerable talk among political commentators during the summer of 2001 that he would be a one-term president like his father. After September 11, that speculation turned into talk about whether a Democratic candidate had any chance of winning in 2004. Although the days of Bush's stratospheric popularity ratings were over by the beginning of

2003, his public approval ratings jumped a second time after the start of the Iraq War, and again after the capture of Saddam Hussein. These increases were not as dramatic as after September 11—only about a dozen points—but they initially convinced many political observers that Bush would lead his party to victory in 2004.

10-3 A Rally, but around Whom?

Almost all political commentators described the public's response to the September 11 attacks as a rally in support of President Bush and his policies. Indeed, almost all political science analyses of the rally-'round-the-flag effect

have focused exclusively on the public's approval of the president. Did the American public rally only around President Bush? Or did other American political leaders experience similar surges in popularity? If the latter is the case, then focusing solely on Bush's approval ratings is misleading.

The one political science study to look beyond presidential popularity turned up evidence suggesting that the president is not the only beneficiary of the rally-'round-the-flag effect. Suzanne Parker, a political scientist at Florida State University, examined a series of polls taken in Florida after the Gulf War began and found that public approval for Congress, trust in government,

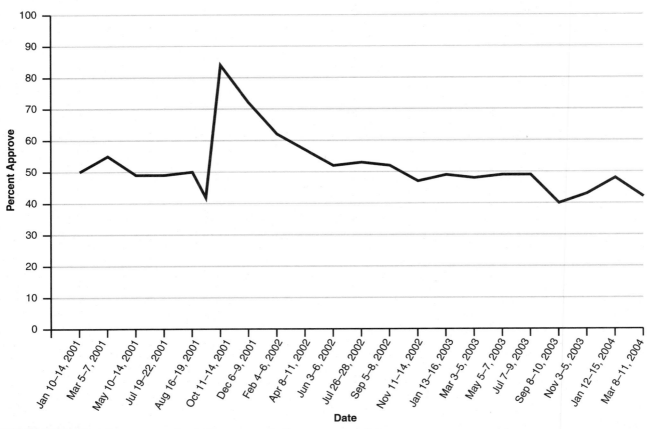

Figure 10-2	Public approval of Congress. *Polling question:* "Do you approve or disapprove of the way Congress is handling its job?"

Source: CNN/USA Today/Gallup Poll.

and economic optimism all increased. If the pattern Parker found in Florida during the Gulf War holds for the rest of the nation and for other crises, the rally effect might more accurately be described as a surge of patriotic support for the president, Congress, and other institutions of government. That could alter any conclusion we can draw about the impact of a rally on the next election.

To get a handle on this issue in the context of September 11, Figure 10-2 presents the results of CNN/*USA Today*/Gallup polls that asked the question, "Do you approve or disapprove of the way Congress is handling its job?" The data parallel the pattern of approval for George Bush. Congress

began 2001 with a 50 percent approval rating. Approval increased 5 percentage points by April and then began a slow decline throughout the rest of spring and summer. By early September, it was only 42 percent. After September 11, public approval of Congress shot up to 84 percent at its peak. Congress's approval ratings actually rose slightly more than did Bush's (42 versus 38 percentage points). Like Bush's approval rating, Congress's approval rating fell throughout the rest of 2001 and 2002, and briefly surged during the Iraq War, and again when Saddam Hussein was captured. Throughout that period, President Bush's approval rating generally stood about 10 percentage points higher than that of

Congress. By the end of 2002, 50 percent of the public approved of the job Congress was doing.

The surge of support was not just for the institution of Congress. As Figure 10-3 shows, similar questions showed more favorable ratings for the Democrats and Republicans in Congress, and for their leaders—Democratic Senate Majority Leader Tom Daschle and Republican House Speaker Dennis Hastert. In the months leading up to September 11, the public looked at the Republicans less favorably than they looked at the Democrats; after September 11, they looked upon Republicans more favorably (with the exception of a brief period during the summer of 2002). In the case of party leaders,

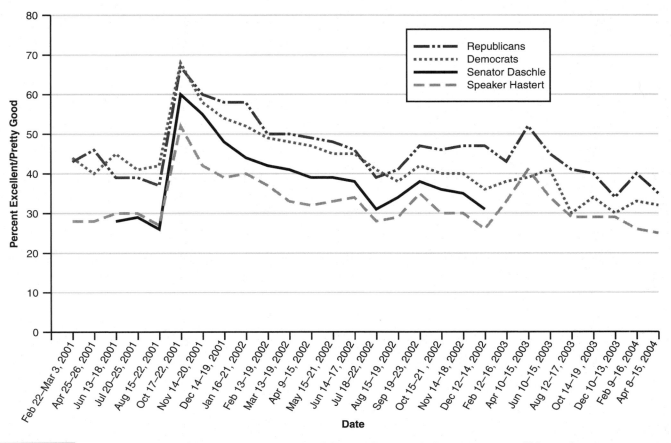

Figure 10-3 Favorable opinions of Democrats and Republicans. *Polling questions:* "How do you rate the job [Democrats/ Republicans] in Congress are doing: excellent, pretty good, only fair, or poor?" "How do you rate the job [Senate Majority Leader Tom Daschle/House Speaker J. Dennis Hastert] is doing: excellent, pretty good, only fair, or poor?"

Source: The Harris Poll, as reported at PollingReport.com, http://www.pollingreport.com/congjob.htm.

the opposite is true. Daschle gained more than Hastert. Details aside, the key points are that the public rallied behind both parties immediately after September 11 and that new support gradually ebbed over the following months.

Trust in the federal government also rose. A *Washington Post* poll conducted in April 2000 asked, "How much of the time do you trust the government in Washington to do what is right? Would you say just about always, most of the time, or only some of the time?" Only 30 percent said "just about always" or "most of the time." That low level of trust was typical in most of the 1980s

and 1990s. But when the same question was asked in a September 25–27, 2001 poll, 64 percent said "just about always" or "most of the time"—a huge jump in confidence in the federal government.

People were also more willing to proclaim their satisfaction with the direction of the country in the aftermath of September 11. A *USA Today*/CNN/Gallup poll asked, "In general, are you satisfied or dissatisfied with the way things are going in the United States at this time?" For most of 2001, about 50 percent reported being satisfied, although that number dropped to only 43 percent in early September. After the

attacks, 61 percent said they were satisfied with the way things were going. Over the next six months, the responses fluctuated in the 60–75 percent range.

Perhaps most surprising, polls showed increased economic optimism. Given the potentially devastating economic impact of September 11, this outlook seems to defy common sense. Yet, that was how Americans reacted. Gallup asked two questions every month: "How would you rate economic conditions in this country today—as excellent, good, only fair, or poor?" and "Right now, do you think that economic conditions in the country as a

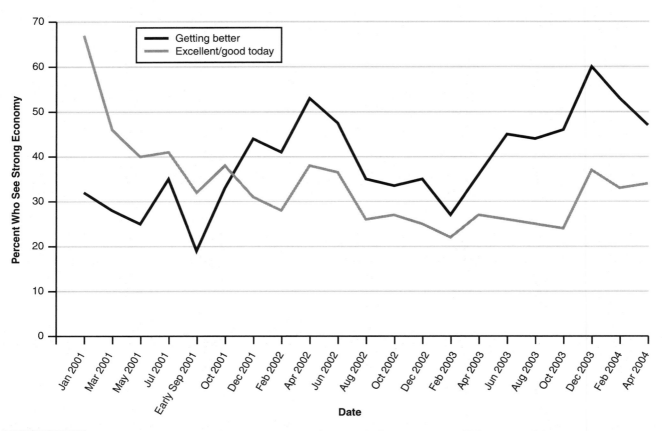

Figure 10-4 Public assessment of economic conditions. *Polling questions:* "How would you rate economic conditions in this country today—as excellent, good, only fair, or poor?" "Right now, do you think that economic conditions in the country as a whole are getting better or getting worse?"

Source: Gallup Polls, as reported at PollingReport.com, http://www.pollingreport.com/consumer.htm

whole are getting better or getting worse?" Figure 10-4 presents the results for the Bush administration from 2001 through May 2004. The percentage of people believing that economic conditions were excellent or good started high when Bush was inaugurated, but fell throughout his first months in office until it reached a low point of only 32 percent at the beginning of September 2001. In the Gallup poll conducted immediately after the September 11 attacks, that number jumped to 46 percent. The trend question—whether economic conditions are getting better or worse—also hit a low point in early September 2001, a mere 19 percent, and bounced up to 28 percent after the attacks.

Both measures showed a drop in optimism by November. As the war in Afghanistan played out in the spring of 2002, however, Americans were more likely to believe that the economy was improving. Not until the summer of 2002 did economic optimism fall back to the low levels of the early months of the Bush administration. Luckily for Bush—or perhaps because of strong campaigning by Bush and his Republican allies—November 2002 saw a brief surge of economic optimism. That surge was well timed for the midterm elections.

Although Americans felt relatively optimistic about the economy throughout most of President Bush's first two years in office, their optimism was not

matched by economic indicators. Aside from the historic slump in the stock market, the unemployment rate climbed—from 4.2 percent in the first month of his administration to 6.0 percent in December 2002. That trend of rising unemployment did not harm Bush's popularity enough to allow the Democrats to pick up seats in the House or Senate. However, the economy's overall health remained a serious worry for the Republican Party heading into the 2004 elections.

Given the evidence in Figures 10-2, 10-3, and 10-4, we can see that the rally-'round-the-flag effect is far more than a rally around the president. There was certainly a surge of public support after September 11, but it was for the nation and its leaders, not just for the president. George Bush gained, but so did his political opponents.

10-4 September 11's Impact on 2002

The 2002 elections were held in the afterglow of the September 11 attacks. President Bush's popularity had fallen from the heady levels of the days immediately after the attacks, but it remained relatively high throughout the fall of 2002. In fact, Gallup found in its last pre-election poll that 63 percent of the public said they approved of the job Bush was doing as president—a figure that matched his highest popularity before September 11. Bush achieved that level of support in his second month in office, during his so-called "honeymoon" period. The September 11 attacks helped extend that honeymoon.

Bush capitalized on the September 11 attacks and the subsequent war in Afghanistan during the campaign. Although Democrats attempted to turn the nation's attention to the floundering economy and other domestic problems, President Bush managed to keep the war against terror on the front pages and in the minds of voters. The growing talk of invading Iraq to prevent Saddam Hussein from building weapons of mass destruction was a key element in that effort. During the last six weeks before the election, President Bush relentlessly talked about the war on terror and the potential war in Iraq. On Election Day, the nation's newspapers even carried a story, based on a Pentagon leak, describing how a CIA Predator drone had destroyed a carload of Al Qaeda fighters in Yemen. That story, coupled with all the others coming out of the White House, focused the nation's attention on foreign policy. When voters thought about President Bush's handling of foreign policy and the war on terror, they approved. That approval helped carry his party to victory in November 2002.

10-5 The Iraq War

The war that President Bush threatened in fall 2002 became a reality on March 19, 2003. The Iraq War showed once again that Americans rally around the president in times of national crisis. Three days after the war began, Gallup found that President Bush's public approval rating had jumped from 58 percent to 71 percent. As Figure 10-1 shows, support stayed at that level for the remainder of the war.

However, the 13-point increase that President Bush received in public support at the start of the Iraq War was much smaller than the 35-point increase he enjoyed immediately after September 11. It was also smaller than the 24-point jump his father received at the start of the 1991 Gulf War. The modest nature of the Iraq rally reflected a deep partisan split over the wisdom of the war. More than 9 out of 10 Republicans supported the decision to go to war, but only half of Democrats did.

That partisan divide stood in particularly sharp contrast to the experience of the Gulf War. Then, overwhelming majorities of members of both parties closed ranks behind the president, despite being deeply split on the eve of war. The lower levels of Democratic support for the Iraq War reflected disagreement over the wisdom of preemptively attacking another invading country, doubts about the sincerity of the administration's diplomatic efforts at the United Nations, and bitterness over the way Bush and other Republicans had questioned Democrats' patriotism in the run up to the war.

As happened with the 1991 Persian Gulf War and after September 11, the public's rally 'round the flag in 2003 extended beyond the White House. In late March and early April 2003, the public gave higher marks to Congress and expressed greater optimism about the country's future. A *New York Times*/CBS poll found that Congress's approval rating jumped 7 percentage points in the first days of fighting. As Figure 10-4 shows, the percentage of the public rating economic conditions in the country as excellent or good jumped 11 points. The percentage of the public saying that economic conditions in the country were getting better jumped 16 points.

The Iraq rally, then, like the rallies that followed the Gulf War and September 11, was about more than just the president. It reflected a surge of patriotic support for the government and country as a whole.

10-6 September 11's Impact on 2004

How are September 11 and the Iraq War likely to affect the 2004 elections? Much depends on which party succeeds in focusing the campaign debate on the issues that put it in the best possible light. The Republicans want voters to go to the polls thinking about the war against terrorism and broader defense and security issues. Since the Vietnam War, the public has given Republicans much higher marks than Democrats on foreign policy and

Table 10-1 — Public Views of Republicans and Democrats on Selected Issues

Polling Question: "Do you think the Republican Party or the Democratic Party would do a better job of dealing with each of the following issues and problems?"

Issue or Problem	Republicans	Democrats	No Difference	No Opinion
Terrorism	60%	30%	5%	5%
Foreign affairs	52%	40%	4%	4%
Taxes	44%	48%	4%	5%
Economy	44%	48%	4%	4%
Federal budget deficit	39%	50%	7%	5%
Education	41%	50%	5%	4%
Health care costs	34%	55%	4%	6%
Environment	35%	57%	3%	5%

Source: Gallup/CNN/USA Today Poll, January 9–11, 2004.

defense. As the survey results in Table 10-1 show, Republicans hold double-digit leads over Democrats on issues such as foreign affairs and terrorism. These public attitudes, combined with President Bush's performance following September 11, potentially make national security a winning agenda for Republicans.

The Democrats, in contrast, want the public to be thinking about domestic issues when they vote. Table 10-1 shows that most voters regard the Democrats as the stronger party on health care, education, and the economy. Moreover, post-September 11 polls show that the public has not changed its views on any of these issues. They like George Bush because of the way he has responded to the attacks, not because of his health care policies or his proposal for privatizing Social Security. If the Democrats can persuade the average voter to think of those domestic issues when voting, they should be in a good position to win back their majorities in the House and Senate.

Another consideration for the 2004 elections—as it is for all elections—is the economy. The economy was weak before the September 11 attacks, and it worsened in their aftermath. Political observers everywhere remember the fate of George Bush's father. Despite sky-high approval of his handling of the Gulf War, the elder Bush lost his reelection bid—largely because the country was in recession throughout much of 1991 and 1992. The elder Bush had 89 percent public approval in March 1991 and only 38 percent of the vote in November 1992. One political analyst explained the outcome by saying, "On election day 1992, only 8 percent of the voters said that foreign policy had been an important consideration in their choice of a presidential candidate." Heading into the 2004 campaign, that was the younger Bush's fear.

Indeed, at the start of 2004, there were signs that history might be repeating itself. Economists talked of a "jobless economy," as statistics showed that the overall economy was growing but that employment levels were not. Political controversy grew over the extent and consequences of "outsourcing," the practice by which U.S. firms subcontracted work to companies outside the United States. (Opening up call centers in India to handle customer service calls from American consumers confused about how to operate their computers or looking to make airplane reservations was one much-talked-about example of outsourcing.) By late spring, however, the numbers on job growth had turned positive, as firms began to hire new workers. Administration officials quickly took credit for the good news, arguing that the president's tax-cut policies had been responsible for stimulating an economic rebound. The high price of gasoline, however, remained a serious concern for Republicans.

But just as White House officials began breathing a sigh of relief on the economy, the policy they had once touted as President Bush's trump card—the Iraq War—looked to be a potential political albatross. The insurgency against the American occupation of Iraq that had ebbed and flowed during the summer and fall of 2003 worsened in early 2004. More American troops died in Iraq in April 2004 than had died liberating the country a year earlier. The publication of photographs of American soldiers abusing Iraqi prisoners created additional political problems for the White House. In May 2004, 58 percent of Americans said they disapproved of the way President Bush was handling the situation in Iraq, and 52 percent said that the war had not been worth fighting.

So six months ahead of the 2004 elections, the race for the White House looked to be a toss-up. Many possible events could change the public's assessment of President Bush, making it impossible to say who will win the presidency in 2004. But if President Bush does benefit over the long term from September 11 and the Iraq War, it will almost certainly be because the public approves of the way he was conducting himself as they went to the polls, rather than because America was attacked or Saddam Hussein ousted from power. Rallies around the flag historically have had limited durations because people move on with their lives. As tragic as September 11 was, and as impressive as the U.S. military victory in Iraq was, they were no different. With time, they faded from political relevance. And the president will be judged on what he is doing, rather than what he has done.

Readings for Further Study

Mueller, John E. 1973. *War, Presidents, and Public Opinion.* New York: John Wiley.

Parker, Suzanne L. 1995. "Toward an Understanding of 'Rally' Effects: Public Opinion in the Persian Gulf War." *Public Opinion Quarterly* 59 (Winter): 526–46.

Teixeira, Ruy. 2001. "Diffident Democrats." *American Prospect.* November 5: 21–23.

Site name: PollingReport.Com

URL: http://www.pollingreport.com/

A regularly updated compendium of polling results on a wide range of issues from an array of polling organizations.

Site name: Brookings Institution—America's Response to Terrorism

URL: http://www.brookings.edu/dybdocroot/fp/projects/terrorism/polling.htm

Links to 15 major polling organizations as well as figures charting trends on several of the most commonly asked polling questions about September 11.

Site name: The Gallup Organization

URL: http://www.gallup.com/

Access to some of the Gallup Organization's polling data and a feature that allows you to sign up for a weekly email analyzing the latest poll results.

Websites to Check Out

Note: As we went to press, these sites were functional using the URLs provided. Check out the online text for the most up-to-date URLs.

Who Won and Who Lost?

Interest Group Politics after September 11

James M. Lindsay

The National Council of La Raza, the League of United Latin American Citizens, and other Latino organizations had much to cheer when Mexican President Vicente Fox visited Washington, D.C., early in September 2001. Latinos were surpassing African Americans as the largest minority in the United States, and American politics was changing as a result. President George W. Bush, calculating that the Latino vote would be critical to future Republican electoral success, had set out to refashion U.S.-Mexican relations that had been marked by suspicion for more than a century and a half. Even more important, Bush had vowed to work with Congress to expand the number of Mexicans who could come to the United States as guest workers and enable many of the millions of Mexicans living in the United States illegally to gain legal residence. For Latino groups, two of their major policy objectives appeared within reach.

September 11 changed everything. Improved relations with Mexico tumbled down the list of U.S. foreign-policy priorities. Interest in making it easier for Mexicans to cross America's southern border gave way to efforts to tighten border security. Immigration issues remained on the political agenda but with an entirely new focus. Washington scrambled to find ways to keep potential terrorists out, not to find ways to enable illegal immigrants to become legal residents.

The dramatic reversal in the fortunes of Latino interest groups after September 11 highlights an important lesson about interest group politics in the United States. A group's ability to get its way depends on much more than its internal attributes, that is, how many members it has, how much money it has in the bank, and how politically skilled its leaders are. Interest groups are also hostage to fate. The political environment in which they operate can make their jobs easier or harder. One moment, an interest group can be like a runner going downhill with the wind at her back. But a foreign-policy crisis, a downturn in the economy, or a switch in which party controls Congress can turn what was a pleasant downhill run into a tough uphill struggle.

So which interest groups won or lost as a result of September 11? The winners, not surprisingly, were groups whose agenda fit the Bush administration's new focus on the war on terrorism. The losers were groups that benefited from the status quo that had existed before the twin towers at the World Trade Center collapsed. But there were also some surprising survivors that persevered with their agendas, despite unfavorable changes in the political landscape.

11-1 Winners

September 11 set back Latino groups. But the terrorist attacks created new opportunities for other interest groups. Three winners stand out: anti-immigration organizations, defense contractors, and security companies.

11-1a Anti-Immigration Groups

The same trends that made Latino groups optimistic in mid-2001 frustrated groups trying to restrict immigration. The Federation for American Immigration Reform (FAIR), Project USA for an Immigration Time Out, Americans for Immigration Control, and similar groups had made little headway in persuading Congress to reduce immigration levels, to adopt tougher laws against illegal immigration, or to revamp the Immigration and Naturalization Service (INS) so it could better enforce existing laws. Only about a dozen or so lawmakers belonged to the Congressional Immigration Reform Caucus. President Bush publicly praised the contributions that immigrants made to the United States.

By late September 2001, however, the political tide had turned in favor of anti-immigration groups. Even though all of the nineteen hijackers had entered the country legally on tourist, business, or student visas—not on immigration visas—membership in the Immigration Reform Caucus swelled to more than five dozen. Members competed with each other to offer legislation designed to tighten border security and revamp the INS. A once-uncontroversial bill to allow more than 200,000 illegal immigrants to remain in the United States while their applications for permanent residency were being processed was derailed in Congress. Most important, passage of an immigration amnesty and new guest-worker program—two policy initiatives that looked to be sure things in August 2001—were dead in the water.

11-1b Defense Contractors

During the 2000 presidential campaign, George Bush criticized the Clinton administration for neglecting the U.S. military. So defense contractors expected that his presidency would mean a windfall for them. Their hopes were quickly dashed. Rather than turning the defense spending spigot wide open, Bush initially said, "There will be no new money for defense this year." That position proved unpopular with the services and with Democrats and Republicans on Capitol Hill. By mid-summer, Bush had reversed himself and added about $30 billion to his de-

fense budget request, an increase of about 7 percent.

This added spending still left defense contractors facing a grim reality: There was not enough money in the budget to fund all the weapons programs the Pentagon had under development. The prospects for another big spending increase were dim. President Bush's tax cut and the country's recession had wiped out most of the federal government's projected budget surplus. Running a budget deficit to finance greater defense spending looked like political poison. Some programs would have to hit the chopping block. That meant companies would lose business they had counted on.

September 11 turned things around. Fears of deficit spending evaporated, and support for defense increases grew. In February 2002, President Bush proposed raising the annual defense budget by $48 billion to $379 billion in 2003, the largest spending increase since the Reagan defense buildup in the early 1980s. Congress eventually agreed to add $38 billion to the defense budget. In February 2003, President Bush asked for $399.1 billion for defense. Equally important, Bush proposed to continue increasing defense spending until it reached roughly half a trillion dollars in 2008, or about 50 percent more than the United States spent when he came to office. And this was before counting the costs of the war with Iraq and the subsequent peacekeeping and nation-building operations.

Although such increases might seem necessary to fund the war on terrorism, only a small portion of the new spending—about $10 billion a year—goes directly to combating terrorists. Most of the new spending simply

funds programs the Pentagon was pursuing before September 11. Indeed, although Bush vowed during the campaign to kill weapons systems designed for a cold war military, by the midpoint in his term, he had canceled only one (the Crusader, the Army's 155mm self-propelled howitzer). Defense contractors who had feared they would have to shut down production lines sighed a breath of relief.

11-1c Security Companies

September 11 made security a top priority for the U.S. government and created an opening for security firms. One top lobbyist told the *National Journal*, "Money is available in relatively prodigious amounts for anything related to defense or homeland security. The budget rules are being thrown out the window." So a company like Ancore, a California-based security firm, tried to interest the Federal Aviation Agency in adopting a neutron-scanning device that can distinguish a bottle of wine from a bottle of liquid explosives inside baggage. And many companies turned to the members of Congress representing the districts in which they were located for support in pushing their proposals.

11-2 Losers

Latino organizations are not the only interest groups whose work suddenly got harder after September 11. For instance, the restaurant, hotel, and agricultural industries that had sided with Latino groups in fighting for amnesty and guest-worker programs—in their case because a reliable supply of low-wage workers means bigger profits—also saw one of their major political objectives frustrated. But they were not alone. Colleges and universities, Arab-American and Muslim-American groups, and Arab governments also saw the political terrain shift underneath their feet.

11-2a Colleges and Universities

September 11 prompted a flurry of interest in beefing up the federal government's ability to track foreign students in the United States. Several of the hijackers had attended American flight schools, and one had entered the country on a student visa to study English but had never enrolled in class. The question of what foreign students did after they entered the country, however, was not new. Efforts to tighten the student visa system had begun years earlier, after it was learned that one of the terrorists involved in the 1993 bombing of the World Trade Center had used a student visa to enter the United States. In 1996, Congress ordered the INS to have a student-tracking system in place by 2003.

However, the INS made only halting progress in getting the system up and running. Why? Stiff opposition from U.S. colleges and universities. They saw the tracking system as a threat to the roughly $12 billion in tuition that they collect from foreign students each year, money critical to enabling many colleges and universities to balance their books. So they mobilized in opposition. As the *Washington Post* described it, "As many as two dozen higher-education groups and large universities drafted harshly worded letters to Congress, the White House, and the INS, protesting various parts of the program as 'unreliable,' 'ill-conceived,' 'a looming disaster,' and 'an obvious and inevitable train wreck.'" By mid-2001, colleges and universities were on the verge of persuading Congress to repeal the entire student-tracking program.

The repeal never happened. In October 2001, Congress passed the USA Patriot Act, which among other things, gave the INS the money it needed to get the system up and running. The bill also extended the tracking system to cover not just students at four-year colleges but also those attending flight, language, and vocational schools. More changes in the student-tracking program may be in the offing. The newly created White House Office for Homeland Security is reviewing student visa policies, and it has directed a special task force "to institute tighter controls and ensure that student visas are being issued appropriately." Faced with this shift in attitudes in Washington, colleges dropped their opposition to tracking foreign students.

11-2b Arab-American and Muslim-American Groups

America has a long history of ethnically and religiously based interest groups. The 1990s saw the emergence of the newest such participants in American political life—Arab-American and Muslim-American groups. The growing visibility of organizations such as the Arab-American Institute and the Council on American-Islamic Relations reflected the rising number of Americans who are of Arab descent or practice the Islamic faith. The groups sought what Irish Americans, Jewish Americans, and others had sought before them. They wanted government to recognize and respect their contributions to American life. They wanted an end to what they perceived as discriminatory treatment. And they wanted more say over U.S. foreign policy; in their case, they especially wanted to reduce what they saw as America's bias toward Israel.

At the start of 2001, many Arab-American and Muslim-American groups believed they were gaining ground. George Bush had actively wooed the Arab Americans during the 2000 campaign. The result? Bush won a far larger share of their votes than any previous Republican presidential candidate. Given the closeness of the election, it is neither surprising nor far-fetched that some Republican political strategists credited Arab Americans with helping push Bush over the top. Many Arab Americans and Muslim Americans expected him to return the favor.

September 11 derailed those hopes. The fact that the September 11 hijackers were Arabs who claimed to be acting on behalf of Islam, coupled with the many stories about how the attacks were cheered throughout the Middle East, made most Americans look less favorably on the Arab and Islamic worlds. (Attitudes toward Arab and Muslim Americans, however, remained relatively positive.) The progress that Arab- and Muslim-American groups had been hoping to make in shifting Washington to a more critical stance toward Israel evaporated. And with the growing frequency of Palestinian suicide bombers in late 2001 and throughout 2002, the Bush administration stood even more firmly behind Israel, to the point of washing its hands of Yasir Arafat, the Palestinian leader.

Arab- and Muslim-American groups also lost ground at home on one of their main domestic issues, ending the practice of racial profiling—that is, singling out people for law enforcement investigation on the basis of their ethnicity or race. The Bush administration responded to September 11 by asking 5,000 men from the Middle East to submit to voluntary interviews with the FBI to see whether they could provide any leads on terrorists in the United States. Arab and Muslim groups argued that these interviews were not really voluntary and were intimidating their communities. These complaints did not move the administration; in early 2002, it began interviewing several thousand more Middle Easterners living in the United States and announced that it would intensify efforts to find and expel Middle Easterners who had been ordered deported for visa violations. The administration also began to require male visitors from most Islamic countries to undergo a special registration with the INS that included being fingerprinted, photographed, and interviewed under oath.

11-2c Arab Countries

Although often overlooked in discussions about interest groups, foreign governments operate in the United States as a type of government interest group. Embassies devote considerable energy to representing their countries' interests to Congress and the executive branch. Countries also hire lobbyists and public relations firms to advance their interests and polish their image. Some of the most devoted practitioners of government interest group activity have been Middle Eastern countries.

After September 11, Arab countries experienced a sea of change in their relations with Washington. Saudi Arabia experi-

enced perhaps the most abrupt reversal. Fifteen of the nineteen hijackers came from Saudi Arabia. Critics charged that the Saudi monarchy had bought peace for itself at home by encouraging virulent anti-Americanism and that it had done little to prevent wealthy Saudis from funding Al Qaeda's operations. The criticism intensified when Saudi Arabia's rulers refused to allow the U.S. military to stage operations against Afghanistan from bases on its soil. With some prominent Americans talking openly about targeting Saudi Arabia in the war on terrorism, Riyadh hired two leading Washington lobbying firms to quell anti-Saudi sentiment in the United States.

11-3 Surprise Survivors

Unfavorable political developments don't always doom interest groups. Consider two of America's most troubled industries—steel and textiles. George Bush campaigned as an ardent proponent of free trade and criticized those seeking to protect American companies from foreign competition. With his public approval ratings jumping to 90 percent after September 11, Bush seemed to be in an unassailable political position to push his free trade policies. Yet, following the attacks, he took steps to shield the steel and textile industries from foreign competitors.

11-3a Steel Industry

The U.S. steel industry has been declining for decades. Pittsburgh, once synonymous with steel, is no longer home to any steel plants. Employment in the steel industry has fallen to fewer than 200,000 workers, less than one tenth of 1 percent of the U.S. workforce. The industry's critics

argue that its problems are self-inflicted. Companies failed to control their costs and modernize their plants. Steel industry executives and steel workers placed the blame elsewhere—on cheap steel from overseas. In early 2002, they wanted the Bush administration to impose steep tariffs (that is, taxes) on imported steel. That would raise the cost of imported steel, making American steel more competitive.

The idea of protecting the steel industry was not popular in an administration populated with proponents of free markets. President Bush's economic advisers argued that he had campaigned against raising taxes and that protecting the steel industry would reward its bad business practices. Foreign-policy advisers warned that imposing tariffs would alienate America's trading partners, invite retaliation against American manufacturers, and strain the anti-terrorism coalition. Steel-consuming industries—including makers of tractors, home appliances, and automotive parts—argued that the tariffs would raise their business costs, making them less able to compete internationally and reducing their profits. None of this deterred the major steel companies or the United Steelworkers Union. In March 2002, they got much of what they wanted—a 30 percent tariff on imported steel. (The tariffs were eventually found to violate international trade rules, and in December 2003 the Bush administration announced it was scrapping them.)

11-3b Textile Industry

When President Bush pressed General Pervez Musharraf to join the U.S.-led war on terrorism, the Pakistani president asked for one thing in return—greater access to the American market for Pakistani textiles. Although textiles is a small and dying industry in the United States, employing fewer than 400,00 people, it is Pakistan's major industry. Musharraf calculated that better access for Pakistani textile exports would help the Pakistani economy and deflect criticism at home over his decision to ally with the United States against fellow Muslims in Afghanistan.

The Bush administration initially looked ready to grant Musharraf's request. Most officials judged it a small price to pay, given Pakistan's pivotal role in defeating the Taliban. But the American textile lobby, led by the American Textile Manufacturers Institute, had no interest in being stuck with the bill. It lobbied sympathetic members of Congress to oppose giving Pakistan trade breaks. In October 2001,

Senators Jesse Helms (R-N.C.) and Fritz Hollings (D-S.C.) sent the administration a letter warning that American textile workers "must not be made pawns in efforts to build an international coalition." This pressure prompted the Bush administration to backpedal. It eventually extended breaks to Pakistani textiles that amounted to only about one-tenth of what General Musharraf had requested.

11-3c Keys to Survival

Why were the steel and textile industries able to survive what should have been an adverse political environment for them? The answer lies in America's geopolitical map, which September 11 did not change. President Bush was elected despite failing to win the popular vote, and only one seat in the Senate and six seats in the House separated Republicans and

Democrats. From that vantage point, the steel and textile industries assumed disproportionate importance. Steel workers are a major force in Pennsylvania and West Virginia—two states likely to be up for grabs in 2004—and textile jobs are concentrated in North and South Carolina—two states with tight congressional races. For Bush's political advisers, and ultimately the president himself, keeping voters in those states happy was itself a major objective. Even though Bush was riding high in the public opinion polls, alienating the textile and steel workers might have meant giving Democrats control of both houses of Congress, as well as a good shot at retaking the White House in 2004. September 11 changed many things, but not the Bush administration's interest in maintaining Republicans' hold on power.

Readings for Further Study

Confessore, Nicholas. 2002. "Borderline Insanity."
Washington Monthly 34 (May): 44–49.

Foer, Franklin. 2002. "Fabric Softener." *New Republic*.
March 4 and 12: 19–21.

Power, Stephen. 2003. "War on Terror Has Lawmakers
Battling to Score the Best Deals." *Wall Street Journal*,
January 24.

Websites to Check Out

Note: As we went to press, these sites were functional using the URLs provided. Check out the online text for the most up-to-date URLs.

Site name: National Council of La Raza

URL: http://www.nclr.org/

An extensive source of information about applied research, policy analysis, and advocacy involving issues important to Hispanic Americans, including education, immigration, housing, health, civil rights enforcement, and foreign policy.

Site name: Project USA

URL: http://www.projectusa.org

A variety of resources arguing that the United States should severely restrict immigration.

Site name: United Steelworkers of America

URL: http://www.uswa.org/

Extensive materials arguing for the need to protect the U.S. steel industry from unfair foreign competition, plus other information about one of America's most prominent unions.

Congress after September 11

James M. Lindsay

Members of Congress had few experiences to prepare them for September 11. Its only precedent in U.S. history was the Japanese attack on Pearl Harbor in 1941, which happened long before most senators and representatives were born. Most members had lived through the U.S. entrance into and exit from the Vietnam War. But that had transpired over the course of a decade, and American civilians were never targeted for attack. Members had also watched the United States triumph in the Gulf War. That conflict, however, began with an Iraqi invasion of Kuwait that had nowhere near the impact on the American psyche that the collapse of the twin towers at the World Trade Center did.

So members of Congress could count themselves as fortunate. They had spent much of their careers—indeed, most of their lives—grappling with the problems that arise from peace and prosperity. But in the aftermath of September 11, they suddenly found themselves on unfamiliar terrain. They had to confront the problems that arise from war and insecurity. Above all, they had to find a way to conduct their legislative business that both fit with their personal beliefs and served their political interests.

Given how much the political terrain changed after September 11, it is not surprising that the way Congress operates changed in the days and weeks following the attacks as well. Members put aside old problems and tackled new ones. They tempered their partisan instincts. And they acted with a speed seldom seen in Washington. The dramatic nature of these changes, coupled with the fact that they helped President George W. Bush accomplish his goals, prompted claims that Congress had become a rubber stamp for White House initiatives. The truth was more complex than that. Members of Congress deferred to President Bush in some areas, but not others. Their deference reflected a mix of principled belief and practical politics.

As Americans gained emotional distance from the attacks on the World Trade Center and the Pentagon, political life on Capitol Hill slowly began to revert to more normal patterns. Members of Congress, however, still face one important question. What should they do now to protect America's system of government in the event that terrorists seek to obliterate Congress? If members fail to act, they could leave the country vulnerable to a political catastrophe unlike any in U.S. history.

12-1 The Impact of September 11

September 11 had a profound and visible impact on the business of Congress. In the span of a few hours, the nation's political agenda was transformed. Members of Congress did not cease to be Democrats and Republicans. They did, however, put much of their partisan wrangling aside, at least temporarily. And an institution known for gridlock showed that it could act with surprising dispatch.

12-1a A New Agenda

September 11's most obvious impact was on Congress's agenda. When members of Congress returned to Washington after Labor Day, they expected to resume debate on a long list of domestic political issues—campaign finance reform, a patient's bill of rights, and Medicare reform, to name just a few. All of these issues were hardy perennials in American politics; members had been arguing over them for months if not years. By contrast, few members planned to devote much time to foreign policy. The subject had seldom come up when they were back in their districts and states during the August recess. If there is any fundamental rule of congressional life, it is this—members focus on issues their constituents care about.

September 11 turned the planned political agenda on its head. Domestic issues that once seemed pressing were put on hold. Questions about homeland security and defense and foreign policy took center stage. Should Congress authorize the president to use military force against those responsible for the terrorist attacks? (It did.) Should it rewrite the nation's anti-terrorism laws? (It did.) Should it overhaul the whole process of providing airport security? (It did.) And no one was asking about the price tag for all these new initiatives. In the aftermath of the terrorist attacks, the hottest topic during the summer of 2001—how could Congress preserve the federal budget surplus?—disappeared from the political agenda.

12-1b The New Bipartisanship

September 11 produced a second immediate change in the way Congress operates: It prompted, at least initially, a new bipartisanship. Most Americans have long disliked what they see as excessive squabbling between Democrats and Republicans in Washington. George Bush tried to capitalize on this sentiment during the 2000 presidential campaign by promising to change the tone of politics in the nation's capital. Nonetheless, during his first eight months in office, partisan squabbling, sometimes aided and abetted by the White House itself, continued to rule the day.

Partisanship took a back seat, however, after September 11. Democrats and Republicans alike

rallied around the president. The most obvious sign of the new bipartisanship was Congress's passage on September 14 of a resolution authorizing President Bush to use "all necessary and appropriate force" against those responsible for the terrorist attacks. It passed with only one dissenting vote. But the willingness to cooperate extended to other initiatives as well. Democratic and Republican leaders in Congress worked closely together and with the White House to provide emergency funding to respond to the attacks. And just as important, though perhaps less noticeable to the average American, the two houses of Congress worked "bicamerally." Disputes between the House and Senate can often be as intense as those between Democrats and Republicans—especially when a different party controls each chamber, as was the case after September 11.

The new bipartisanship did not mean that all partisan disputes ended, though when debate did arise it often broke down along unusual lines. For instance, criticism of the White House proposal to strengthen the nation's anti-terrorism laws—which eventually culminated in passage of the USA Patriot Act—came from a coalition of liberal Democrats and conservative Republicans. These members of Congress were accustomed to battling each other on issues such as abortion, government regulation, and tax policy. But in this case, they were united by their mutual suspicion of giving the executive branch too much power to investigate the activities of Americans.

12-1c The New Decisiveness

The third change that September 11 brought to Capitol Hill in the fall

of 2001 was a new urgency to pass legislation. Congress has long angered proponents of change—and pleased advocates of the status quo—because it usually moves slowly. During times of peace and prosperity, members of Congress believe they have the luxury—and the responsibility—to take their time evaluating legislative initiatives. Members demand the right to be heard, seize opportunities to score political points, and look for ways to change bills more to their liking. What results is "gridlock" to some and "deliberation" to others.

In the days and weeks immediately following September 11, however, decisiveness replaced deliberation as the watchword. Members felt a sense of urgency to act. They worried that moving slowly might leave the United States and the American people vulnerable to more attacks. As former Representative Bill Frenzel describes it, "The normal diversions that add so much time to the legislative process—including budget restrictions, partisanship, parochialism, and members' philosophical leanings—were not ignored, but they were reduced." Members understand that their decisiveness has a cost. "As a lawmaker," Frenzel says, "when you pass bills in an emergency, you know you're going to make mistakes. The reality is that the emergency warrants quick and sometimes imperfect work, but it is more important to get bills passed in order to help the nation move forward."

12-2 A Congressional Rubber Stamp?

The bipartisanship and decisiveness that characterized Congress's behavior in the months immediately following September 11 clearly benefited President Bush. Before the terrorist attacks, his prospects for persuading the House and (especially) the Senate to follow his legislative lead looked doubtful. After the attacks, he had considerable success winning support on Capitol Hill. Does that mean that September 11 turned Congress into a rubber stamp for the president's initiatives?

No. To begin with, President Bush's track record on Capitol Hill improved after the attacks, but it was not perfect. On a number of issues Congress balked at what President Bush proposed to do. It refused to grant his request that the White House be given a blank check to decide how emergency funds would be spent. It scaled back his proposed anti-terrorism legislation, demanding among other things that its key provisions expire in 2005 unless Congress acted to renew them. It insisted, over White House objections, that the federal government assume the responsibility for airport security. The Senate blocked action on President Bush's plan to stimulate the economy, which had weakened even before the attacks. It also fought with the White House over how much freedom the administration should have to hire and fire workers in the new Department of Homeland Security.

There was, however, one area where members of Congress clearly were reluctant in the first eighteen months after September 11 to question President Bush. That was on his conduct of the war on terrorism. Virtually no one opposed his decision to declare war on terrorism in general or on Al Qaeda in particular. No members offered legislation to cut off funding for military operations in Afghanistan. The administration's

decisions to send U.S. military advisers to Georgia, the Philippines, and Yemen to provide anti-terrorism training were applauded rather than booed. And Congress voted by a large margin and with surprisingly little debate to give the president authority to wage war on Iraq.

Three factors account for Congress's robust support for the president, especially on the conduct of the war. The most important one in the early days of the crisis is probably the one that drew the least attention: Members of Congress genuinely agreed with what the president proposed to do. The enormity of what happened on September 11, the fact that civilians were deliberately targeted, and Osama bin Laden's intention to keep attacking until America withdrew from the Islamic world all simplified the issue for most people. Indeed, members were just like their constituents, who also showed remarkable unanimity on the need to strike back at Al Qaeda and the governments that sheltered them. And as long as the war on terrorism went well—and it largely did during its first eight months—most members saw no need to question U.S. policy.

A second factor that helped drive congressional support for the president's decisions was a genuine belief on the part of many members that during a crisis it is in the country's best interests that Congress defer to presidential leadership. Just as too many cooks spoil the soup, wars by committee are difficult to run. Domestic debates may also have the perverse effect of encouraging the adversary to fight because it believes America is divided. So many members believe that the only responsible course of action they can take during

wartime is to give the president considerable leeway to plot the nation's strategy.

The third factor is the one that elicited the most discussion but which was probably the least important in the immediate aftermath of September 11—electoral politics. When the president is at 80 percent approval in the public opinion polls—as George Bush was for months after the terrorist attacks—it is difficult for most members to criticize the White House on its military strategy. That is especially true for Democrats facing a Republican president. Ever since the Vietnam War, Democrats have positioned themselves as "softer" on defense than Republicans. This stance helps when the public believes Washington is exaggerating the threats facing the country; it hurts when the public believes Washington needs to do more to protect the United States. For Democrats, then, criticizing President Bush's handling of the war on terrorism in the absence of clear evidence that his strategy was not working would play to the stereotype that they were not prepared to stand up for America.

If political calculations were not the main reason that Congress initially rallied around President Bush, their importance grew over time as the immediate crisis ebbed and talk turned to "phase two" in the war on terrorism. In late February 2002, Senate Majority Leader Tom Daschle (D-S.D.) reiterated his support for the war in remarks to journalists. But he added that the White House needed to give Congress a "clearer understanding" of where the war on terrorism was headed and that he believed that efforts to expand the war lacked "a clear direction." He also said that the United States had to find top

Taliban and Al Qaeda leaders, including Osama bin Laden, "or we will have failed."

Congressional Republicans quickly jumped all over these seemingly mild remarks. (President Bush himself had said two months earlier that he wanted bin Laden captured "dead or alive.") Senate Republican leader Trent Lott accused Daschle of "trying to divide our country while we are united." House Majority Whip Tom Delay called Daschle's remarks "disgusting." Representative Tom Davis (R-Va.) invoked the technical definition of treason when he said Daschle's "divisive comments have the effect of giving aid and comfort to our enemies by allowing them to exploit divisions in our country." None of these comments persuaded Daschle to retract what he said. But it was telling that virtually none of his Democratic colleagues came to his defense. They were silent, even though many had voiced similar concerns in private.

It is easy to understand why Republican leaders would want to paint Democrats as unpatriotic, and why Democrats would go to great lengths to avoid doing or saying anything that would give that charge substance. The war on terrorism was popular, and seats in Congress were almost evenly divided between the two parties. A political party seen to be lacking in enthusiasm for the war could find itself on the losing end at the next election, and perhaps for many more in the years to come. That calculation influenced many Democrats on the run up to the Iraq War. Most of them swallowed their reservations about the wisdom of war, deciding that, in this instance at least, discretion was the better part of valor.

As the costs of occupying Iraq became clear, however, many Democrats (and more than a few Republicans) began to wonder whether the country's broader interests had been served by a Congress that declined to debate the White House's national security proposals. Administrations dislike being asked tough questions about what they intend to do. But they often benefit from it. Forced to think hard about their policies, to address hidden assumptions, and to confront potential dangers, they are likely to make better choices. Historians will long debate whether the Bush administration would have made smarter choices in Iraq after the fall of Baghdad if members of Congress had been less deferential to the White House.

12-3 The Return to Normalcy

Many Americans no doubt hoped that the less partisan, more decisive Congress that emerged after September 11 would stick around. But by the summer of 2002, all signs suggested that, when it came to domestic policy, life on Capitol Hill was inexorably reverting to what it had been on September 10.

This return to normalcy was visible in Washington's evolving political agenda. The debates over domestic policy that had been put on hold months earlier resumed. Congress passed a campaign finance bill. The Senate defeated President Bush's proposal to open the Arctic National Wildlife Refuge for oil exploration. Members wrangled over the fate of the patient's rights bill. Congress's return to these and other domestic policy issues was

natural. They had been major issues before September 11 because they affected the lives and well-being of millions of Americans.

At the same time, signs of renewed partisanship abounded. The divisions on campaign finance reform and drilling in the Arctic National Wildlife Refuge broke down largely on party lines. The two parties could not agree on whether to pass legislation to stimulate the economy. Senate Republicans complained that Democrats were refusing to allow President Bush's judicial nominations to come for a vote. Senate Republicans and Democrats also split over how much freedom President Bush should have to disregard union work rules as he put together the new Department of Homeland Security. This drift back toward life as it existed on September 10 is not surprising. The philosophical and political differences separating Democrats from Republicans were simply too strong—and the next congressional election too near—for the two to put all their differences aside.

Finally, the decisiveness that Congress displayed in September and October 2001 gave way to gridlock—or deliberation, depending on one's perspective. Efforts to build a consensus on reorganizing the intelligence community to avoid the mistakes that contributed to September 11 broke down. Optimism that headway might be made in resolving major health care issues proved misplaced. The 107th Congress even called it quits in November 2002 without completing work on one of its basic tasks—passing annual appropriations bills. The reason for the slowdown was simple. As months passed without another terrorist attack, members of

Congress again began to feel comfortable taking time to look more carefully at what they were being asked to approve. Sometimes, they did not like what they saw.

The 108th Congress that opened in January 2003 almost immediately lapsed into gridlock. The session began with a dispute between Senate Republicans and Democrats over how to allocate committee seats and budgets. This quickly turned into substantive disputes over White House proposals for a tax cut and an overhaul of Medicare. As the two parties headed into their presidential nominating conventions in the summer of 2004, they had, with the exception of a bill creating new prescription drug benefits for seniors, failed to strike a compromise on the major legislative differences separating them. September 11 may have reminded Americans of what they had in common. It did not, however, end deep-seated policy disagreements between the two major parties.

12-4 The Unthinkable

Congress may have returned to business as usual by 2002, but at least one important question prompted by September 11 remained unfinished. It involved the fourth hijacked plane, which crashed in western Pennsylvania. No one knows the plane's intended target. Many speculate that it may have been Congress itself. What would have happened if United Airlines Flight 93 had crashed into the Capitol building?

The answer to that question is troubling. On the morning of September 11, the House and Senate were in session. Both chambers were filled with representatives and senators. Had Flight 93 crashed into the Capitol building, dozens of members—

perhaps even hundreds—could have been killed. The human tragedy of such a catastrophe is obvious. But the consequences could have been even more far reaching, possibly even culminating in the loss of one of our three branches of government.

Why? Because neither the U.S. Constitution nor any statute in the law books provides for keeping Congress running in the face of a catastrophic attack. Some constitutional rules could even make it difficult to get Congress back into business quickly. For example, Article I provides that a bill can become a law only if majorities in both chambers vote yes. By tradition, the number of votes that constitutes a majority is based on the number of living and duly sworn members in each chamber. It is not based on the number that shows up to vote. So if an attack hospitalized a substantial portion of Congress, it might not be able to meet and conduct its business.

Ironically, an attack that killed substantial numbers of lawmakers, rather than merely incapacitating them, would be less disruptive because the number of votes needed to reach a majority is calculated based on *living* members. But a massive death toll would create a different problem, namely, how to replace members. The Constitution requires that all House vacancies be filled by special election. Under existing laws, it would be months before these elections could be held. In the meantime, the House would be run by what might be a small fraction of its intended membership.

The Constitution does not impose an election requirement on Senate seats, so Senate vacancies are easier to fill. Some states require elections; others give the

governor authority to appoint replacements. Even here, though, the result could be undesirable. If the governor and the deceased senator hail from different parties, then gubernatorial choice could dramatically shift the partisan balance in the Senate. And if the Senate death toll is high, it is conceivable that Americans could end up with a Senate in which a majority of its members is unelected.

None of these scenarios is appealing. As Norman Ornstein, a Washington political commentator, observes, "Among the last things the United States needs in the aftermath of a terrorist attack is the enduring absence of national leadership—or the necessity, for an extended period of time, for a president or a literal handful of lawmakers to act in sweeping ways in their absence (i.e., the equivalent of martial law)." That outcome is hardly compatible with our ideas about democratic government. It would be even worse if the obliteration of Congress occurred simultaneously with the assassination of the president and senior executive branch officials.

The problem that members of Congress face today is that there is no simple fix to the havoc that a terrorist attack could wreak on our system of democratic government. A constitutional amendment is likely necessary, but what that amendment (or any ordinary legislation) should say is a matter of debate. Should it redefine what constitutes a majority during a period of national emergency? Should it provide for interim appointments to the House and Senate until special elections can be held? Should it provide for emergency powers to be delegated to congressional leaders if large numbers of members are killed or incapacitated? And what constitutes a "national emergency" or "large numbers"?

For two-and-a-half years after September 11, Congress put off debate on how to fix the problem that a major terrorist attack could create. Finally, in April 2004, the House passed a bill allowing for special House elections in the event a terrorist attack killed 100 or more of its members. Under the proposed legislation, within ten days of the declaration of "emergency circumstances," political parties could nominate one candidate in each congressional district with a vacancy, and the special election would be held within 45 days. Critics argued that 45 days was too short a time in which to hold meaningful elections and too long a time to go without a fully staffed House. They argued instead for a constitutional amendment that would empower state governors to make temporary appointments to the House, thereby allowing more time to organize a new election. Proponents of a constitutional amendment hoped their approach would win supporters on the other side of Capitol Hill. In any event, the Senate did not move quickly to address the continuity in government issue.

Congress's reluctance to address the question of what should happen after a major terrorist attack is not surprising. Like most people, members of Congress do not like to think about the unthinkable. And because September 11 has receded into the past, the sense of urgency and fear that many members felt in the first hours after the attacks has faded as well. But if Congress fails to grapple with the unthinkable, it will leave the country open to a potentially catastrophic interruption of its system of government.

Readings for Further Study

Binder, Sarah, and Bill Frenzel. 2002. The Business of Congress after September 11. Brookings Institution *Policy Dialogue*, No. 1. February. Available at http://www.brookings.edu/dybdocroot/comm/policybriefs/pd01.htm

Dionne, E. J., Jr., Bruce Katz, James M. Lindsay, Thomas E. Mann, and Peter R. Orszag. 2003. After the Midterms: Congress, the President, and Policymaking in 2003.

Brookings Institution *Policy Brief*, No. 115. February. Available at http://www.brookings.edu/dybdocroot/comm/policybriefs/pb115.pdf

Continuity of Government Commission. 2003. *Preserving Our Institutions: The First Report of the Continuity of Government Commission*. Available at http://www.continuityofgovernment.org/pdfs/FirstReport.pdf

Websites to Check Out

Note: As we went to press, these sites were functional using the URLs provided. Check out the online text for the most up-to-date URLs.

Site name: Congress.org
URL: http://www.congress.org
A privately run website that provides a comprehensive and searchable guide to the U.S. Congress, along with a feature that allows you to email your elected representatives and to read what other Americans think.

Site name: Continuity of Government Commission
URL: http://www.continuityofgovernment.org/home.html
The Continuity of Government Commission, which was launched in fall 2002, is studying what steps should be taken to preserve the continuity of U.S. government institutions in the event of a catastrophic attack.

Site name: Roll Call Online
URL: http://www.rollcall.com
The website of the daily paper for Capitol Hill provides some news, analysis, and commentary in the free portion of its site.

The Bush Presidency after September 11

Cary R. Covington

Americans have long held conflicted attitudes toward the presidency. The framers, fresh from overthrowing tyrannical British rule, were deeply suspicious of executive authority. So they wrote a Constitution that checked presidential power. Yet in times of trouble, Americans have put aside these fears of executive tyranny and called for a strong leader who would work energetically to solve national problems and protect national interests.

The lesson here is clear: What Americans want from their presidents depends on the climate of the times. During times of peace and prosperity, we favor a presidency with limited powers. But when crises arise, we swing like a pendulum to favor a more robust conception of the office. Presidents who fail to offer strong leadership in such times endanger the success of their presidencies.

President George W. Bush and his advisers understood these lessons. They knew that the September 11 attacks on the World Trade Center and the Pentagon created a crisis of historic proportions, simultaneously increasing Bush's political resources and heightening public expectations for his leadership.

How did the attacks on September 11 change the expectations and political resources available to President Bush? How, in the subsequent eighteen months, did he use his resources to meet those expectations?

13-1 Heightened Expectations

President Bush spent his first seven months in office focused primarily on domestic policy. His top legislative priority was persuading Congress to cut income tax rates. He succeeded. He also worked with Congress to pass legislation overhauling the federal government's programs to assist education. Administratively, Bush used his powers to fulfill several campaign promises on domestic policy. He established the Office of Faith-Based and Community Initiatives to facilitate cooperation between private religious charities and government; blocked and revoked environmental and health and safety regulations that he believed placed excessive burdens on business; and repealed protections for organized labor that the Clinton administration had created.

In comparison, Bush approached foreign policy relatively cautiously during the spring and summer of 2001. He announced early on that the United States would no longer participate in international negotiations to complete work on the Kyoto Treaty on global warming. But he did not propose a rapid deployment of a missile defense system, or move decisively to target Al Qaeda for having attacked the *USS Cole* in October 2000, or, at least initially, propose a major increase in defense spending. The decision to focus on domestic issues first was deliberate. President Bush remembered that his father had been repeatedly accused of being more interested in what happened abroad than what happened at home. The younger Bush concluded that the American public would ultimately judge him on how well he handled domestic affairs.

September 11 changed those calculations. Bush knew almost instantly that the public, and history, would now judge his presidency by how he responded to the attacks. The presidency always comes to the forefront when the country faces threats to its national security for the reason that Alexander Hamilton pointed out more than two centuries ago in Federalist Paper #70: "decision, activity, secrecy, and dispatch will generally characterize the proceedings of one man in a much more eminent degree than the proceedings of any greater number." At no time are these qualities more greatly valued than when the nation's security is at risk.

President Bush's decision to frame his response in terms of a "war on terrorism" underscored the significance of the stakes involved. Presidents have often used the "war" metaphor to lend urgency to their policy proposals. Lyndon Johnson waged a "war on poverty." Richard Nixon urged a "war on crime." Gerald Ford called for a "war on inflation." Jimmy Carter called the energy crisis the "moral equivalent of war." By describing the September 11 attacks as an act of a war requiring military action, rather than as a crime requiring a police response, Bush highlighted the magnitude of the task before the nation and so justified his leadership role in responding to the attacks.

13-2 The Bush Presidency Gains Strength

September 11 strengthened Bush's presidency in four ways. First, it eliminated any lingering questions about the legitimacy of his presidency. Second, it justified the exercise of unilateral presidential powers. Third, it shifted the public's attention from domestic issues toward foreign-policy issues. Fourth, it sent Bush's public approval skyrocketing and discouraged critics from challenging his decisions. Each development strengthened Bush's hand, creating a "window of opportunity" for him in leading the nation as he sought to root out terrorism

and fulfill his other campaign promises.

13-2a A Challenged Presidency Legitimized

The first effect of the attacks was to put to rest questions about the legitimacy of Bush's presidency. He had assumed the presidency only after a protracted dispute in Florida and an unprecedented intervention by the U.S. Supreme Court. That controversy did not sit well with many Americans. Some members of the House of Representatives walked out when the Electoral College votes were officially counted to register their disapproval of his election. Opinion polls conducted before Bush's inauguration showed that 40 percent of the public believed he had not been legitimately elected. At the end of Bush's first One Hundred Days, the period most likely to produce a presidential honeymoon and create the public's most favorable impression of the new president, more than one third of those surveyed continued to question the legitimacy of his presidency.

These questions evaporated after September 11. The public responded to the attacks as it does to virtually any event that it perceives as a threat to the nation's security: It rallied around the president. This produced an enormous boost in Bush's public approval ratings and silenced those who had previously criticized his legitimacy or abilities as president. Press coverage became much more respectful, and several newspaper columnists who criticized Bush's decisions in the first hours after the attacks were fired. Thus, events bestowed upon Bush what he had not been able to generate for himself: pub-

lic acceptance of and even trust in his leadership.

13-2b Expanded Scope for Action

The second effect of the attacks was to enable Bush to use unilateral powers that would have seemed excessive in more normal circumstances. The Constitution, statutory laws, and historical practice give the president many important powers. During ordinary times, however, political constraints hinder their efforts to exercise that authority to its maximum extent. These constraints evaporate during a crisis. Actions that once seemed excessive suddenly seem necessary. The public and political opponents find they can live with a president who pushes his authority to the maximum.

13-2c Domestic Policy Gives Way to Foreign Policy

The third effect of September 11 was to change the nation's political agenda. Domestic-policy issues retreated into the background as foreign-policy issues came to the forefront. That helped Bush. Although he had gotten his tax cut and education packages through Congress, many of his other domestic-policy initiatives were foundering. His initiative to give public funds to faith-based organizations that were providing social services to the needy attracted criticism not only from secularists but also from religious groups. His decision to oppose a variety of environmental regulations the Clinton administration had proposed and to push to open the Arctic National Wildlife Reserve for oil drilling stoked public fears that he was anti-environment. Indeed, polls showed that on many domestic issues, the public had greater confidence that Democrats would protect their interests than President Bush would. September 11 pushed these growing concerns to the side. Terrorism and national security became the public's immediate focus. And on that score, Americans had greater confidence in Republicans than Democrats.

13-2d Sky-High Popularity

The final and perhaps most striking effect that September 11 had on Bush's presidency was on his public approval ratings. Like most modern presidents, Bush's popularity had declined during his first eight months in office. As Figure 13-1 shows, his job approval ratings dropped from a peak of 63 percent in early March to 51 percent by the first week in September. Though Bush could say that his fall had been modest compared to other presidents over the same time period, he also began his presidency less popular than every one of his ten predecessors since World War II.

The terrorist attacks changed all that. Bush's approval ratings immediately jumped to 86 percent. By early October they stood at 90 percent. Both the 39-percentage point jump in his approval ratings and his 90 percent level of support are records for presidents.

High public approval ratings matter because they can make it easier for presidents to persuade Congress to pass their legislative initiatives. While it is generally safe to oppose an unpopular president, it is politically risky to oppose a popular one. That goes double during wartime. Opponents worry the public will see their criticisms as unpatriotic. So popularity gives presidents a tool that they can use to accomplish their goals.

But popularity does not guarantee presidents more influence. In particular, presidents whose popularity is high because of a foreign-policy crisis usually find it difficult to translate that popularity into influence on legislation that is not directly tied to that crisis. The experiences of the first President George Bush are instructive in this

regard. His public approval ratings soared with America's victory in the Gulf War. He then sought to translate this popularity into congressional approval of his domestic-policy agenda. However, with both houses controlled by the Democrats and a presidential election on the horizon, Congress turned a cold shoulder to his requests. Thus, popularity gives presidents the opportunity to exercise influence rather than a guarantee of influence.

13-3 President Bush Responds

President Bush clearly benefited politically from September 11. The terrorist attacks opened a window of opportunity for strong presidential leadership, and he seized it. But the duration and scope of that opportunity proved to be limited. On terrorism and related issues, Bush was a virtually unquestioned leader. On other policy issues, however, his ability to dominate policymaking was much less secure and eroded over time.

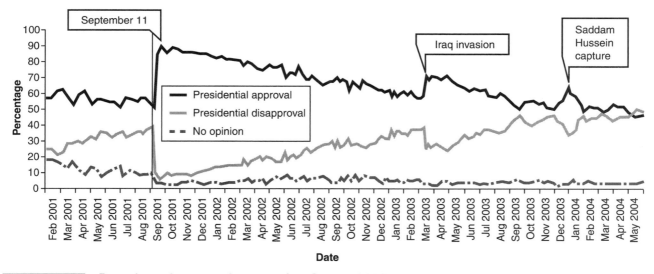

Figure 13-1 Presidential approval ratings for George W. Bush. *Polling question:* "Do you approve or disapprove of the way George W. Bush is handling his job?"

Source: Gallup Poll and CNN/*USA Today*/Gallup Poll.

Bush took several steps in the months immediately following September 11 to address the threat to the United States. He used his unilateral administrative powers to sign more executive orders in the first three and one-half months after the terrorist attacks than he had during the first eight months of his presidency. Many of his orders were widely endorsed, as when he ordered the airline industry to strengthen cockpit doors, or when he called the military reserves into action. Other directives were controversial, though. His orders establishing military tribunals and freezing the assets of anyone suspected of aiding the Al Qaeda network provoked protests. Yet, none of the orders were blocked on the grounds that Bush lacked the authority to act. During a crisis, presidents are expected to respond, and the public gives them great latitude to do so.

Bush also took the lead in seeking new laws to respond to the attacks. Congress moved with remarkable speed to enact several of his initiatives, including bills to authorize him to use force against those responsible for the attacks, strengthen the nation's counterterrorism laws, help New York City and the airline industry recover from the attacks, and improve the nation's border security. In February 2002, he proposed, and Congress subsequently approved, the largest defense spending increase in two decades. In October 2002, Bush persuaded Congress to vote overwhelmingly to approve a resolution giving him authority to use military force as he saw fit against Iraq.

Congress sometimes tinkered with Bush's legislative proposals on terrorism and national security. In the main, however, it accepted them. Congress's cooperative spirit reflected to a considerable extent its own sense of the need to act quickly and its agreement with the White House on the merits. But it also reflected a clear calculation that the political costs of being seen as obstructing what the president was trying to accomplish in the country's hour of need could be enormous.

However, Bush had much more difficulty leading on issues unrelated to terrorism. One top Bush priority was legislation opening the Arctic National Wildlife Reserve for oil exploration. The House approved the idea, but the Senate rejected it. Bush's judicial nominations made very little headway in the Senate in 2002. His budget proposals for fiscal year 2003 languished when the House and Senate could not agree on funding levels for most government agencies.

One reason Bush encountered increased congressional resistance in 2002 to his legislative agenda was that his public approval ratings had fallen from the peaks they had reached immediately after September 11. As Figure 13-1 shows, a year after the attacks, the percentage of the public approving of his performance in office had fallen to 66 percent, while the level of disapproval had climbed to 30 percent. Emboldened by the downward trend in the president's approval ratings, congressional Democrats began to assert themselves even on terrorism-related issues. For example, in early fall 2002, they held up passage of Bush's proposal to create a Department of Homeland Security because workers in the new agency would not enjoy the same civil service protections as other federal workers.

13-4 The Midterm Surprise

President Bush realized that he could give new life to his diminishing advantage if he could persuade American voters to make Republicans the majority party in the Senate as well as the House. Presidents find it much easier to enact their agendas when their own party controls both houses of Congress. For example, following the September 11 attacks, Republicans regularly used their narrow majority in the House to pass Bush's initiatives. In contrast, Democrats, who controlled the Senate by a single vote, frequently used their majority status to block what the president wanted to accomplish. Bush knew that if Republicans retained control of the House in the November 2002 midterm elections and seized control of the Senate as well, he would be in a much more powerful position in the second half of his term than he had been in the first half.

The results of previous midterm elections did not offer Bush much reason to be optimistic that he could restore Congress to Republican control. As Table 13-1 shows, the president's party lost seats in the first midterm election of every presidency from Harry Truman through Bill Clinton. The numbers for the Senate were only slightly more encouraging. The president's party gained seats on only three of nine occasions. The conventional wisdom was clear: Presidents are seldom able to influence midterm elections in their favor. Voters tend to view congressional elections as local rather than national events.

But Bush had formidable resources. Despite the erosion of his public approval ratings from their once astronomical heights, he was one of only two post–World War II presidents more popular with the American public heading into the midterm elections than at the start of his term. (His father was the other.) His 67 percent approval rating in October 2002 was higher than that of any other president at a comparable point in their terms. In addition, the public continued to express much greater confidence in his leadership in the war on terrorism than in his presidency in general.

Bush sought to exploit these advantages. He campaigned vigorously on behalf of Republican congressional candidates, going as far as to launch a grueling 10,000-mile, seventeen-city, fifteen-state campaign swing on the eve of Election Day. Everywhere he stopped, he urged voters to give him a Republican Congress that would be more helpful and sympathetic to his efforts to fight terrorism. No president in memory had so publicly staked his reputation on being able to influence the outcome of a midterm election.

Contrary to most expectations, the public was receptive to Bush's appeals. The November 2002 elections produced a historic shift in partisan control of Congress. Republicans increased the size of their majority in the House, the only time a president's party had done so in a first term since World War II. More impressive (and more important to Bush), the Republicans also claimed majority status in the Senate, something that no president's party had ever done in a

| Table 13-1 | Midterm Election Seat Changes in the House and Senate for First-Term Presidents, 1946–2002 |

President	Seat Change in the House	Seat Change in the Senate
Harry S. Truman	−31	−5
Dwight D. Eisenhower	−18	−1
John F. Kennedy	−5	+2
Lyndon B. Johnson	−48	−4
Richard M. Nixon	−12	+1
James E. Carter	−16	−3
Ronald W. Reagan	−27	+1
George H. W. Bush	−7	−1
William J. Clinton	−54	−10
Average Change, Truman through Clinton	−24	−1.5
George W. Bush	+6	+2

Source: Peverill Squire et al., *Dynamics of Democracy*, 3rd ed. (Cincinnati, OH: Atomic Dog Publishing, 2001), Appendix L, updated by the author.

first-term midterm election. The result was a unified Republican government in Washington for the first time in fifty years.

13-5 The Iraq War

The 2002 midterm election both "institutionalized" and broadened the window of opportunity that September 11 created for President Bush. With Republicans now controlling both the House and Senate, he received a more sympathetic hearing for his legislative proposals than when control of Congress was divided. Indeed, the effects of the midterm elections on Capitol Hill were evident even before the victorious candidates were sworn into office. In a lame-duck session of Congress, Senate Democrats dropped their opposition to the president's proposals on civil service protection and agreed to pass the legislation creating the Department of Homeland Security.

Bush's 2003 State of the Union address reflected his new political strength. The first half of his address presented an array of domestic policy initiatives, ranging from more tax cuts to Medicare and Social Security reform that would have been less likely had Democrats retained control of the Senate. The second half of the address discussed the nation's security. The president outlined his growing concern about the danger that Iraq posed, and he insisted he was willing to confront that danger even if the United Nations refused to authorize military action.

President Bush eventually made good on his threat. On March 19, 2003, U.S. forces, aided by British troops and small contingents of soldiers from Australia and Poland, invaded Iraq. Bush's decision to go to war once again ratcheted up the expectations and opportunities for his presidency. Wars can make or break presidencies. Abraham Lincoln and Franklin Roosevelt are generally acknowledged as two of our greatest presidents. Their reputations were grounded in their wartime successes. In contrast, Lyndon Johnson saw Vietnam undo his otherwise successful presidency.

President Bush justified his decision to go war on the grounds that Iraq posed an unacceptable threat to the United States. He and his advisers argued that Saddam Hussein's government possessed massive quantities of weapons of mass destruction, weapons they might give to terrorists. Administration officials also contended that the Iraqi people would welcome the American invasion because it would end a tyrant's rule and put Iraq on a path to democratic government.

Opponents denounced the war as unnecessary and foolhardy. They believed that America's overwhelming military threat would deter Iraq from attacking the United States or giving weapons of mass destruction to terrorists. Critics also worried that the war would produce chaos rather than democracy in Iraq. That, in their view, would destabilize the Middle East and in all likelihood increase the terrorist threat to the United States.

By any calculation, then, the decision to attack Iraq represented a substantial political gamble. Once the bombs began falling on Baghdad, the American public again rallied around President Bush. As Figure 13-1 shows, however, the rally was smaller than it had been after September 11. His public approval ratings jumped only about a dozen points. The modest nature of the rally reflected a deep partisan split over the wisdom of the decision to go to war. Although more than nine out of ten Republicans

immediately supported it, only half of Democrats did. Americans who opposed the decision to go to war believed that the administration should have let weapons inspectors continue their work or waited until the United Nations authorized military action before going to war.

Although the American military victory in Iraq boosted Bush's public approval ratings, this greater popularity did not automatically give him increased say over domestic policy. Just as was the case after September 11, Congress was willing to defer to Bush's judgments on what to do abroad but not to his proposals on what to do at home. Indeed, the day after the Iraq war began, the Republican-controlled Senate voted for a second time to reject his proposal to drill in the Arctic. It later voted to reduce by half the size of his proposed tax cut.

13-6 The Future of the Bush Presidency

Although the Iraq War was popular with Americans in April 2003, a year later, it was starting to become a political liability for President Bush. As the death toll from the U.S. occupation mounted through the winter and spring of 2004, many Americans began to worry that the United States had made a mistake in invading Iraq. Although Bush insisted that he intended to stay the course in Iraq, public sentiment favoring a quick American exit was rising. By May 2004, 40 percent of Americans supported withdrawing U.S. troops from Iraq in order to avoid further U.S.

casualties, even if that meant that civil order would not be restored there. With the public souring on Iraq, Bush's public approval ratings dropped below 50 percent, as Figure 13-1 shows.

The American public's trepidations about Iraq and Bush's declining public approval ratings created a political opportunity for Democrats. Many of them had felt muzzled since September 11 in criticizing Bush's foreign policy for fear of looking unpatriotic. Now that they had an opening, they were delighted to argue that he had committed a foreign-policy blunder of epic proportions. They also pounced on the opportunity to argue that Bush, like his father, had been too concerned with events overseas and, as a result, had neglected important problems here at home.

Whether Iraq would ultimately cost Bush his reelection, however, was unclear. Although in May 2004 a majority of the public disapproved of his handling of Iraq policy, Senator John Kerry, the Democratic nominee, did not immediately benefit. Polls showed the two men to be in a dead heat, and the public gave Bush substantially higher marks for leadership, and, surprisingly, for his ability to handle the situation in Iraq. Bush also had some good news going his way. Economic data in the spring of 2004 showed the economy to be picking up steam. A strong economy typically helps the incumbent president. All told, the 2004 elections looked to be a tough race, where events in the final weeks of the campaign could prove decisive.

Readings for Further Study

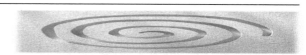

Mayer, Kenneth R. 2001. *With the Stroke of a Pen*. Princeton: Princeton University Press.

Neustadt, Richard. 1990. *Presidential Power and the Modern Presidents*. New York: Macmillan.

Simendinger, Alexis. 2004. "Power Plays." *National Journal*. April 17: 1166–1174.

Site name: The White House

URL: http://www.whitehouse.gov

The official White House web page contains an exhaustive collection of materials from the Bush presidency, including speeches, policy initiatives, and executive orders.

Site name: Federal Register—Orders

URL: http://www.archives.gov/federal_register/executive_orders/executive_orders.html

The official source for all presidential executive orders issued since Herbert Hoover. This site provides details on the orders George W. Bush has issued, both before and after the terrorist attacks.

Site name: Washingtonpost.com Politics

URL: http://www.washingtonpost.com/wp-dyn/politics/

This website contains the *Washington Post*'s coverage of American politics, with pages devoted to the Bush administration and the elections, among other topics.

Websites to Check Out

Note: As we went to press, these sites were functional using the URLs provided. Check out the online text for the most up-to-date URLs.

Solution or Sideshow?

The New Department of Homeland Security

James M. Lindsay

Tonight, I propose a permanent Cabinet-level Department of Homeland Security to unite essential agencies that must work more closely together. . . . The reason to create this department is not to increase the size of government, but to increase its focus and effectiveness. . . . This reorganization will give the good people of our government their best opportunity to succeed by organizing our resources in a way that is thorough and unified.

—President George W. Bush,
Address to the Nation, June 6, 2002

For nearly 200 years, the United States was blessed with a level of security that was the envy of the world. This is not to say that it never became embroiled in wars. It did. But unlike most countries, which have repeatedly experienced devastating wars on their home soil, the United States fought most of its wars on foreign soil. To borrow the locker room metaphor that military officers often use, the United States historically played "away games." One consequence of this history was that when it came to protecting America, the U.S. government created a bureaucratic structure that was primarily designed to defeat threats before they reached our shores. Considerably less attention was paid to creating agencies whose primary mission was preventing and responding to attacks on American soil.

September 11 shattered that mindset. America now faces the prospect of playing "home games." With this realization, Washington shifted to the question of how best to organize the U.S. government to provide for homeland security—the task of preparing for, preventing, protecting against, and responding to attacks on American soil. No one argued that government reorganization would provide a silver bullet against terrorism. But most recognized that failing to get the organizational structure right would make the war on Al Qaeda harder to win. As President Dwight D. Eisenhower once noted, "although organization cannot make a genius out of an incompetent . . . disorganization can scarcely fail to result in inefficiency and can easily lead to disaster."

Washington's eventual answer to the question of how best to organize itself for homeland security was to create a new cabinet agency, the Department of Homeland Security (DHS). The department's creation reflected a mix of politics and policy. The idea for DHS was initially championed by Senate Democrats looking to do good and score political points at the White House's expense. President Bush eventually stole the idea and used it against Democrats in the 2002 midterm elections. Now that DHS has become the nation's fourteenth cabinet agency, it is up to the Bush administration to make it work. That is a difficult task.

14-1 The Office of Homeland Security

President Bush's initial response to September 11 was to create a new Office of Homeland Security (OHS) in the White House. His pick to run OHS was his close friend, Tom Ridge, the governor of Pennsylvania. Ridge had impressive credentials. He was a decorated Vietnam War vet and a former member of Congress, in addition to being a popular two-term governor of Pennsylvania. Bush had seriously considered him as a potential running mate in 2000.

The executive order spelling out Ridge's duties also created a Homeland Security Council (HSC). The HSC is composed of the president, vice president, secretary of treasury, secretary of defense, attorney general, secretary of health and human services, secretary of transportation, director of the Federal Emergency Management Agency (FEMA), director of the Federal Bureau of Investigation (FBI), director of the Central Intelligence Agency (CIA), and director of the homeland security office.

The HSC is consciously modeled after the National Security Council (NSC), which was created at the end of World War II to advise the president on foreign and defense policy. As spelled out in the founding executive order, the HSC is "responsible for advising and assisting the President with respect to all aspects of homeland security. The Council shall serve as the mechanism for ensuring coordination of homeland security–related activities of executive departments and agencies and effective development and implementation of homeland security policies." OHS, in turn, staffs the HSC, much as the NSC staff support the work of the NSC. Although the homeland security adviser is tasked with coordinating the federal government's homeland security activities, he does not have authority to tell federal agencies what to do or how much to spend. Instead, much like the NSC adviser, his primary power for getting things done is the power of persuasion.

14-2 The Critics Weigh In

Not everyone applauded the Bush administration's approach to organizing for homeland security. Critics complained that a White House coordinator could not begin to meet the challenge facing the country. Senator Joseph Lieberman (D-Conn.), who was Al Gore's running mate in 2000, summarized the doubts about what Ridge could realistically do: "I fear that as an advisor who

lacks a statutory mandate, Senate confirmation, and budget authority, he will not be as effective as we need him to be. Governor Ridge deserves to have at least the power he enjoyed as Governor of Pennsylvania. Clearly, appointing a homeland coordinator with only advisory authority is not enough."

Lieberman and many others in Congress wanted to give the homeland security adviser more legal authority. More important, they argued that a new Cabinet-level department of homeland security should be created. This new agency would combine the Federal Emergency Management Agency (FEMA), several large agencies such as the Customs Service that had responsibility for border security, and several small programs designed to protect the country's critical infrastructure. The assumption underlying the proposal to create a new department was straightforward: Putting the major agencies responsible for homeland security under one roof would make it easier to coordinate their activities and thereby improve the country's security.

President Bush resisted Lieberman's effort to create a new homeland security agency, arguing that such a large-scale reorganization was both unnecessary and dangerous. In March 2002, Ari Fleisher, the White House spokesman, said that "creating a cabinet department doesn't solve anything." He went on to insist that "the White House needs a coordinator to work with the agencies, wherever they are."

Bush administration officials, and outside experts who shared their skepticism of the benefits of creating a new cabinet department, argued that the proposal rested on the appealing but mis-

taken assumption that greater centralization would make the American people safer. In their view, making the homeland safe from attack rested instead on doing exactly the opposite—decentralizing authority. Customs agents need to know what to look for at the border, Coast Guard cutters need to know which ships to interdict, and Immigration and Naturalization Service (INS) officers need to know whom to bar from entering the country. Hospital emergency room doctors need to know what symptoms indicate possible exposure to a biological attack. Trying to cram these diverse agencies, and their diverse missions, into a single organization could actually make the government less effective in battling terrorism, not more.

A second criticism of proposals to create a new department was that so many government agencies had a role in homeland security that it was impossible to put them all under one roof. Intelligence agencies such as the CIA and National Security Agency try to track terrorists before they reach our shores; border control agencies such as the Border Patrol, Coast Guard, Customs Service, and INS try to keep out unwanted visitors and cargo; law enforcement agencies such as the FBI, Secret Service, and Drug Enforcement Agency try to catch terrorists who might be operating in the United States; and emergency response agencies such as FEMA, the Centers for Disease Control and Prevention, and the Pentagon's Joint Task Force for Homeland Defense respond to attacks. Some agencies with critical homeland security responsibilities would by necessity remain outside any homeland security department, meaning that the problem of coordinating the efforts of different cabinet agencies would remain.

A third criticism was that formally consolidating agencies does not guarantee effective integration. Congress created the Department of Defense (DoD) in 1947, but in the view of many defense experts, it took nearly forty years and several reform efforts before the Pentagon began working as intended. Likewise, the Department of Energy was created in 1977 to bring a variety of nominally related government programs into a single organization. A quarter of a century later, however, its integration remains far from complete and its effectiveness is often questioned.

14-3 A Course Correction

President Bush's announcement on June 6, 2002, that he would ask Congress to create a homeland security department came as a surprise. Doubly surprising was the fact that the president's reorganization plan dwarfed anything being considered on Capitol Hill. His plan proposed merging 22 agencies, employing nearly 170,000 workers, and spending more than $35 billion annually. To top it all off, the president wanted Congress to pass the legislation authorizing the reorganization—which would be the most ambitious and complex government reshuffling since the creation of DoD—by the end of the year.

Why the about-face? President Bush said in his nationwide address that he was endorsing reorganization because "as many as a hundred different government agencies have some responsibilities for homeland security, and no one has final accountability." His advisers added that he had seen the limitations of the

traditional way of doing business and had decided that change was necessary.

The president's critics dismissed the claim that he had been persuaded of the merits of reorganization. They contended that he had embraced the idea for purely political reasons. In May 2002, the Senate Governmental Affairs Committee, which Senator Lieberman chaired, had approved a reorganization bill of its own. The idea was picking up some Republican support, and it looked as though the White House would suffer a major political defeat. At the same time, the administration was being buffeted by a string of news stories that questioned its competence in the weeks leading up to September 11. Reporters had uncovered evidence about how miscommunication and squabbling between and within the CIA and FBI had contributed to the government's failure to uncover the terrorist plot. Indeed, President Bush announced his reorganization proposal the night before the much-awaited congressional testimony by an FBI agent on how FBI headquarters had failed to pursue possible leads that might have uncovered the September 11 plot.

14-4 The Politics of Reorganization

President Bush's proposal caught Washington off guard and created political dilemmas for both Republicans and Democrats. Many congressional Republicans privately disliked the idea of creating a new cabinet department. For months, they had defended the administration's refusal to undertake a major reorganization. Making matters worse, many Republicans believed the plan

would lead to a bigger, more costly, more intrusive federal government—an outcome they had long fought to avoid. Anticipating these objections, Bush said in his announcement that the plan was not intended to increase the size of government and that "by ending duplication and overlap, we will spend less on overhead, and more on protecting America." Even though experts dismissed the president's claim as unrealistic, most Republicans quickly recognized that political necessity dictated that they support their party's leader.

Democrats faced a different problem. By embracing the idea of a new Cabinet department, Bush had stolen an issue that they had planned to use against the White House in the fall elections. Worse yet, most Democrats knew that after demanding the creation of a homeland security department for months, they could not suddenly denounce it as a bad idea. So Democrats could only applaud the president's change of heart and hope that voters remembered it had been a Democratic idea first. Richard Gephardt, the leader of the House Democrats, went even further. He tried to top Bush's announcement by committing Democrats to passing a reorganization bill by September 11, 2002, the first anniversary of the terrorist attacks.

Congress ultimately failed to meet Gephardt's deadline. The stumbling block was not the substance of President Bush's proposal. Many legislators on both sides of the aisle certainly had reservations about the specific organizational changes in the Bush plan. Under different circumstances, lawmakers might have substantially revised the proposed merger. But with House and Senate leaders determined to act quickly, these reservations were quashed. By early August, each chamber had prepared legislation that largely reflected the basic outlines of the organization the White House wanted to create.

The stumbling block instead was over process. President Bush wanted the freedom to strip workers in the new department of the civil service protections they had previously enjoyed. He and his advisers argued that leaving the traditional civil service regulations in effect would stifle the reorganization and reduce the department's overall effectiveness. The president's request was popular with Republicans for an additional reason. They saw it as a way to reduce the power of the heavily unionized federal workforce.

It was just this possibility that made the president's request unacceptable to Democrats. They insisted that the president was asking for far more discretion than he needed and that his claim that civil service protections would undermine the department's effectiveness impugned the patriotism of federal workers. Many Democrats found the president's demand for discretion especially galling coming as it did only months after unionized police officers and firefighters gave their lives at the World Trade Center. With unions forming a core constituency of the Democratic Party, most Democrats believed they had to fight the president's proposal.

The dispute over civil service protections set the lines for a stark political clash. Republican strategists welcomed Democratic opposition. They calculated that many voters would see the Democrats as putting union interests before the national interest and, as a result, vote Republican in the congressional midterm races. By contrast, Democratic strategists calculated that the issue would energize union supporters and help generate a strong Democratic turnout in November.

Election Day results bore out the arguments of Republican strategists. In most congressional races, the dispute over civil service protections barely figured. But it was a prominent issue in several close Senate races, perhaps none more so than Democrat Max Cleland's efforts to win reelection to Georgia's Senate seat. His Republican challenger, Saxby Chambliss, relentlessly used Cleland's defense of civil service protections to question his patriotism. Although Cleland had lost three limbs fighting in Vietnam and his opponent never served in the military despite being of draft age during that war, the charges stuck, and Chambliss won.

14-5 The Organization

The 2002 elections decided the question of civil service protections. Congress reconvened shortly after Election Day in a lame duck session. Democrats conceded defeat and agreed to legislation establishing a new department largely along the lines that President Bush had requested.

DHS opened for business on January 24, 2003. Tom Ridge was sworn in that day as its first secretary. On March 1, 2003, DHS assumed formal control of the bulk of the agencies it was scheduled to absorb. It absorbed all its planned units on September 30, 2003. With the merger process completed, DHS now has more than 180,000 employees—making it the third largest Cabinet department after DoD and the Veterans Adminis-tration—and an annual budget of more than $35 billion.

Figure 14-1 presents the basic organization of DHS. The heart of the department is the four policy directorates, each headed by an under secretary. The largest directorate is Border and Transportation Security. It has more than 100,000 employees and a budget exceeding $18 billion. It includes people and missions from the Customs Bureau (formerly in the Department of the Treasury), the Transportation Security Administration (which was created immediately after September 11 and was initially lodged in the Transportation Department), and the law enforcement parts of the Immigration and Naturalization Service (Justice Department). The Border and Transportation Security directorate's main task is to allow legitimate people and goods into the country and keep terrorists and terrorist weapons out.

A second directorate is Information Analysis and Infrastructure Protection (IAIP). This directorate began with only about 1,000 employees. Unlike Border Security and Transportation, it is less about merging existing agencies than about building new government capabilities. Before September 11, the federal government had taken only rudimentary steps to protect the nation's critical infrastructure—the food, water, energy, financial, and information networks on which the U.S. economy depends. The new unit is responsible for identifying vulnerabilities in America's critical infrastructure and determining the best ways to protect these networks. A key to accomplishing this task is the unit's ability to integrate and assess information about potential terrorist threats from intelligence and law enforcement sources.

A third directorate is Science and Technology. It began its organizational life with only a few hundred employees who had worked in small offices transferred

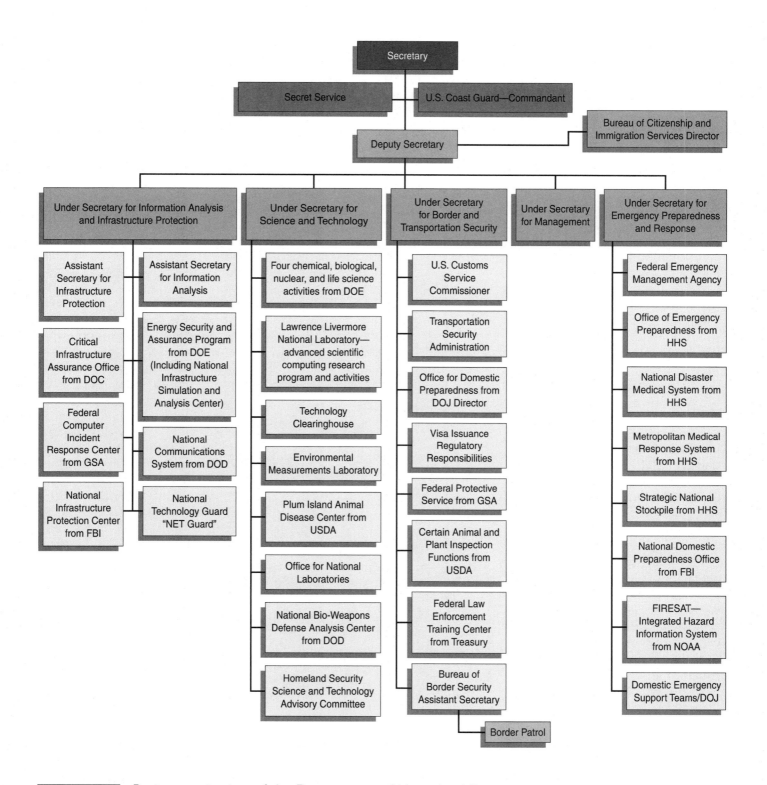

Figure 14-1 Basic organization of the Department of Homeland Security.

Source: O'Hanlon, Michael E., Peter R. Orszag, Ivo H. Daalder, I. M. Destler, David L. Gunter, James M. Lindsay, Robert E. Litan, and James B. Steinberg. 2003. *Protecting the American Homeland: One Year On.* Washington, D. C.: Brookings Institution Press.

from DoD and the Department of Energy. Like the Information Analysis directorate, most of its capabilities have yet to be built. The Science and Technology directorate's primary responsibility is to help develop new technologies that can detect, defeat, and mitigate chemical, biological, radiological, and nuclear attacks. When the directorate is fully operational, much of its work will be devoted to mobilizing other parts of the federal government to do the actual scientific investigations.

The fourth directorate is Emergency Preparedness and Response. It has about 6,000 employees and a budget of $6 billion. The core of this directorate is FEMA, which as its name suggests, is the federal government's lead agency in responding to disasters. It continues to devote much of its work to responding to natural disasters, such as those caused by hurricanes, tornadoes, and floods. There were two main arguments for folding FEMA into DHS. One was to make responding to terrorist attacks a higher priority within FEMA. The other was to take advantage of the expertise and networks that FEMA has developed over the years in working with state and local governments, which will play important roles in responding to any terrorist attack. Several other, much smaller programs and offices (most of which are in the Department of Health and Human Services) were merged into the Emergency Preparedness and Response directorate along with FEMA.

In addition to these four directorates, DHS absorbed several other agencies. One is the Coast Guard, which previously had been part of the Department of Transportation. The Coast Guard, which has lead authority for monitoring exit from and entry into U.S. ports, coordinates its work with the Border Security and Transportation Directorate but reports directly to the secretary of homeland security. The Secret Service, which comes over from the Department of the Treasury, also reports to the secretary. The Bureau of Citizenship and Immigration Services, which is essentially those parts of INS that weren't folded into the Border Security and Transportation directorate, reports directly to the deputy secretary for homeland security.

14-6 Be Careful What You Wish For

President Bush got the large homeland security department he wanted. He also got the mammoth task of putting it into operation. As it turned out, it was a lot easier to propose integrating twenty-two agencies than to actually do it.

The reviews that DHS received on its first birthday were at best mixed. On the positive side of the ledger, the department cited several major successes. It had created US-VISIT, a program that registers all foreigners as they enter the United States. It had also begun educating the American public about how to prepare for an emergency and had posted sensors in major American cities in an effort to get early warning of any terrorist attack that used biological weapons.

Critics, by contrast, pointed to a long list of DHS missteps. DHS's management team experienced substantial turnover. Senior officials who resigned during the first year included the deputy secretary (the number two post at DHS), the department's chief financial officer, and Ridge's own chief of staff. The first director of IAIP resigned shortly after he angered members of Congress by testifying that his directorate had hired only a quarter of its proposed staff "because we do not have the [office] space for them."

DHS also failed to make much progress on several high-profile initiatives. One of the main reasons for creating the IAIP directorate was that it would match intelligence about potential threats with information about vulnerabilities in the United States. But IAIP's director confessed in September 2003 that it might take five years to complete a threat-and-vulnerability assessment. DHS likewise had the task of merging the terrorist "watch lists" compiled by different government agencies into a master list. Despite DHS's public promises during 2003 that the master watch list would "soon" be ready, no such list existed at the start of 2004, and the task of compiling it had been quietly given to the FBI.

The creation of DHS also did not end turf battles among federal agencies, and in fact, it may have added to the problem. A major division emerged between DHS, which claimed it was responsible for making the country secure, and the Justice Department, which insisted that it was responsible for stopping terror attacks. The rivalry between the two departments sometimes led the federal government to speak with two, contradictory voices. In May 2004, for instance, Ridge told a morning news show that he had seen no information that justified raising the color-coded national alert system from yellow to orange. Later that day, Attorney General John Ashcroft held a press conference to warn that seven suspected Al Qaeda operatives had possibly entered the country intent on launching a major attack. Homeland Security officials later told journalists that the intelligence that prompted the attorney general to issue his warning was neither new nor specific. Representative Christopher Cox (R-Calif.) expressed the frustration of many members of Congress when he said diplomatically that Ashcroft's "news conference and Secretary Ridge's earlier public statements conveyed the perception that the broad and close consultation we expect may not have taken place."

None of these growing pains came as a surprise to anyone who had followed previous governmental reorganizations. Creating new agencies and reorganizing old ones can be a challenging task. Take the case of the Transportation Security Administration (TSA). In its first year of existence, TSA went through two directors and missed many of the performance deadlines that Congress set for it.

Ridge faced a particularly challenging task at DHS. According to a study done by the Brookings Institution, a nonpartisan think tank in Washington, D.C., the twenty-two agencies being merged came with a vast array of largely incompatible management systems, including at least 80 different personnel systems mixed in and among agencies. There were, for example, special pay rates for the Transportation Security Administration, the Secret Service, and the Biomedical Research Service; higher overtime rates for air marshals, Secret Service agents, and immigration inspectors; Sunday, night, and premium pay for the Secret Service, Customs Service, and immigration inspectors; and foreign language awards and death benefits for Customs officers. Ridge and his advisers also had to settle numerous issues that might seem trivial to people outside DHS but that were critical to people inside it. One such case in-volved whether the officers in Immigration and Customs Enforcement, the investigative arm of the Border and Transportation Security directorate, should carry the 9-mm pistol that Customs officers used or the 40-caliber pistol that INS officers used. Not surprisingly, each group fought to make its preferred gun the department's standard.

At the same time, even as Ridge and his subordinates sought to create new capabilities within DHS, they also had to overhaul many of the department's existing capabilities. Some of the agencies being merged—the Coast Guard comes immediately to mind—had reputations for being well run. Others were broken organizations that were notorious for performing their missions poorly. The INS topped most experts' lists of agencies in trouble. Among other things, it sent visa renewal notices to two of the September 11 hijackers—six months after they flew planes into the World Trade Center. No one thought that separating INS's law enforcement and service functions, as DHS did, would by itself fix the problems that plagued that organization.

But the problems at DHS may reflect more than the inevitable mistakes that accompany any reorganization. Critics argued that they also reflected the fact that President Bush focused his attention in the war on terrorism primarily on offensive efforts to kill terrorists overseas, and thereby regarded efforts to secure the American homeland as decidedly less important. Rand Beers, who served as the Bush administration's top counterterrorism official, resigned his post in 2003 because of what he alleged was the White House's refusal to make homeland security a top priority. (Beers, a career civil servant, later became a top foreign-policy adviser to Senator John Kerry.) Senator Lieberman, in looking at what had happened to his original idea, complained, "The fact is, we have not yet seen the kind of focused leadership, nor the resources, needed to fulfill the promise of the Homeland Security Act as we envisioned it two years ago."

Whatever priority Bush put on homeland security, several of his decisions undercut the effectiveness of DHS. The most prominent decision of this sort came even before DHS became operational. In his 2003 State of the Union Address, Bush surprised Congress by announcing the creation of the Terrorist Threat Integration Center (TTIC). Staffed by officials from the FBI and a range of intelligence agencies and based at the CIA's headquarters in Langley, Virginia, TTIC was tasked with developing a comprehensive picture of the terrorist threat to the United States by consolidating and analyzing information gathered at home and abroad about terrorism—precisely the mission that the IAIP directorate was created to handle. TTIC's deputy director later said with some understatement, "There is a degree of ambiguity between our mission and some other analytic organizations within the government."

The confusion over the respective roles of TTIC and IAIP, like the turf battles between DHS and Justice and dispute over what kind of gun Immigration and Customs Enforcement officers should carry, highlights the fact that DHS is better thought of as a work in progress than a finished product. So don't be surprised if in a few years Congress revisits the issue and decides to reorganize the reorganization.

Readings for Further Study

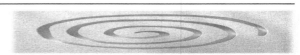

Crowley, Michael. 2004. "Bush's Disastrous Homeland Security Department." *New Republic*. March 15: 17–21.

Department of Homeland Security. 2004. "Fact Sheet: A Better Prepared America: A Year in Review." Undated. Available at http://www.dhs.gov/dhspublic/display?theme=52&content=3610

Gorman, Siobhan. 2004. "On Guard, but How Well?" *National Journal*. March 6: 472–76.

Websites to Check Out

Note: As we went to press, these sites were functional using the URLs provided. Check out the online text for the most up-to-date URLs.

Site name: The Department of Homeland Security
URL: http://www.dhs.gov
The homepage of the Department of Homeland Security contains a wide variety of information about the homeland security mission, as well as a biography of Governor Ridge and a review of the department's responsibilities.

Site name: FirstGov
URL: http://www.firstgov.gov/Topics/Usgresponse.shtml
Designed to be "your first click to the U.S. government," FirstGov provides links to the entire array of federal agencies involved in homeland security, as well as links to state agencies.

Site name: Homeland Security Institute
URL: http://www.homelandsecurity.org/
A comprehensive resource on homeland security with links to current news, upcoming events, state resources, suggested readings, federal agencies, a virtual library, and notable quotes, among other offerings.

Trying Terrorists:
Military Commissions and the American Legal System

Timothy M. Hagle

President George W. Bush responded to September 11 by committing the United States to a worldwide war on terrorism. The war got off to a good start. U.S. troops captured Taliban and Al Qaeda fighters in Afghanistan. FBI agents fanned out across the globe and helped arrest suspected terrorists in places as diverse as Bosnia, Pakistan, and Singapore. These successes raised an immediate policy question for the Bush administration: What should it do with the suspected terrorists it catches in its war on terrorism?

President Bush had the option of trying suspected terrorists in federal civilian courts. That is what the United States had done in previous terrorist cases, including the 1993 bombing of the World Trade Center. In his Military Order of November 13, 2001, however, Bush created another option by announcing that foreign (but not American) citizens detained in the war on terrorism could be tried before military commissions—or, as they are commonly called in the press, military tribunals. He reserved for himself the right to decide which suspects the commissions would try.

President Bush's announcement angered many civil libertarians. More than 700 American law professors signed a letter calling the military commissions "legally deficient, unnecessary, and unwise." The criticisms did not break down neatly along party lines, though. Leading Democratic politicians, such as former vice presidential candidate Senator Joseph Lieberman (D-Conn.), endorsed the use of commissions. Some Republicans, such as William Safire, a former speechwriter for President Richard Nixon, called the idea a blunder.

Much of the initial criticism reflected the fact that President Bush's executive order provided little detail about how the commissions would operate. What it did say was that "it is not practicable" for military commissions to follow "the principles of law and rules of evidence generally recognized in the trial of criminal cases in the United States." Critics worried that suspected terrorists would be denied legal rights, such as the presumption of innocence and the right to counsel, that are the hallmarks of a fair trial.

President Bush left it up to the Department of Defense to specify how the military commissions would operate. After consulting with outside legal experts, including some who had criticized the original directive, Secretary of Defense Donald Rumsfeld released Military Commission Order No. 1, on March 21, 2002. It stipulated that many of the safeguards common to civilian criminal trials (such as the right to legal counsel) would apply to the military commissions as well. Although this order addressed some of the critics' concerns, they complained that the commissions remained a bad idea that harmed U.S. interests.

So why did President Bush decide to create special military commissions? Does he have the power to make such a decision? Where do the military commissions mimic the procedures of civilian criminal courts and where do they diverge? The answers to these questions shed light on why the idea of military commissions triggers such passionate debate.

15-1 Why Military Commissions?

The Bush administration offered a mix of principled and pragmatic reasons for deciding to try accused foreign terrorists before military commissions rather than in federal civilian courts. Administration officials argued that terrorists were "unlawful combatants" whose attacks rose above the level of mere crime and should be recognized as such. Vice President Dick Cheney was blunt on this score: Terrorists "don't deserve the same guarantees and safeguards that would be used for an American citizen going through the normal judicial process." The use of military commissions "guarantees that we'll have the kind of treatment of these individuals that we believe they deserve." This approach has the weight of history behind it. Wars are fought under well-understood rules that John Dean, a legal counselor to President Nixon, has pointed out do not "include providing Miranda warnings when capturing an enemy, nor employing the niceties of the Federal Rules of Criminal Procedure when punishing them."

At the same time, administration officials argued that proceeding through federal civilian courts—and abiding by all the costly and cumbersome procedures that would entail—could defeat the purposes of justice. No doubt with memories of the O. J. Simpson trial in mind, officials worried that terrorist suspects could drag out an ordinary trial and create a media circus. The intelligence agencies would be reluctant to discuss secret information in open court for fear of revealing, and losing, their sources—a development that could increase the risk that America would be caught unaware by a future attack. Moreover, given that groups like Al Qaeda had shown no qualms about killing civilians, terrorists might seek to intimidate civilian

jurors and judges. This fear is not idle speculation: The federal judge who presided in the trials of the suspects in the 1993 World Trade Center bombing is still under 24-hour protection by U.S. marshals, and may be for the rest of his life.

Critics of military commissions countered with their own mix of principled and pragmatic arguments. They contended that by declining to use the federal civilian courts, the administration was raising questions about America's commitment to its basic values. They argued that comments like those Vice President Cheney made suggested that the United States did not want justice; it wanted kangaroo courts where the outcomes would be preordained. Such courts would undercut the U.S. claim that it is a nation governed by the rule of law.

Critics further argued that while federal civilians courts may be more costly and cumbersome than military commissions, the United States has for years used them successfully to prosecute terrorists. Indeed, at the time of the September 11 attacks, four men convicted of participating in the 1998 bombings of the U.S. embassies in Kenya and Tanzania were awaiting sentencing by the federal district court in Manhattan, just blocks from the World Trade Center. The fact that these trials proceeded through ordinary legal channels gave the resulting convictions considerable credibility, both at home and abroad. Moreover, the critics argued, by resorting to military commissions, the United States would undercut its long-standing policy of criticizing countries that try accused terrorists in courts that ignore fundamental legal rights.

15-2 Are Military Commissions Constitutional?

Does the president of the United States have the authority to create special military commissions and to order individuals to stand trial before them? The answer is not immediately obvious. The Constitution says nothing directly about such a presidential power, and Articles I and III specifically give Congress the power to create new courts.

Despite the lack of an explicit constitutional authorization, administration lawyers insist that President Bush is acting within his powers. They point out that military commissions have a long history in the United States, first being used during the presidency of George Washington. A military tribunal tried John Wilkes Booth's co-conspirators in the assassination of Abraham Lincoln. Moreover, the Supreme Court's ruling in *Ex parte Quirin* (1942) suggests that presidents have the power to establish military commissions to try unlawful combatants.

Quirin involved Nazi saboteurs during World War II. In June 1942, a German submarine secretly deposited Richard Quirin and three other German nationals off the coast of Long Island, New York. A second German submarine dropped off four more saboteurs just south of Jacksonville, Florida. All landed wearing German military uniforms, but changed into civilian clothes and traveled to nearby cities. Two of the men decided almost immediately to give themselves up. As a result of their confessions, all eight were arrested within days. President Franklin Roosevelt, as president and commander in chief, immediately appointed a military commission to try the men for plotting sabotage.

As their trial before the military commission progressed, Quirin and his fellow defendants asked the Supreme Court to review the procedures under which they were being tried. Quirin's attorneys argued that trial by military commission was inappropriate because the United States had not been invaded and the civilian courts were still operating. Nonetheless, the Court ruled on July 31, 1942, that "the military commission was lawfully constituted." Four days later, all eight men were convicted and sentenced to death by electrocution. Roosevelt commuted the sentence to life in prison for the two Germans who had revealed the plot. The other six were executed on August 8, less than two months after coming ashore.

One aspect of *Quirin* is especially relevant today. President Bush's Military Order specifically excludes U.S. citizens from being tried before a military commission. (That is why John Walker Lindh, the so-called American Taliban, was tried in federal court.) But that exclusion is not a constitutional requirement. One of the eight Germans in *Quirin* was a naturalized American citizen who had returned to Germany shortly before the war began. The Supreme Court ruled that the fact an enemy belligerent held U.S. citizenship did not shield him from trial before a military commission, nor did it give him the right to access to civilian courts.

Critics of military commissions have complained that *Quirin* was wrongly decided. They have also argued that it does not apply to President Bush's proposed military com-

missions because in declaring war on Germany, Congress had explicitly authorized the use of military commissions. Congress has not explicitly authorized the use of military commissions in the wake of September 11 (though it did pass a resolution authorizing the president to "use all necessary and appropriate force against those . . . persons he determines planned, authorized, committed, or aided the terrorist attacks"). Still, efforts to challenge the constitutionality of the military commissions are likely to fail, if only because courts usually defer to past rulings. Indeed, as long as terrorists are held overseas, U.S. courts may refuse to hear any lawsuits challenging the constitutionality of military commissions on the grounds that their authority ends at America's border. That is why the Bush administration decided to detain Taliban and Al Qaeda members at Guantanamo Bay in Cuba, rather than bring them to the United States.

Nevertheless, accused terrorists are not restricted to challenging the constitutionality of the military commissions. They can also try to challenge the particular procedures the commissions follow. If American courts agree to hear such legal challenges, and that is a big "if," these lawsuits may have a greater possibility of succeeding.

15-3 Military Commissions Versus Civilian Courts

Military commissions are not the same as civilian courts, but the two are not entirely dissimilar either. Perhaps most important, both must assume that the accused is innocent until proven guilty and that guilt must be

shown beyond a reasonable doubt. The similarities go further. The accused in a trial before a military commission will be able to obtain witnesses and evidence to use in his or her defense. Witnesses for both the defense and the prosecution will be under oath and subject to direct- and cross-examination. Corresponding to the Fifth Amendment right against self-incrimination, the accused cannot be forced to testify at his or her trial. The accused is protected against double jeopardy—he or she cannot be tried twice before a commission for the same offense. The accused may negotiate a plea agreement with the prosecution and make a statement or present evidence during sentencing proceedings.

There are also important differences between military commissions and civilian courts, as Table 15-1 illustrates. Some of these differences involve constitutional rights we consider fundamental to our system of justice. Still, the commission procedures tend to minimize the effect of the differences, and they do not leave the accused without protection.

15-3a Commission Membership and Selection

Military commissions will consist of at least three, but no more than seven members. The secretary of defense will select the members, who must be military officers, though not necessarily lawyers. They may be on active duty, in the National Guard or reserves, or retired personnel recalled to active duty. Each commission will have a presiding officer to head the proceedings. Presiding officers must be judge advocates; that is, they must be military lawyers. In this commission, compared to a civilian court, the presiding officer is effectively the

Table 15-1   Federal Civilian Criminal Courts Versus Military Commissions

Jury/Commission Membership and Selection	Right to Counsel	Right to a Public Trial	Rules of Evidence	Vote Required to Convict	Right to Appeal
Federal Civilian Criminal Courts					
Twelve members are chosen at random from the community.	The defendant chooses his or her own lawyer. The government provides one if the defendant cannot afford one.	Trials are held in public with rare and limited exceptions.	Strict rules of evidence apply. No hearsay testimony is allowed. Rules regarding legal search and seizure must be followed.	Unanimous verdicts are required to convict and impose sentence in all cases.	Defendant has the right to appeal to the U.S. Court of Appeals. The U.S. Supreme Court has discretion on whether to hear further appeals.
Military Commissions					
Three to seven military officers are selected by the secretary of defense. Seven members are required for death penalty cases. The presiding officer must be a judge advocate (military lawyer).	The defendant is provided a military lawyer but can request that a different military lawyer serve as counsel. The defendant can choose to have a civilian attorney, but not at government expense.	Trials are open to the public unless the presiding officer decides that the proceedings need to be closed to protect secret information, the safety of participants, or national security interests.	Evidence can be admitted if it has "probative value to a reasonable person." Hearsay evidence is permitted, and traditional search and seizure requirements are not in effect.	A two-thirds vote is required to convict in all cases but capital ones. Those involving the death penalty require a unanimous vote for conviction and sentencing.	Defendant has the right to appeal to review panel consisting of three military officers, appointed by the secretary of defense. No sentence is final until the president approves it.

Sources of Information for Military Commissions: Department of Defense, Military Commission Order No. 1, March 21, 2002, available at http://www.defenselink.mil/news/Mar2002/d2002032lord.pdf, and Department of Defense, "Fact Sheet: Department of Defense Order on Military Commissions," March 21, 2002, available at http://www.defenselink.mil/news/Mar2002/d2002032lfact.pdf.

judge and all the members of the commission are the jury.

Jury trial, of course, is the hallmark of our civilian legal system. The job of the jury is to determine the facts and, ultimately, the guilt or innocence of the accused. For serious offenses, juries in civilian criminal cases consist of twelve members. The accused can waive the right to a jury and, with the consent of the prosecution, have a trial only before a judge. This is known as a "bench trial." In a bench trial, the judge assumes the jury's role of factfinder. In both jury and bench trials, the accused has the right to an impartial factfinder.

One criticism of military commissions concerns the impartiality of their members. Although the Military Commission Order says that commissions must be impartial in their proceedings, critics argue that members of Al Qaeda or the Taliban who have sworn to kill all Americans could not receive a fair trial before a commission composed of military officers. Although one could make the same argument regarding civilian juries, there may be a greater perception of impartiality in the civilian courts because of the ability of the defense to participate in the jury selection process.

In this regard, commission members are more like a panel of judges hearing a case than a jury. The parties in civilian courts have no say in the selection of the judge, with the limited exception of circumstances in which a judge has demonstrated a lack of impartiality and may be removed for cause. Along these lines, the Military Commission Order provides for the removal of commission members for "good cause." Military commissions will likely follow the established procedures for regular courts-martial (military courts used to try military personnel accused of violating military law), which allow the defense to object to members for a lack of impartiality. Moreover, at a practical level, the amount of scrutiny the commissions will attract significantly diminishes the chances that a clearly biased officer will be allowed to serve.

15-3b Right to Counsel

The Supreme Court has held that someone charged with a crime in a civilian court has the right to an attorney. In addition, if the accused cannot afford counsel of his or her own choosing, one will be appointed at government expense. Those being tried before a military commission also have the right to counsel, and one will be provided at government expense, but with certain important differences.

The Military Commission Order establishes an Office of the Chief Defense Counsel (OCDC). The OCDC is primarily responsible for coordinating and overseeing the overall defense efforts on behalf of those being tried subject to President Bush's directive. This includes assigning one or more military officers who are also judge advocates to conduct the defense in each case before a commission. As with defense attorneys provided at government expense in civilian trials, Detailed Defense Counsel (DDC) must zealously defend the interests of the accused within the bounds of the law and without regard to personal opinion.

The accused can request a different military officer who is a judge advocate as a replacement for the DDC. If this alternate officer is available, he or she will assume the original DDC's duties. The accused can request that the original DDC stay on to assist in his or her defense. Any alternate DDC is also provided at government expense.

As in the civilian courts, the accused may choose to have a civilian attorney, but with certain differences. First, the government will not pay for a Civilian Defense Counsel (CDC). This limitation may not be significant, however, because many civilian attorneys may be willing to donate their services, or certain groups may be willing to pay the accused's legal expenses.

Second, CDCs must meet certain qualifications, such as being a U.S. citizen, being admitted to the practice of the law in the state or federal courts, not having been subject to any disciplinary action by a court, and so on. A particularly important qualification is that the CDC must be eligible for access to information classified at the SECRET level or higher.

Third, even if a CDC meets the necessary qualifications, the commission may exclude him or her if it goes into closed session. The commission may also deny the CDC access to evidence it considers particularly sensitive. For this reason, the DDC will remain on the case should the accused choose a CDC to be his or her main attorney.

Finally, the presiding officer has the authority to maintain the dignity and decorum of the proceedings. The same is true of civilian judges, but one can safely assume that presiding officers will be less tolerant of defense attorneys who attempt to try their cases in the media. Some groups may complain about stricter limitations on such activities, but the limitations should not affect CDC performance in the trial itself.

15-3c Right to a Public Trial

The right to a public trial is one that the accused and the public share in the civilian courts. The Supreme Court has held that trials need to be open unless the prosecution or the defense can demonstrate a compelling reason to close them. Such reasons include the ability of the accused to get a fair trial or national security concerns. There may also be reasons to close a portion of a trial, such as when a particular witness testifies (e.g., the child victim in a sexual molestation case). Again, usually the trial can be closed only after the trial judge holds a hearing on the matter.

The Military Commission Order specifies that trial proceedings are to be open to the press and the public, unless the presiding officer determines that the proceedings need to be closed. The trial may be closed to protect classified or sensitive information; the safety of the participants (witnesses, commission members, counsel, and the accused); intelligence sources, methods, and activities; or national security interests. Both the accused and a CDC may be excluded from closed sessions of the commission. The DDC, however, may not be excluded from any trial proceeding. The CDC and DDC may not disclose information presented in a closed proceeding to anyone not present at the proceeding. Decisions to send commission proceedings into closed session trial will likely attract criticism, especially if the accused and CDC are also excluded. Again, however, closed proceedings are not unknown at civilian trials.

15-3d Rules of Evidence

The procedures governing the use of evidence in military commissions differ from those in civilian courts in two primary ways. First, civilian criminal cases rely on very strict rules of evidence. They include the general prohibition against the use of hearsay—that is, unverified information that a witness has learned from someone else—as well as requirements for how physical evidence is obtained (to protect against unlawful searches) and who possesses it (to prevent tampering). In contrast, military commissions will consider evidence if the presiding officer decides it would "have probative value to a reasonable person." This looser standard means that the evidence will be admitted as long as it tends to prove or disprove some element of the case. Technical violations or irregularities in the gathering or handling of the evidence will not lead to its exclusion, provided that the presiding officer finds it to have value.

The second difference involves decisions to close portions of the proceedings. Even when the proceedings are closed to the public in civilian trials, the accused has a right to hear all the evidence, and with very narrow exceptions, to know the identity of witnesses giving testimony. As noted above, though, the accused may be excluded during closed sessions of a military commission to protect information or witnesses. The Bush administration justifies the use of secret testimony on the grounds that it spares the prosecution from having to make the difficult choice that civilian prosecutors often face between revealing sensitive sources of information or letting defendants go free.

A conviction and death sentence based on the use of secret evidence in a closed proceeding is the situation that raises the greatest fear among civil libertarians. It is also the one aspect of trials by military commissions that is likely to resonate unfavorably with the public. Even the most ardent supporters of military commissions may find it difficult to defend.

15-3e Vote Required to Convict

All federal criminal prosecutions require twelve-member juries and unanimous verdicts. (Some states have less stringent standards for low-level crimes.) In the case of the three-to-seven-member military commissions, a two-thirds vote is sufficient to convict in all cases except those involving the death penalty. A unanimous vote is required to impose a death sentence.

Administration officials note that the U.S. military uses the two-thirds standard in regular courts-martial. Moreover, it is a higher standard than the one used for summary courts-martial involving low-level violations of military law. Summary courts-martial use only one officer, who acts as judge, whereas military commissions require no fewer than three members regardless of the offense. Consistent with procedures for ordinary courts-martial, commissions will likely have the maximum number of seven members for more serious offenses, particularly those where punishment may mean death.

In civilian criminal cases, it is usually left for the jury to decide during its deliberations how to conduct its votes. The jury may decide to vote by a show of hands or by secret ballot. After a verdict is reached and announced in court, however, the jury may be polled to ensure that a unanimous verdict was reached. Members of military commissions will vote on both guilt and sentence by using secret, written ballots. The secret votes are intended to minimize the possibility that senior officers will unduly influence junior officers. The individual votes of the commission members will not be made public.

15-3f Right to Appeal

A defendant convicted in a civilian trial has a constitutional right to ask higher courts to review the case. Courts of appeal are usually composed of panels of three or more judges who examine the trial proceedings for clear errors of law or fact. A majority of these judges is needed to either affirm or reverse the verdict of the trial court. Review procedures vary among the state and federal court systems. In most cases involving serious offenses, and especially in death penalty cases, a convicted defendant has a right to an initial review by an appellate court. Beyond that, however, there typically is no right to an appeal. The U.S. Supreme Court and the highest state courts generally have discretion to decide which appeals they want to hear.

Conviction and sentencing by a military commission will not become final until the president approves them. In practice, the president is likely to delegate his review authority to the secretary of defense. He will create a review panel consisting of three military officers, at least one of whom is a judge. The presiding officer of the commission will authenticate the trial transcript and send it either to the official who appointed the commission (for a purely administrative review) or directly to a review panel. The panel will examine the trial transcript in secret. It has the authority to ignore a commission's minor violations of established procedures if, in its judgment, they do not materially affect the trial's outcome. A majority vote of the panel is required to either forward the case to the secretary of defense or to return it to the commission for further proceedings. The secretary of defense reviews the case and either returns it for additional proceedings or forwards it to the president for review and final decision (unless the president has designated the secretary of defense to perform final review in a particular case).

A review panel cannot change a finding of not guilty to guilty. A review panel, the secretary of defense, or the president may, however, change a finding of guilty to not guilty. Any of the three may also reduce a guilty finding to one of guilty to a lesser-included offense. Any of the three may also mitigate, commute, or suspend the sentence. The president's decision or, if he delegates his authority, the secretary of defense's decision, is final.

The finality of the president's decision means that those convicted by a military commission do not have access to the federal civilian courts for additional review, and no military commission cases will go to the Supreme Court. This is unlike state criminal trials where those found guilty can petition the federal courts for review (either by the Supreme Court directly, or the lower federal courts via a petition for a writ of habeas corpus) if they believe their constitutional rights were violated. Critics complain that this lack of independent civilian review violates a fundamental tenet of the American judicial system. They argue that because the secretary of defense and military officers work for President Bush, their impartiality will be unduly swayed by his repeated references to members of the Taliban and Al Qaeda as "evildoers."

The fact that the Bush administration has not provided for independent civilian review does not mean that the federal courts might not step in anyway. Those convicted may file petitions for writs of habeas corpus in federal courts, essentially asserting that they are being held illegally. The important question, of course, is whether the courts would agree to hear such petitions, let alone grant them. (If a court grants a writ of habeas corpus, it is ordering the prisoner's release.) Given the administration's insistence that military commissions are essential, the courts' traditional deference to the president's constitutional powers in foreign affairs, and the Supreme Court's decision in *Quirin,* the likelihood that any court will grant a writ of habeas corpus is slim.

15-4 Continued Debate

By adopting many of the legal protections that guide civilian criminal trials, Military Commission Order No. 1 narrowed the differences separating the Bush administration from its critics. Even if the administration makes further concessions, the debate over military commissions will persist because of fundamental disagreements about how to handle suspected terrorists. The administration and its supporters believe that military commissions are the most appropriate trial venue given what Al Qaeda and other terrorists are trying to do. Conversely, critics argue for trying accused terrorists in ordinary criminal courts precisely because terrorism seeks to challenge the notion of rule of law. Procedural changes cannot bridge this gap.

For all the ink that has been spilled arguing the merits of military commissions, how often they will be used remains an open question. More than two-and-a-half years after President Bush announced the creation of military commissions, the administration had yet to bring any accused terrorist before a tribunal. In fact, it had moved in the opposite direction. The administration decided to try both Zacarias Moussaoui, a French national of Moroccan descent accused of being part of the September 11 conspiracy, and Richard Reid, a British national accused of bringing a "shoe bomb" aboard an American Airlines flight, in federal district court. Opponents hope that these decisions mean that the idea of using military commissions has quietly been shelved. (Critics also argue that the decisions disprove the administration's contention that the commissions are needed to protect jurors and judges and to avoid disclosing secret information.) At a minimum, the controversy surrounding military commissions makes it likely that they will be used only for high-level members of the Taliban or Al Qaeda.

That could be an ironic result. Why? Because most Taliban and Al Qaeda fighters might be best served by a trial before a military commission. Military officers may be more sympathetic to a defendant's claim that he was merely following orders. Conversely, federal law gives the Justice Department some discretion over where to prosecute defendants. In the cases of Moussaoui and John Walker Lindh, it filed its charges in the U.S. District Court for the Eastern District of Virginia. That is no accident. That court draws its jury pool from a relatively conservative community populated with military veterans, Pentagon workers, and federal employees. Such juries historically have been sympathetic to prosecutors and comfortable with imposing the death penalty. Moreover, the U.S. District Court for the Eastern District of Virginia is also known as the "rocket docket" because it tends to dispose of its cases faster than normal. The faster pace usually favors the prosecution.

Readings for Further Study

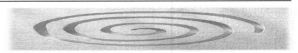

Dean, John. 2001. "The Critics Are Wrong: Why President Bush's Decision to Bring Foreign Terrorists to Justice before Military Tribunals Should Not Offend Civil Libertarians." November 23. Available at http://writ.news.findlaw.com/dean/20011123.html

Katyal, Neal K., and Laurence H. Tribe. 2002. "Waging War, Deciding Guilt: Trying the Military Tribunals." *Yale Law Journal* 111 (April): 1259–1310.

Rehnquist, William H. 1998. *All the Laws But One: Civil Liberties in Wartime.* New York: Alfred A. Knopf.

Websites to Check Out

Note: As we went to press, these sites were functional using the URLs provided. Check out the online text for the most up-to-date URLs.

Site name: Avalon Project at the Yale Law School

URL: http://www.yale.edu/lawweb/avalon/avalon.htm

A comprehensive collection of documents in law, history, and diplomacy from the eighteenth century to the present. Among many other collections, the site includes an extensive set of documents relating to the Nuremberg War Crimes Trials.

Site name: FindLaw's Tribunal Forum

URL: http://writ.news.findlaw.com/tribunals.html

In addition to a wealth of information about legal issues, FindLaw posts commentaries by a wide array of legal authorities on the merits of military commissions.

Site name: Legal Information Institute—Cornell Law School

URL: http://www.law.cornell.edu

A comprehensive web resource in the field of law containing a wide range of Supreme Court rulings (including *Ex parte Quirin*), statutes, regulations, and other legal materials.

Still Not Washington's Job Alone:

American States and the Terrorist Threat

Peverill Squire

The jetliners that crashed into the twin towers of the World Trade Center and into the Pentagon on September 11 made immediately clear the threat that terrorism poses to America's security. But although the Constitution makes it the federal government's responsibility to provide for the common defense, the police, firefighters, rescue, and health care workers who came to the aid of the victims that morning were overwhelmingly state and local government employees, not federal government employees. This observation highlights an important but underappreciated fact about the American governmental system: National security is the responsibility of the federal government, but most of the men and women who guard and protect us, who actually provide much of our homeland security, work for state and local governments.

The essential state and local role in providing homeland security is understood in Washington. During a Senate Governmental Affairs Committee hearing in December 2001, for example, the committee's chair, Senator Joseph Lieberman (D-Conn.) noted,

In America's war against terrorism, city, county, and state governments and workers bear primary responsibility for providing our citizens with the services and safety they need. The local role is much deeper and broader than emergency response. State, county, and city agencies are the primary providers of public health, transportation, and social support services. And as the daily law enforcement presence in our communities, they play a lead role in helping to prevent terrorist acts from happening in the first place.

Some simple statistics back up what Senator Lieberman had to say. In 2000, the federal government had 88,496 full-time employees who were authorized to carry firearms and to make arrests. Of them, only about 13 percent worked for the Federal Bureau of Investigation. (Far more worked for the Immigration and Naturalization Service and the Federal Bureau of Prisons.) In contrast, the number of state and local law enforcement officers exceeded 660,000. The disparity between the number of federal versus state and local emergency responders is even greater. The federal government employs very few firefighters and emergency medical technicians. State and local governments employ more than 1 million firefighters and

more than 155,000 emergency medical technicians. Thus, much of the burden of stopping terrorists who are operating on American soil and responding to the consequences of any attacks they might launch falls on the shoulders of state and local government.

But just how ready are state and local governments for the new task of homeland security? Much like the federal government, they are struggling to adapt to the post-September 11 world. They have had to update their laws to cover crimes that previously had been unthinkable. They have also had to find the money to pay for the new homeland security mission. The price tag is steep. By some estimates, the states faced $4 billion in new expenses in 2002 alone. Yet, it is obvious that if the states fail to increase their preparedness, America's vulnerability to, and the consequences of, future terrorist attacks will remain unacceptably high.

16-1 Initial State Responses

Many state governments responded quickly to September 11. Not surprisingly, New York State took the lead. Governor George Pataki called the state legislature into special session on September 17 to consider a package of anti-terrorism bills that he claimed would be the toughest in the nation. Many of the ideas contained in the legislation had been offered earlier in the year but had languished for a lack of support. Now they had irresistible political momentum. The bills passed on the same day they were offered on near-unanimous votes without any hearings or amendments. The governor signed them into law within hours. The speed with which New York acted is remarkable. In comparison, the U.S. Congress took until the end of October to pass comparable anti-terrorist legislation.

The laws that New York passed represent a substantial attempt to address the problem of terrorism at the state level. The legislation defined terrorism in sweeping terms: any criminal act that aimed to intimidate or coerce a civilian population, influence governmental policy, or affect the conduct of a governmental agency. Anyone convicted of committing terrorist acts faced a maximum sentence of life in prison. The legislation also made it a crime to make terrorist threats, make false bomb threats or pull fire alarms under false pretenses, assist in terrorist crimes, or obstruct criminal investigations of terrorist crimes. Each of these crimes also came with severe penalties. Making false bomb threats, falsely pulling a fire alarm, or making any terrorist threat could earn up to seven years in prison. Soliciting a terrorist act or contributing more than $1,000 to an organization deemed to be a terrorist group could result in up to fifteen years in prison. And the death penalty

was mandated for any murder committed during a terrorist crime.

Before passing its anti-terrorism legislation, however, New York state legislators had to answer a question facing state legislators across the nation: Why pass anti-terrorism legislation when most such acts are covered by federal legislation? New York state legislators understood that much of their legislation was legally redundant; even the Assembly speaker who supported the bills noted that they "may very well be overkill." But passing the bills allowed the legislators to take a public position opposing terrorism and demonstrate to their constituents that they were taking action. A state anti-terrorism bill also would fill any cracks in federal law through which a terrorist act might fall, particularly cases involving actions occurring entirely within a state's borders.

New York's anti-terrorist legislation set the tone for most of the bills that state legislatures considered during the remainder of 2001. One of the states that moved quickly to follow New York's lead was Florida, where several of the alleged September 11 terrorists had resided and attended flight school. Governor Jeb Bush, brother of President George W. Bush, signed eleven anti-terrorism bills into law in December 2001. The bills strengthened penalties for terrorist crimes, allowed state judges to authorize wiretaps that followed crime suspects around the state rather than being attached to a single device, and created penalties for contaminating food and water with biological poisons. The new laws also toughened regulations protecting crop dusters, created seven regional domestic terrorism task forces,

and established a statewide counterterrorism center.

During the last few months of 2001, not all the action at the state level took the form of new laws. Governors in most states used their executive powers to take action to improve security even in the absence of new legislation. In Iowa, for example, Governor Tom Vilsack ordered a security review of state government buildings. Additional security measures were taken for the state capitol, and National Guard troops were deployed to guard the state hygienic laboratory, where samples of suspicious materials were tested.

State governments continue to respond to the threat of terrorism. By the beginning of 2003, 19 states had created a state office, bureau, or agency of homeland security. Other states gave new homeland security responsibilities to existing departments. And 37 states formed task forces of one sort or another to assess their preparedness in dealing with terrorism.

16-2 Paying for Homeland Security

Most of the actions that states took to make themselves and their citizens less vulnerable to terrorist attack required money. In California, for example, tighter security measures and overtime cost the California Highway Patrol alone as much as $1 million a day during the weeks following September 11. Iowa spent almost $3 million over the last four months of 2001 for new homeland security measures. Police overtime expenses totaled $3 million in West Virginia during the same time period. And the anthrax scare also created unanticipated costs for the states. The Alabama state health department, for example, spent $110,000 testing suspicious powders, while Idaho had to spend $30,000 for the same reason.

These sudden costs would have created a problem for states under any circumstances. None of them had put money aside for responding to a possible terrorist attack, so they had to find money to cover their unanticipated expenses. But these unexpected bills came at a particularly bad time for the states. Even before September 11, the unprecedented economic expansion of the 1990s had slowed sharply. Slower economic growth meant less tax revenue and greater pressure on state budgets.

The terrorist attacks only made this revenue problem worse, as the nation's economic downturn accelerated. Hawaii was particularly hard hit. Its economy depends heavily on tourism. But airline travel was shut down temporarily after the attacks. When the airlines resumed flying, few Americans were interested in traveling. Hawaii estimated that its economy suffered $1 billion in losses. And the budget pressures on the state did not come just from the sudden need to pay attention to homeland security. The spike in unemployment that occurred after September 11 meant that states also had to dig deeper into their pockets to pay the higher social service costs.

State governments scrambled to rearrange their budgets to finance the homeland security mission. But, by the start of 2003, their budgets were in their worst shape in several decades. Collectively, they were some $50 billion in deficit. Homeland security needs had to compete with education, welfare, and prisons for scarce public dollars. And, whereas the costs states have to

pay for expenses such as unemployment insurance will drop as their economies pick up steam, homeland security is not a one-time expense. For years to come, states will have to set parts of their budget aside to redress their vulnerabilities and to develop their capabilities to respond to any attack. That will mean greater budgetary competition for all the other government missions.

16-3 More Deliberate State Responses in 2002

Because the majority of state legislatures are part-time organizations, most of them met for the first time following September 11 only in 2002. This meant that unlike the U.S. Congress or the state legislatures in New York and Florida, legislators in most states had several months to absorb what had happened and to reflect on the possible policy consequences. Not surprisingly, this additional time for thought led legislators in some states to develop different responses to the terrorist threat than those adopted by Congress and by their counterparts in New York and Florida.

In Iowa, for example, state legislators began their 2002 legislative session considering an anti-terrorism package similar to the one passed in New York. But as the session wore on, legislators began to back away from the expansive language that New York had used. An odd coalition of interest groups—uniting the Iowa Civil Liberties Union and labor groups on the political left with gun rights organizations and pro-life groups on the political right—argued that some traditional political activities might qualify as terrorist acts under the language of the bill. So Iowa legisla-

tors added a provision that explicitly excluded picketing and other forms of public demonstrations as instances of terrorism. And Iowa legislators, who had resisted reinstating the death penalty several times over the previous decade, rejected an attempt to impose a death penalty for murders committed during a terrorist act. In the end, the anti-terrorism package that Iowa adopted differed substantially from the original proposal, mostly in ways acceptable to civil libertarians.

Several other state legislatures followed similar trends. In the predominantly Democratic Maryland state legislature, liberal legislators worried about broad definitions of terrorism. But their concerns were also shared by their most conservative Republican colleagues. One GOP legislator, for example, fretted, "I do realize that we're at war, but we can't take the chance that we're curtailing our liberty." She went on to add, "Today, it may be Al Qaeda; tomorrow it may be anti-abortion protestors." And in the Idaho state legislature—one of the most heavily Republican state legislatures in the country—members similarly rebelled against expansive definitions of terrorism, noting that teenagers who falsely pull fire alarms might be construed to be terrorists. Significant resistance to broad definitions of terrorism surfaced among legislators in California and Washington State as well.

But not all state legislatures shared these fears. Many passed their own tough anti-terrorism bills. Legislators in South Dakota, Utah, and Virginia, for example, were comfortable with broad definitions of terrorism. Indeed, South Dakota legislators were comforted by the comments of

Deb Bowman, their state's homeland security coordinator. She assured them that no innocent people would be caught up in the new law because, "When we see terrorism, we know what it is."

By the end of 2002, at least 32 states had amended their criminal codes to include new provisions covering terrorist acts. In about a third of those states, certain terrorist acts were made eligible for the death penalty. Several states passed laws dealing specifically with the use of weapons of mass destruction, whereas others toughened statutes dealing with those who might support or assist terrorists. Finally, numerous states passed laws punishing terrorist hoaxes. Several of these laws require those convicted of the offense to pay for the economic costs of their acts.

16-4 Other State Government Actions

One point that became evident after September 11 is that state efforts to deal with potential terrorist threats will be an ongoing activity. Although public attention focused on state legislative debates on antiterrorism bills, state governments undertook many other important but less conspicuous actions. A number of states, for example, removed information from their websites that might be useful to terrorists. The New Jersey Department of Environmental Protection removed maps of the state's reservoirs, as well as information about hazardous chemicals kept at 33,000 businesses around the state. Pennsylvania removed information about toxic waste sites and mining operations. Florida removed links to pages with information about crop dusters. Washington State deleted information disclosing where its emer-

gency management center is located.

Several of the September 11 hijackers had fraudulently obtained driver's licenses, prompting states to tighten their procedures for granting licenses. A number of states passed laws requiring applicants to submit more than one piece of identification with their application for a driver's license. Many states now require applicants who are not American citizens to provide proof that they are in the United States legally before they receive a license. Minnesota now issues noncitizens a driver's license in a different color from those given to American citizens. Several states tied the date the license expires to the date an applicant's immigration visa expires. Finally, several states integrated technological advances into their driver's licenses. Georgia and West Virginia, for example, now incorporate biometric identifiers, such as thumbprints, and information about the retinal structure of a person's eye. Connecticut is now issuing licenses with sophisticated data encryption embedded in them.

In another action motivated in part by the terrorist threat, seven states joined the Emergency Management Association Compact (EMAC) after September 11, bringing the total number of states in the compact to 47, plus the District of Columbia, Puerto Rico, and the Virgin Islands. Only California, Hawaii, and Wyoming remain outside the compact. The EMAC is an agreement among the signatory states that makes it easy for states to send personnel and equipment to help another state experiencing an emergency, when additional police and rescue personnel are desperately needed. Under the

compact, a state that receives out-of-state assistance is legally obligated to pay the cost of that aid. States join the EMAC because it greatly facilitates the rendering of timely help when catastrophes occur, as all of them are now aware can happen. Indeed, the compact is credited with playing a critical role in allowing member states to quickly assist the states affected by the September 11 terrorist attacks.

Another compact among the states gained greater prominence after September 2001. The Interstate Compact on Adult Offender Supervision, which was originally created in 1937, is designed to coordinate the monitoring and supervision of criminal parolees and probationers living or traveling in states other than where they were convicted and sentenced. A new compact was developed in 1998 to meet the needs of a changing criminal justice system. In June 2002, thirty months after the new compact began, it became operational when its 35th member (Pennsylvania) joined. By May 2004, every state but Massachusetts and Mississippi had joined. The compact commits the states to, among other things, collect and analyze standardized information about parolees and probationers.

Finally, the federal government is helping state and local governments prepare for potential terrorist attacks. The federal Department of Health and Human Services provided $1.1 billion to be spent during the 2002 fiscal year to assist states in developing plans for responding to potential bioterrorism, expanding public health laboratories, enhancing the readiness of hospitals to handle large numbers of victims, and improving communications among public health officials and hospitals. President Bush's 2003 budget requested $3.5 billion in grants to assist state and local government. But by some calculations, Congress included only $800 million in new spending for these purposes in the final budget bill. The money will be used to help communities conduct emergency planning, purchase equipment, train personnel, and run exercises to test their readiness for real attacks.

16-5 Conclusion

After September 11, state and local governments attempted to respond to the terrorist threat. These responses took diverse forms. State legislatures passed laws designed to make sure terrorist acts are covered by state laws. Governors reviewed their state's bureaucratic structures to determine whether they could respond appropriately in the event of a terrorist attack, and, more important, if they are equipped to prevent such

attacks in the first place. A multitude of other state and local agencies, such as public health laboratories and fire departments, struggled to assess and improve their own policies and capabilities. State and local governments were not wholly unprepared before September 11, but the terrible events of that day pointed out how much people rely on their efforts to protect and to serve them. Should another attack occur, state and local government would once again be on the front lines.

Readings for Further Study

Gavin, Robert. 2002. "Frenzy to Adopt Terrorism Laws Starts to Recede." *Wall Street Journal.* March 27.

Kettl, Donald F. 2002. "Connecting the Dots." *Governing Magazine* 15 (October): 13. Available at http://www.governing.com/archive/2002/oct/potomac.txt

Walters, Jonathan. 2001. "Safety Is Still a Local Issue." *Governing Magazine* 15 (November): 12. Available at http://www.governing.com/archive/2001/nov/potomac.txt

Websites to Check Out

Note: As we went to press, these sites were functional using the URLs provided. Check out the online text for the most up-to-date URLs.

Site name: National Conference of State Legislatures

URL: http://www.ncsl.org/programs/cj/terror.htm

A wealth of information about issues, including terrorism, that are being debated in the nation's fifty state legislatures.

Site name: National Emergency Management Association

URL: http://www.nemaweb.org

News updates on state actions to develop emergency management capabilities, as well as a report on trends in state terrorism preparedness.

Site name: Stateline.org

URL: http://www.stateline.org/stateline/?pa=issue&sa=showIssue&id=541

A daily compendium of news stories about state decisions on a host of issues, including anti-terrorism policies and programs.

The Mystery of the Vanishing Surplus:

Who Took It and Where Did It Go?

James M. Lindsay

What a difference a year makes. In January 2001, the U.S. government took pride in having finally put its financial house in order. For most of the three previous decades, it had spent more each year than it took in as revenue. This deficit spending persisted regardless of which party controlled the White House or Congress. But as George W. Bush was sworn in as the forty-third president, Washington was looking forward to running a $313 billion annual budget surplus, which would put the federal budget in the black for the fourth year in a row. And the annual surpluses figured to go higher in the years ahead. Economists were projecting that the federal government would run up a $5.6 trillion budgetary surplus over the ten-year period from 2002 to 2011 (see Figure 17-1a). That surplus would enable Washington to pay off essentially all of the public debt—or at least all of it that could be paid off early—by 2009. Things were going so well that economists were left hunting for reasons why having a government firmly in the black might be bad.

The budgetary picture looked far less impressive in January 2002 (see Figure 17-1b). The actual budget surplus for 2001 had turned out to be only $127 billion, nearly $200 billion less than anticipated. Forecasts for 2002 and 2003 indicated that the federal budget would slip back into a deficit for the first time since 1997. These same projections held that the budget would rebound into the black later in the decade. Even then, the annual surpluses would be much smaller than previously projected. In the new projections, the cumulative surplus between 2002 and 2011 would be only $1.6 trillion.

Thus, in only one year, roughly $4 trillion in projected surpluses vanished. To put that number in perspective, consider this: $4 trillion is greater than the entire gross domestic products of Australia, Denmark, Ireland, Italy, Mexico, South Africa, and South Korea—combined.

Who is responsible for the vanishing surplus? Several suspects have been named: the Bush administration's income tax cut, the country's economic recession, Congress's inability to control its appetite for new spending, and the war on terrorism. Who is to blame—or perhaps more accurately, who the public comes to blame—could have major consequences for American politics in the next several years.

17-1 So What?

Why should we care what happened to projected surpluses? After all, the national debt quintupled in size between 1980 and 2000 as the federal government's budget books gushed red ink. But the 1980s and 1990s were also decades of tremendous economic prosperity. So if we can have massive deficit spending and economic growth, why be frightened of small deficits that will eventually turn into surpluses?

Answers to that question usually point to two concerns. The first is that deficit spending can retard economic growth. When the federal government spends more than it takes in, it makes up for the shortfall by borrowing money. In doing so, the government competes with other borrowers for funds, which drives up interest rates. Higher interest rates, in turn, can discourage firms from investing in new factories and technologies, thereby diminishing economic growth.

This argument has empirical support. Economic growth was particularly robust in the second half of the 1990s, a time when the government's annual deficits were falling rapidly—as were interest rates. Of course, current projections suggest that the

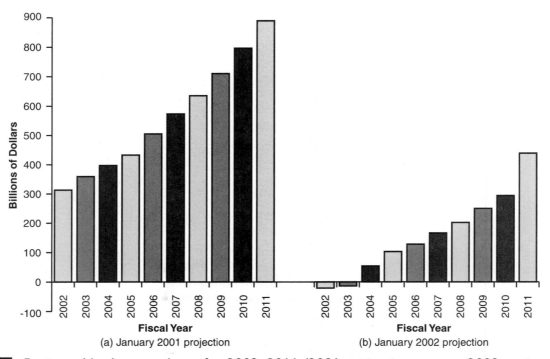

Figure 17-1 Projected budget surpluses for 2002–2011 (2001 projections versus 2002 projections). *(a)* In January 2001, the Congressional Budget Office projected that the federal government would generate annual budget surpluses totaling $5.61 trillion between 2002 and 2011. *(b)* The new projections issued in January 2002 indicated much smaller surpluses.

Source: Congressional Budget Office.

federal government's deficits will be small and last only a few years—so any depressing effect on the economy should be small. But if those projections prove wrong, and the deficits are large and persistent, the economic harm could be substantial.

The second and more prominent concern today, though, is that the vanishing surplus means Washington is not paying down its national debt as rapidly as it needs to in order to prepare for the consequences of the graying of America. Beginning later this decade, the first Baby Boomers, the most populous generation in U.S. history, will begin to retire. This unprecedented demographic transition has tremendous budgetary implications. Baby Boomers will go from paying the taxes that

fund the federal government's retirement and medical care programs to being the beneficiaries of these programs.

Social Security is the program that causes the most concern. To see why, one needs to recognize that it is a pay-as-you-go program. That is, today's workers pay special payroll taxes—called FICA on your pay stub—that pay the benefits of today's beneficiaries. Historically, revenues from payroll taxes have exceeded the annual costs of Social Security benefits. Indeed, the large surplus generated by payroll taxes explains why the overall federal budget is so close to being in the black. The January 2002 projections calculated that when Social Security revenues are put aside, the federal budget deficit would

hit $181 billion, and the federal budget would not return to a surplus until 2010.

Now here's the catch. Economists project that unless current laws are changed, or the average lifespan suddenly gets much shorter, the Social Security surplus will begin to shrink by the end of the decade as more and more Baby Boomers retire. By 2015, the number of retirees will be so large that the annual cost of paying Social Security benefits will exceed annual revenues from Social Security payroll taxes. The Social Security deficit will rapidly worsen each year thereafter, exceeding more than $400 billion by 2025. (The problem is actually worse because other federal spending tied to the graying of America, such as paying for retirees' health care costs, will go up in a similar fashion.) Moreover, these projections are pretty solid, certainly more solid than most budgetary projections. Why? Because they are based on established demographic trends. Tomorrow's elderly are alive today.

2 Here's how what happens to Social Security a decade from now plays into today's budgetary debates. If annual payroll taxes eventually do fall short of annual Social Security payments, then the government must make up the shortfall. It can do so by dipping into general tax revenues, cutting benefits, raising payroll taxes, or borrowing money. The first three choices are all painful. Dipping into general tax revenues takes funds away from other government programs. Cutting benefits angers retirees, and raising taxes upsets workers. Both groups vote, and politicians are usually reluctant to alienate voters.

3 That leaves borrowing as the most appealing solution to any shortfall in Social Security. But the government's capacity to borrow is not unlimited. And borrowed money comes at a cost, namely, interest payments. That is why so many people were happy in 2001 to see the projected $5.6 trillion budget surplus. They hoped that the money would be used to pay down the national debt. That would give the country an extra cushion should it need to borrow heavily in the future to finance the retirement of the Baby Boomers.

Given the potential economic stakes, it is not surprising that the political stakes are high in debates over the vanishing surplus. If either the Democrats or Republicans are blamed for having squandered the surplus, they could be vulnerable to charges that they have jeopardized Social Security, which is one of the federal government's most popular programs. Conversely, if either Democrats or Republicans succeed in fixing blame for the vanishing surplus on the other party, they could have a powerful issue to take to the polls.

17-2 The Suspects

So who was responsible for the vanishing surplus? Several suspects stood out:

1 • **The Tax Cut.** George W. Bush campaigned on one central pledge in the 2000 presidential campaign—cutting income taxes. The rationale Bush offered for his tax-cut proposal varied over time. It was initially justified as necessary to sustain the economic boom of the 1990s. Later, it was hailed as a way to jump-start a slowing economy. And occasionally, it was justified on the grounds that limiting government revenue would reduce Congress's ability to increase government spending. Whatever the rationale, in 2001, President Bush made good on his campaign pledge. Less than four months after taking office, and to the surprise of the many observers, he persuaded Congress to slash federal tax rates. Yet, lower tax rates can mean lower government revenues and small budget surpluses (or bigger deficits).

• **The Recession.** The federal budget projections released in January 2001 came out in the glow of economic good times. The U.S. economy had grown rapidly in the 1990s, and the stock markets had hit all-time highs. Things were so good that economists were eagerly debating whether we were witnessing the birth of a "New Economy," one in which information technology had revolutionized the economy, dramatically increased productivity, and ended the boom and bust of the business cycle. Only two months later, much of this euphoria was gone. By March 2001, the U.S. economy had entered a recession. Many companies began laying off employees. Some went bankrupt. The stock market, which had been faltering in the second half of 2001, continued a sharp downward slide. None of this was good news for the federal treasury. When economies slide into recession, tax revenues almost always go down.

• **The War on Terrorism.** In January 2001, Americans were basking in an unprecedented era of peace and prosperity. The Cold War was distant memory. It had been more than nine years since the Soviet Union had been tossed onto the ash heap of history. The United States was an unchallenged superpower, a colossus bestriding the globe. The news media were heavily geared to "lifestyle" news and stories about dot.com millionaires, not foreign threats. September 11 changed all that. By October, the United States was embroiled in a war in Afghanistan. Money spent on smart bombs and cruise missiles is money that won't be going to the surplus.

• **Increased Domestic Spending.** The projection of a $5.6 trillion surplus came with fine print—a warning that the projection assumed that domestic spending would not rise faster than the projected inflation rate. But neither members of Congress nor the president are bound by that fine print. They are first and foremost politicians who respond to what voters want. And voters wanted many things. Parents and teachers wanted more education spending. Farmers wanted more government support for agriculture. Environmentalists wanted more to be done about environmental hazards. Some of those calls for increased spending ended up in the 2002 budget. And greater spending means smaller surpluses (or bigger deficits).

17-3 The Verdict

So who was guilty? The Congressional Budget Office's January 2002 budget projection supplies the answer. (CBO is a nonpartisan agency. Its director was appointed by Republicans when they controlled Congress. So there is no reason to believe that CBO's numbers are tilted against either party or against the Bush administration. Similar projections by private groups produce similar numbers.) As Figure 17-2 shows, all of our suspects contributed something to the $4 trillion in vanishing surpluses, though they did not play equal roles.

The single biggest culprit was the tax cut. It was responsible for 41 percent of the $4 trillion reduction in the surplus. The tax cut reduced the projected surplus in two ways. The obvious way is that lower taxes mean less government revenue. This direct cost of the tax cut was $1.3 trillion. But tax cuts also have an indirect cost. Lower revenues mean less of the national debt can be paid off, and

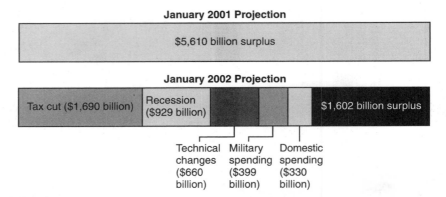

January 2001 Projection

$5,610 billion surplus

January 2002 Projection

Tax cut ($1,690 billion) | Recession ($929 billion) | | | | $1,602 billion surplus

Technical changes ($660 billion)   Military spending ($399 billion)   Domestic spending ($330 billion)

Figure 17-2   Why the 2001 projection changed. The tax cut and a weaker economy help explain why the Congressional Budget Office's projection for the total federal surplus between 2002 and 2011 fell by $4 trillion between January 2001 and January 2002.

Source: Congressional Budget Office.

a higher-than-projected national debt means that the U.S. Treasury has to pay more in interest. The indirect, debt-related cost of the tax cut ran about $400 billion.

The recession had the second largest impact on the projected surplus. The CBO officially placed the cost at $929 billion, or 23 percent, of the $4 trillion drop in the projected budget surplus. Because the economy had weakened, CBO had to lower its assumption about how rapidly the economy would grow in the near term. It also used slightly less optimistic assumptions about economic growth later in the decade. The CBO reports that about three-quarters of the $929 billion revenue loss associated with the recession comes as a direct result of lost revenue. The rest of the decline is the result of the indirect cost associated with not having the national debt shrink as rapidly as anticipated.

But the cost of the recession may actually be larger. For methodological reasons, CBO puts all changes in its projections that are not the result of changes in legislation or changes in its

economic forecasts in a category labeled "technical changes." In 2002, CBO concluded that technical changes accounted for $660 billion, or 16 percent, of the $4 trillion decline in the projected surplus. These technical changes to revenues stemmed primarily from new projections about proceeds from capital gains taxes (that is, taxes on investments that are sold for profit) and adjustments to account for lower-than-anticipated tax revenues during 2001. Those changes were triggered largely by the weakening of the economy itself, so the actual impact of the recession was closer to $1.6 trillion.

In comparison to the tax cut and the recession, increased defense and domestic spending played a secondary role in the vanishing surplus. The cost of increased defense spending and the resulting increase in interest costs amounted to roughly $400 billion, or 10 percent of the missing $4 trillion. (This figure includes the impact of spending increases for the military that Congress and the president approved before September 11, as well as after it.)

Increased domestic spending, including new spending for the nondefense aspects of homeland security, constitute another $330 billion, or 8 percent of the $4 trillion vanishing surplus.

17-4 That Ain't All

Even if a $1.6 trillion surplus is smaller than a $5.6 trillion one, it still would make a sizable dent in the national debt. That would alleviate the fears of those worried that the vanishing surplus hindered economic growth or prevented Washington from preparing for the graying of America. The problem with this argument, though, is that the $1.6 trillion projected surplus turned out to be just as illusory as the $5.6 trillion projected surplus.

There are three reasons for that. Two have already been mentioned: All long-range budgetary projections make crucial assumptions about future economic growth and government spending. If those two assumptions are off, the projections will be off as well.

That looked to be the case in mid-2004. Contrary to the assumption that CBO made in 2002, the economy did not bounce back quickly from recession. CBO's assumption that discretionary government spending—that is, all spending outside of entitlement programs such as Social Security—would grow no faster than the projected inflation rate also proved wrong. Indeed, less than two weeks after CBO projected the $1.6 trillion surplus,

President Bush unveiled a new budget that included, among other things, the largest increase in defense spending in two decades. And in 2003, Congress and the White House agreed to legislation creating a new prescription drug benefit that was estimated to cost more than half a trillion dollars over the next decade.

The gap between assumptions and reality explains why CBO's March 2004 budget projections looked far more dismal than they did two years earlier. Whereas CBO had projected a budget deficit of $21 billion in 2002 and $14 billion in 2003, the federal government actually ran a deficit of $158 billion in 2002 and $375 billion in 2003. CBO's March 2004 projections forecast that the budget would remain in the red through 2014, the last year in its projections. And while CBO concluded that the size of the deficit would drop sharply beginning in 2012, it projected that the federal government would run a budget deficit of $2.9 trillion between 2002 and 2011—a swing of $8.5 trillion from its projection three years earlier. Again, the 2004 projection assumed government spending would grow at the rate of inflation. Yet, in mid-2004, neither the White House nor Congress looked ready to make the tough choices that would be required to slow government spending.

The third reason that the $1.6 trillion surplus figure looked to be off the mark—and a reason to be wary of even the $2.9 trillion

deficit figure—is that it assumes that the tax law that Congress and the president wrote in 2001 will go into effect exactly as written. This is crucial because some of the tax cuts in that law are scheduled to expire as early as 2004. The entire legislation is scheduled to expire in 2010. Yet, President Bush made clear in his State of the Union addresses in 2003 and 2004 that he wanted Congress to make many of the tax cuts permanent—and to enact a wide-ranging set of new tax cuts. In May 2003, Congress agreed to a tax-cut plan estimated to cost $350 billion over ten years. If Congress agrees to the rest of President Bush's tax-cut agenda, the federal government's budget deficit will grow even larger.

Should we worry that the days of budgetary prosperity are over? Optimists remind us that budgetary projections are notoriously unreliable. In the mid-1990s, everyone was projecting unending budget deficits. By 1998, the federal budget was in the black. Much the same could, and perhaps will, happen again in the next few years after the economy gets back on its feet. But pessimists are more likely to be right. The push for higher levels of government spending, both on defense and domestic programs, is likely to grow, not shrink, in the coming years. And looming just over the horizon is the prospect of paying for the retirement of the Baby Boom generation. So if you are a betting person, bet on red ink.

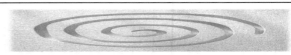

Readings for Further Study

Congressional Budget Office. 2004. *CBO's Current Budgetary Projections*. Washington, D.C.: U.S. Government Printing Office. Available at http://www.cbo.gov/showdoc. cfm?index=1944&sequence=0

Kamin, David, and Richard Kogan. 2004. *Deficit Picture Grimmer Than CBO's March Projections*. Center on Budget and Policy Priorities. June 4. Available at http://www.cbpp.org/6-4-04bud.htm

Office of Management and Budget. 2004. *Budget of the United States Government, Fiscal Year 2005*. Washington, D.C.: U.S. Government Printing Office. Available at http://www.whitehouse.gov/omb/budget/fy2005/budget.html

Websites to Check Out

Note: As we went to press, these sites were functional using the URLs provided. Check out the online text for the most up-to-date URLs.

Site name: Congressional Budget Office

URL: http://www.cbo.gov/

CBO's website contains detailed historical budget data, current budget and economic projections, and updates on the status of appropriations bills.

Site name: Office of Management and Budget

URL: http://www.omb.gov/

OMB, which is part of the Executive Office of the Presidency, maintains a website that contains a wealth of information about the president's proposed federal budget, as well as detailed data on past and projected budgetary expenditures.

Site name: Bureau of the Public Debt—The Debt to the Penny

URL: http://www.publicdebt.treas.gov/opd/opdpenny.htm

The U.S. Treasury Department maintains this site, which not only tracks the current federal debt "to the penny," but also provides information on virtually every aspect of the federal debt.

Government Regulation after September 11

James M. Lindsay

Washington responded to September 11 with a blizzard of actions designed to secure the American homeland against future terrorist attacks. President George W. Bush ordered U.S. forces to wage war against Al Qaeda and Taliban forces in Afghanistan. The White House and Congress agreed on the largest defense spending increase in two decades, and they nearly doubled spending on the domestic aspects of homeland security. They also created the Department of Homeland Security, which brought nearly two dozen federal agencies with homeland security duties under one roof.

Washington hopes that military action abroad, increased spending on defense and home security, and new organizational procedures will spare the United States from experiencing another September 11. But government officials also know that even if they do a better job of stopping terrorists overseas and catching them when they enter the United States, another attack that kills thousands of Americans and disrupts the economy remains a possibility. The openness of American society and the wonders of modern technology make it possi-

ble for very small groups of people to take many lives. And the United States provides a rich list of potential targets. Hundreds of thousands of people work each day in lower Manhattan, inside the loop in Chicago, and in downtown Los Angeles. Nearly ninety college and professional stadiums seat 60,000 or more people. The Indianapolis 500 attracts 250,000 spectators each year, while NASCAR races such as the Daytona 500 regularly attract 100,000 or more fans. Tens of thousands of people flock each day to tourist spots such as Disney World and the Mall of America.

So providing homeland security requires more than rooting out terrorists, tightening borders, and improving communication within government. It also requires making targets less vulnerable to attack. But that poses a problem. Many of the sites that terrorists might attack are owned not by federal, state, or local government but by private firms and individuals. What steps, if any, should government take to persuade these private interests to secure their property against possible terrorist attack? Just as important, who will pay to make sure the TransAmerica building in San Francisco and the Seabrook

Nuclear Power Plant north of Boston are less vulnerable to attack? The federal government? The state government? The property owner? Some combination of all three?

The federal government can take one of five basic approaches to the problem of persuading private property owners to adopt anti-terrorism measures. Each approach has its own strengths and weakness, each raises questions of fairness, and each sticks different groups in society with the price tag. Because no approach is objectively "best," and because the price tag for anti-terrorism measures can be steep, the question of how best to protect private property is a politically volatile issue.

18-1 Do Nothing

The first approach the federal government could take is to do nothing. Such a policy might seem irresponsible at first glance, but it has considerable logic to it. A senior official at the Environmental Protection Agency captured the basic idea when he argued shortly after September 11 that it might be inappropriate to impose federal security standards on chemical plants and refineries: "Industry has a very powerful incentive to do the right thing. It ought to be their worst nightmare that their facility would be the target of a terrorist attack because they did not meet their responsibility to their community." And it's not just a sense of responsibility that could drive companies to do the right thing. If they don't, and an attack occurs, they will pay a price both in terms of the damage done to their property and in terms of the money they can expect to pay to compensate those hurt in the attack. Conversely, leaving firms to deal with the terrorist threat as they see fit has a benefit: Companies will know what works best for them and have an incentive to hold down the costs of anti-terrorism measures.

As a practical matter, the "do nothing" approach will prevail when it comes to protecting most private property. Every McDonald's and every movie multiplex is a potential target of a terrorist attack. But the potential economic and human toll of attacking such targets is likely to be too small—at least when measured against what happened on September 11—and the costs of protecting them too high to justify substantial government action. As Mitch Daniels, the former director of the White House Office of Management and Budget, said in early 2003, "There is not enough money in the galaxy to protect every square inch of America and every American against every conceivable threat that every hateful fanatic in the world might conjure up." So in most cases, the government will leave it up to the property owners to decide what anti-terrorism measures they want to take.

It is less obvious that the do-nothing approach works with targets such as skyscrapers and chemical plants, where the costs of an attack could be sizable. For one thing, just as people "ought" to exercise regularly but often don't, some companies may fail to protect themselves adequately against attack, even though they should. There are many reasons why they may not. They may be irresponsible. They may decide that the odds they will be targeted are too low to bother. They may worry that the necessary counterterrorism measures will cut too deeply into their profits. They may lack experience with terrorism and misperceive their potential vulnerabilities. Finally, they may have noticed that the federal government helped bail out the airline industry after September 11 and decide that they too will be rescued if something terrible happens.

18-2 Assume Private Sector Responsibilities

The second approach the federal government could take might be called the "do everything" option. That is, the government could make private responsibilities governmental ones. For instance, the government could take the job of providing security at plants that produce or process hazardous materials away from the plants' owners. When the federal, as opposed to state, government does this, it is known as "federalizing" private responsibilities.

The "do everything" approach might seem outlandish, but in some instances, it has already happened. Immediately after September 11, many state governors dispatched national guardsmen on a temporary basis to protect nuclear power plants. On a more permanent note, in the fall of 2001, Congress federalized the task of providing airport security. It took the responsibility for screening passengers and checking bags away from the private security firms that had always done the job for the airlines and gave it to the newly created Transportation Security Administration. And it is likely that with some occasional events that have major symbolic importance, such as the Super Bowl and World Series, the federal government will take the lead in providing security.

Still, the do everything option has sharp limits. One is that America is built on free enterprise. So outside of some special cases, of which airport security is one, government proposals to take over responsibilities from individual businesses will run into stiff political opposition. The do everything solution may also be an inappropriate solution for many terrorism problems. For example, experts argue that the air filtration systems that service large office buildings should be secured so that a terrorist could not introduce deadly chemical or biological agents into them. It is hard to imagine the government taking over responsibility for managing air filtration systems in all major office buildings, however. Even if such a task were affordable—and growing federal budget deficits are already crimping spending on homeland security—there is good reason to wonder how many responsibilities government could take on before it would find itself overwhelmed.

18-3 Offer Owners Incentives

Government has several choices in promoting counterterrorism efforts between doing nothing and doing everything. One choice is to entice private owners into making their property less vulnerable to terrorist attack by making it worthwhile for them to do so. This could be done directly by subsidizing—that is, paying part or all of the cost—of anti-terrorism measures. For instance, the government could decide to pay, say, half the cost of protecting air filtration systems against biological attack in all office buildings with more than 5,000 occupants. The government could also entice private owners to protect their property indirectly through tax incentives. For example, the government could give special tax breaks to property owners who install sophisticated air filtration systems in their office buildings.

The federal government has a long history of using direct subsidies and tax incentives to influence private behavior. Subsidies to keep farmers in business and tax credits to encourage people to have children are two well-known examples. Why are subsidies and tax incentives popular? One reason is that people are less likely to object to being encouraged to do something as opposed to being told to do something. With subsidies and tax incentives, firms and individuals get to decide whether they want to take advantage of what the government is offering. If they are not interested, or if they don't think the government is offering enough, they can do what they wish. Farmers can stop farming and people can decide not to have (more) kids.

Although this "you decide" approach may be sensible for agricultural and family planning policy, its applicability to anti-terrorism policy is less obvious. If the subsidies and tax incentives don't persuade private owners to protect their property, society will remain vulnerable to attack. One way to avoid this problem is to provide more generous subsidies and tax incentives. But that drives up the federal government's costs. And if private owners conclude that the government is going to be generous, they will ask for larger subsidies or tax incentives than are needed to change their behavior. In the worst case, the government could end up paying private owners to do what they would have done in any event (just as many people would have children even in the absence of a child-tax credit). The result would be no net decrease in society's vulnerability, just a sizable increase in the federal government's budget.

18-4 Require Insurance

A fourth option government could pursue is to require all major factories, plants, official buildings, and commercial complexes to carry insurance against terrorist attacks. Why insurance? The logic here is that if firms are required to have insurance, then insurance companies will make sure they take steps, such as maintaining a sufficient number of security guards and securing air filtration systems, to minimize their terrorism risk. After all, the more insurance companies have to pay off on their policies, the less money they make. In short, government could create pressure on firms to do what they "ought" to do without assuming for itself the laborious task of monitoring private behavior.

Government has used insurance schemes to change private behavior in other situations. For instance, most state governments require automobile owners to carry liability insurance as a condition for registering their cars. The idea here is that the more reckless you are as a driver, the more you have to pay for insurance, and in turn, the greater your economic incentive to drive responsibly.

But insurance schemes have their own disadvantages. One is how to persuade insurance companies to insure against terrorism. The price tag of a terrorist attack could be enormous, as September 11 makes clear. Insurance companies may be unwilling to put themselves in a position where making good on a policy could push them into bankruptcy. Indeed, immediately following the attacks on the World Trade Center and the Pentagon, many insurance companies stopped providing terrorism coverage, which traditionally had been offered for free as part of most commercial insurance policies. (Because terrorist attacks were largely unknown before September 11, the offer almost never cost insurers any money.) President Bush and Congress sought to overcome that reluctance by enacting a law in November 2002 that, among other things, required insurers to provide terrorism insurance but limited the amount of claims they would have to pay in the event of an attack.

Unfortunately, limiting insurers' financial exposure to terrorist attacks does not solve every problem with insurance schemes. An additional complication is that the market for terrorist insurance lacks the one thing that makes the market for, say, life insurance work so well—a detailed understanding of the risk to be insured against. Tell an insurance company a bit about your age, occupation, and health history, and it has a good idea of how long it can expect you to live and how much to charge you for insurance. Insurance companies don't have the same experience with terrorism. So they are likely to charge inflated prices to minimize their own risk. In 2003, some companies saw the premiums they paid for terrorism coverage more than triple.

A final problem with insurance is that as long as coverage is voluntary, companies can refuse to buy it. This problem grows larger as the cost of premiums rises. Higher premiums mean higher costs for firms. Companies may not be able to pass these costs off to their customers, which would mean lower profits. Insurance industry experts estimate that a majority of commercial policyholders decided against purchasing insurance made available under the November 2002 law. Again, the federal government could always enact a law requiring firms to buy insurance. But because such a mandate would cost companies money, they would likely fight the legislation tooth and nail.

18-5 Regulate Private Behavior

The final option that the government can pursue is to impose anti-terrorism standards on private owners; that is, it can regulate their behavior. Regulation of the private sector is one of government's major functions, and it permeates virtually every facet of our lives. For instance, the federal government regulates how meat packers process their foods, what security procedures airlines must follow, and how hazardous materials are handled and transported. Because the food, airline, and hazardous materials industries

are all potential terrorist targets—which could be said of many other regulated private behaviors—the United States in a way had anti-terrorism regulations in place even before September 11.

Regulations have two advantages. One is that, unlike subsidies or tax incentives, they compel private owners to change their behavior. (This assumes, of course, that the regulations are enforced.) In the case of anti-terrorism policy, where society as a whole remains vulnerable if parts of it are, this is an important benefit. The second advantage is that regulation can ban activities that are judged to be too risky. For example, immediately following September 11, the federal government decided that the standard cockpit door made it too easy for terrorists to hijack a plane. So it ordered the airlines to install reinforced cockpit doors.

Regulations also have disadvantages, however. One is that they are often unpopular with the private interests that are regulated, which can make them politically difficult to impose and enforce. After September 11, for example, the chemical industry succeeded in blocking legislation that would establish minimum security requirements at chemical plants and other industrial facilities that store large amounts of toxic chemicals. Regulations are binding, so private owners are not free to use their assets as they see fit. Many don't like these constraints. (In some cases, though, private interests want to be regulated because such regulation helps them to hold potential competitors at bay.) Another disadvantage with regulations is that determining exactly how much regulation is needed to protect so-

ciety against terrorism is very difficult. There may be a temptation to impose too many regulations, which could impose considerable costs on the private sector.

A third disadvantage is that regulations can be inflexible or inappropriate. Regulations stipulate rules that private actors must abide by. But a rule that makes sense in most instances may not make sense in all instances. For example, regulations might require owners of buildings with a certain minimum occupancy to protect the building's air filtration systems against biological attack. Those protections may be affordable for newer buildings but financially impractical for older ones, forcing owners of those properties either to defy the government or go bankrupt.

Finally, regulations can be difficult to write and counterproductive. For instance, suppose the government decides it is essential to limit the chance of cyber-terrorism against private firms. (The destruction of the computer system of a major U.S. financial company, for example, could have devastating consequences for the American economy.) What kind of regulation should the government write? It obviously has to say something more than, "Thou Shalt Protect Thy Computer Systems." But what else should it say? If the government directs firms to use specific software or hardware fixes, it runs a good chance that firms will do exactly what the regulations require and no more, even if those regulations become outmoded. Those regulations might even discourage firms, or budding young entrepreneurs, from finding innovative solutions to the cyber-terrorism threat because firms are focused on what the government requires, rather than on what works. So the long-term result could be regulations that make society more, not less, vulnerable.

18-6 Is There a Best Option?

The question of what government should do to get private owners to act in ways it prefers is not new. Economists have studied this question for decades, and the gist of their labor is that there is no "best" way to influence private behavior. Part of the reason is that each approach offers a different mix of costs and benefits. For example, are we better off now that the federal government has federalized airport security? Or are we just as vulnerable as we were under the old system with the added twist that now the federal government picks up more of the tab?

Further complicating judgments about these types of questions is that we don't have a good fix on risks of terrorism. We know terrorism has happened, but what is the probability that another case of catastrophic terrorism will occur? Have the Afghanistan and Iraq wars effectively destroyed Al Qaeda and deterred groups that might be contemplating similar attacks against the United States? Or are Al Qaeda operatives regrouping to plan more attacks while other terrorist organizations decide to follow Al Qaeda's lead? We can all guess at the answers to these questions, but no one knows for sure. That matters because the greater we think the risk of another terrorist attack is, the greater the costs the public is willing to bear to protect society and the less inclined it is to let private property owners choose not to protect themselves.

Finally, efforts to pick the "best" approach are bound to stumble over fundamental questions of fairness; that is, who should bear the costs of preventing certain events? Reasonable people can disagree over how to answer this question. For example, why should the owner of a petrochemical plant have to pay to protect itself against terrorist attacks when it is the government's responsibility to provide the common defense? On the other hand, why should society pay to protect a petrochemical plant when its owner is voluntarily engaging in an activity that it knows makes it a tempting target for a terrorist attack?

These tough questions explain why heated political debates over how best to reduce America's vulnerability to terrorism are inevitable. Each of the five major approaches to the problem poses costs and benefits to different parts of society. No one likes to be stuck with the bill, even when the subject is terrorism.

Readings for Further Study

Carr, David. 2002. "The Futility of 'Homeland Defense.'" *Atlantic Monthly* 289 (January): 53–55.

Flynn, Stephen E. 2004. *America the Vulnerable: How Our Government Is Failing to Protect Us from Terrorism.* New York: HarperCollins.

O'Hanlon, Michael E., Peter R. Orszag, Ivo H. Daalder, I. M. Destler, David L. Gunter, James M. Lindsay, Robert E. Litan, and James S. Steinberg. 2003. *Protecting the American Homeland: One Year On.* Washington, D.C.: Brookings Institution Press.

Websites to Check Out

Note: As we went to press, these sites were functional using the URLs provided. Check out the online text for the most up-to-date URLs.

Site name: AEI-Brookings Joint Center for Regulatory Studies
URL: http://www.aei.brookings.org
Two of the nation's leading think tanks maintain a joint website that contains analyses of existing and proposed regulatory schemes, plus links to other websites devoted to regulatory studies.

Site name: Cato Regulatory Studies
URL: http://www.cato.org/research/reglt-st.html
The Cato Institute, the nation's leading libertarian think tank and a vocal supporter of giving market forces wide rein, maintains a website that is highly skeptical of many federal regulations.

Site name: Nuclear Energy Institute
URL: http://www.nei.org/
The official policy organization of the nuclear energy and technologies industry provides information about security at nuclear power plants and about the safety of transporting used nuclear fuel.

Are We Hated?

America's Image in the World

James M. Lindsay

Has the United States become *persona non grata* in the world?

Just asking that question causes most Americans to shake their heads in amazement. They point to the countries around the world liberated by U.S. soldiers; to the millions of people abroad who survived floods, famines, and other natural disasters because of the generosity of the American people; and to the continual stream of immigrants seeking to enter the United States. Why would a country with such a record of good deeds and with such an enduring appeal be widely disliked?

Anyone who travels abroad or watches the foreign news media knows, however, that resentment of the United States has soared in recent years. Al Qaeda represents the extreme manifestation of this phenomenon. "I love Islam. I love Muslims. I love all human beings—except the Americans," says one suspected terrorist. Although very few people around the world would act on such hate, considerable numbers seem to share it. When the World Trade Center towers collapsed, crowds in Beirut and Cairo watching the carnage unfold on television applauded.

Anger at the United States is not limited to Muslims or Middle Easterners. "Why do Americans seem to think that their lives are more valuable than lives outside their borders?" asks a South African. "I think it's fair to say that many Filipinos are now resentful of superpower and supercop America's attempts to impose its standards on the world," says a former chief of staff of the Filipino military. Brazilian soccer players donned Osama bin Laden T-shirts and waved bin Laden flags after September 11.

Resentment of the United States is also not a phenomenon restricted to poor countries. It also surfaces in advanced industrialized democracies. German Chancellor Gerhard Schroeder resuscitated what appeared to be a doomed reelection campaign in fall 2002 by playing to criticisms of the United States. Noh Moohyun did much the same thing two months later in winning South Korea's presidential election. More than eight in ten Canadians believe the United States was wholly or partly responsible for the September 11 attacks.

"Anti-Americanism" is the label often given to the phenomenon in which foreigners dislike the United States. However, in many ways, it is an unhelpful term. Flying planes into commercial buildings and marching peacefully in the streets to denounce the president of the United States are qualitatively different things. At the same time, people can dislike U.S. actions in the world and still like individual Americans. As the German foreign minister Joschka Fischer observes, "This is not anti-Americanism if we disagree on an issue."

All of this suggests several key questions. Exactly who dislikes the United States? What are they angry about? Should Americans care that many people around the globe see Washington as a threat to peace and security, rather than a force for good in the world? And if America's declining image abroad is a problem, what, if anything, should the United States do about it?

19-1 How Is America Viewed Abroad?

The easiest way to gauge how others see America is to look at the results of a standard polling question: Do you have a favorable or unfavorable opinion of the United States? Such polls can provide quick snapshots of sentiment in many different countries. Still, they have some limitations worth noting.

One such limitation is that no one knows what level of favorability signifies a problem. We may all agree that a 90 percent favorability rating signals that all is well, whereas a 10 percent favorability rating is a warning light that screams "Danger!" But what about a 75 percent popularity rating? Or a 50 percent rating? Should analysis of the polling data take into account the nature of U.S. ties to the country in question? Or does a 60 percent favorability rating mean the same thing, regardless of whether it is in an allied country like Germany or a nonallied country like Indonesia?

Another problem with favorability ratings is that they reveal nothing about why people dislike the United States. As we will see in a moment, the list of possible reasons is long. Favorability ratings also reveal nothing about the intensity of people's dislike. Some people may dislike the United States in the same way they dislike broccoli. Not to their taste, but also not worth expending much time or energy worrying over. Someone else's dislike may be rage—an emotion powerful enough to move him or her to violence. Finally, many countries don't allow surveys, and these countries often have troubled relations with the United States. So the polling results do not reflect a random sample of countries in the world, and they may exaggerate America's popularity in the world.

With these limitations in mind, examine Table 19-1, which shows America's favorability ratings in 28 countries. All of the countries were polled before September 11. Follow-up polls were conducted after the terrorist attacks, but none was conducted

Table 19-1	How the Rest of the World Views America (Percent Holding a Favorable View of the United States)					
Region	1999/ 2000	2002	2003	2004	Change 1999/2000– 2002	Change 2002– 2003
Europe						
Bulgaria	76%	72%	—	—	–4%	—
Czech Republic	77%	71%	—	—	–6%	—
France	62%	63%	31%	37%	+1%	–32%
Germany	78%	61%	25%	38%	–17%	–36%
Italy	76%	70%	34%	—	–6%	–36%
Poland	86%	79%	50%	—	–7%	–29%
Russia	37%	61%	28%	47%	+24%	–33%
Slovak Republic	74%	60%	—	—	–14%	—
Spain	50%	—	14%	—	—	–36%
Ukraine	70%	80%	—	—	+10%	—
United Kingdom	83%	75%	48%	58%	–8%	–27%
Central/South Asia						
Pakistan	23%	10%	—	21%	–13%	—
Turkey	52%	30%	12%	30%	–22%	–18%
Uzbekistan	56%	85%	—	—	+29%	—
Western Hemisphere						
Argentina	50%	34%	—	—	–16%	—
Bolivia	66%	57%	—	—	–9%	—
Brazil	56%	52%	—	—	–4%	—
Canada	71%	72%	—	—	+1%	—
Guatemala	76%	82%	—	—	+6%	—
Honduras	87%	80%	—	—	–7%	—
Mexico	68%	64%	—	—	–4%	—
Peru	74%	67%	—	—	–7%	—
Venezuela	89%	82%	—	—	–7%	—
Asia						
Indonesia	75%	61%	—	—	–14%	—
Japan	77%	72%	—	—	–5%	—
South Korea	58%	53%	—	—	–5%	—
Africa						
Kenya	94%	90%	—	—	–4%	—
Nigeria	46%	77%	—	—	+31%	—

Sources: *What the World Thinks in 2002* (Washington, D.C.: Pew Research Center for the People and the Press, 2002), p. 4, available at http://people-press.org/reports/display.php3?ReportID=165; "America's Image Further Erodes, Europeans Want Weaker Ties," Pew Research Center for the People and the Press, Washington, D.C., March 18, 2003, p. 1, available at http://people-press.org/reports/ display.php3?ReportID=175; "A Year after the Iraq War: Mistrust of America in Europe Even Higher, Muslim Anger Persists," Pew Research Center for the People and the Press, Washington, D.C., March 16, 2004, p. 6, available at http://www.people-press.org/reports/pdf/206.pdf.

in the months immediately following the destruction in New York and Washington. This point is important because polls taken in late September 2001 almost certainly would have inflated America's popularity in many countries because the tragedy of September 11 would have been so fresh in people's minds.

Three points in Table 19-1 are worth noting. First, in 1999/2000 and again in 2002, a majority of people in 22 of the 28 countries surveyed viewed America favorably. In a dozen of the countries, more than 70 percent of their population viewed the United States favorably in both years. Again, these data may exaggerate the popularity of the United States. Comparable polling data are not available for Arab and most Islamic countries, and by all accounts, the citizens of these countries take a dimmer view of the United States.

Second, America's favorability ratings vary substantially across countries even at the same point in time. In 1999/2000, 94 percent of Kenyans viewed the United States favorably, whereas only 23 percent of Pakistanis did. Significant variations in favorability ratings even occur within the same region of the world. France and Poland are both European countries, but in 1999/2000, 86 percent of Poles gave the United States the thumbs up, whereas only 62 percent of the French did.

Third, the general trend in America's favorability ratings in recent years has been downward. Roughly two-thirds of the countries surveyed between 1999/2000 and 2002 showed a decline, though in most of those cases, the drop was in the single digits. The same can't be said for the change between 2002 and 2003. The average decline in America's favorability rating for the countries for which we have data was 31 percentage points. In 2004, in only one of six countries surveyed did pollsters find that a majority of the public viewed the United States favorably. Obviously, something happened. But what?

19-2 Why Do They Hate Us?

Efforts to explain America's image abroad and the reasons it might vary over time and place fall into two broad categories: those that blame events and attitudes in the country doing the rating and those that blame the United States. Which set of explanations has the better of the argument is hotly disputed and perhaps impossible to answer. The reasons for disliking the United States can vary tremendously from individual to individual and country to country.

19-2a It's Them

Arguments that blame the people who dislike the United States come in a variety of forms. A common one is that they envy the United States. Some explanations argue that others are envious because America commands the world stage in a way their own countries can't, even if they once did. "Scratch an anti-American in Europe," says one British official, "and very often all he wants is a guest professorship at Harvard or to have an article published in the *New York Times*." Other envy-based explanations point to resentment of America's tremendous wealth. The closest most people in the world come to experiencing the comforts that Americans take for granted is watching Hollywood movies or reruns of *Dallas*. On September 11, 2001, many countries around the world "saw a country hit by terrorism, as some of them had been," writes Fareed Zakaria of *Newsweek*, "but that was able to respond on a scale that was almost unimaginable."

A second set of "it's them" explanations argues that people dislike the United States because it provides a convenient scapegoat for the failures of their own societies. Rather than admit that their own leaders made bad economic and political choices, they prefer to blame the United States. America provides the perfect foil because its power, wealth, and engagement around the world make plausible the idea that it is somehow responsible. After all, few people in Indonesia or Argentina would believe that Honduras or Luxembourg caused their political stagnation and economic collapse.

A third set of "it's them" explanations points to deliberate efforts by foreign governments to stoke hatred of the United States. Some governments have found that criticizing the United States is a tried-and-true method of diverting public attention from their own failures. This is especially true in the Middle East. Egypt receives $2 billion a year from the United States, and its state-run news media denounce the "errors" of the U.S. government and the moral failings of American society. U.S. troops have preserved Saudi Arabia's security for more than a decade, while the Saudi monarchy bankrolls groups that call for America's destruction. Nor is the tendency to criticize the United States for political gain something peculiar to the Arab world, as the 2002 German and South Korean elections show.

A fourth set of "it's them" explanations emphasizes the role of privately owned foreign media. These companies are in business to make money, the argument goes, and they do so by playing to the prejudices of their audiences. Consider the case of the Arab cable network *Al Jazeera*. In its coverage of the Afghanistan and Iraq wars, it emphasized grisly video of civilian deaths, frequently aired unsubstantiated and erroneous claims about U.S. military actions, and seldom provided context for its reports. The intention of the coverage, according to *Al Jazeera*'s critics, was to inflame opinion in the Arab world rather than to inform it. Inflammatory coverage guaranteed larger audiences and more advertising money. In that respect, the news media become an echo chamber—identifying what their audiences want to see and hear and then delivering it to them.

19-2b It's Us

Explanations that attribute hostile feelings toward America to the petty and malicious motives of foreigners find a ready audience in the United States. After all, it flows from the same human emotion that would lead people abroad to scapegoat America. But some explanations of why the United States has a tarnished image abroad argue that the fault lies not overseas but at home.

The "it's us" explanation that tops most people's lists is U.S. foreign policy. Although most Americans see their country as a force for good in the world, many people overseas disagree. A common complaint is that American foreign policy is inconsistent and hypocritical. Washington trumpets the importance of democracy yet over the past half century has

supported authoritarian governments from Greece to the Congo to Chile to South Korea. Another common complaint is that Washington refuses to live by the same rules it imposes on others. It justifies a decision to invade Iraq as necessary to destroy Iraqi weapons of mass destruction, even though it possesses massive numbers of nuclear weapons and a sophisticated biological weapons program that is ostensibly "defensive" in purpose. Likewise, photographs of U.S. soldiers abusing Iraqi prisoners provided powerful evidence for critics who doubted that the United States had invaded Iraq in part to foster democracy there. Even if non-Americans aren't troubled by American inconsistency or arrogance, they may simply disagree with what Washington is trying to do or how it is trying to do it.

A second set of "it's us" explanations moves away from the grand sweep of American foreign policy and blames the current occupant of the White House, George W. Bush. "In Europe this summer," wrote one British journalist in late 2002, "I encountered remarkably little anti-Americanism—but a great deal of anti-Bushism." The problem is one of both style and substance, say the critics. They find his bluntness, his frequent invocation of God, his tendency to cast issues in black-and-white terms, and his lack of interest in the opinions of other countries maddening. They also criticize his administration's concerted efforts to torpedo multilateral efforts such as the Kyoto Accord on global warming and the International Criminal Court.

A third set of "it's us" explanations goes in the opposite direction, blaming not the actions of a single administration or even the actions of successive adminis-

trations over the past half-century, but rather America's very pervasiveness in the world. Globalization—growing economic, social, and political interconnectedness among countries—has been growing at a stunning rate in recent years. In many parts of the world, it is equated with Americanization. One can easily see why. Drop an American in any of the world's major cities, and it won't take him or her long to find the trappings of home—McDonald's, Starbucks, Tommy Hilfiger, and the Gap. Many people overseas see their cultures changing, becoming more "American," and they resent the change.

19-2c All of the Above?

Which of these explanations is right? In a sense, they all shed light on how others see the United States. The reasons people might dislike the United States are complex and vary both over time and across place. It would be very unusual indeed if one single explanation could explain the views of a college student in Beirut, a day laborer in Johannesburg, a street vendor in Mexico City, and a college professor in London.

At the same time, however, these explanations are not all equally good at explaining the sharp changes that have occurred in America's favorability ratings in recent years. Take the "They envy us" argument. American dominance is not a sudden event; the United States has been a superpower for more than half a century and the lone superpower for more than a decade. So envy can't explain why America's favorability rating dropped 31 percentage points between 2002 and 2003. Similar observations can be made about most of the other explanations.

The one explanation that would seem to explain the sharp decline in U.S. favorability ratings between 2002 and 2003 is the Bush administration's foreign-policy choices, and specifically, its decision to invade Iraq. The Iraq War was deeply unpopular with citizens of most countries. Polls conducted by the Pew Research Center on the eve of war found 87 percent of Russians, 86 percent of Turks, 75 percent of the French, and 69 percent of Germans opposed to the war. Only 39 percent of the British public supported Prime Minister Tony Blair's decision to send British troops to fight alongside the United States. So it should not be surprising that U.S. favorability ratings declined.

Yet, if one foreign-policy decision—even a momentous one—can change the U.S. image abroad so drastically, should Americans worry about what the world thinks of them?

19-3 Should We Care?

Optimists in the debate over America's image abroad argue that too much is made of how others view the United States. They note that the United States will never be loved by everyone. Moreover, people abroad will always run hot and cold about American foreign policy. In the late 1960s and early 1970s, the object of ire abroad was the Vietnam War. In the early 1980s, it was Ronald Reagan's nuclear modernization initiative and the NATO decision to deploy medium-range nuclear missiles in Europe. Today, it is Washington's aggressive pursuit of terrorists and tyrants. In sum, the bane of being a superpower is that its decisions inevitably affect others. To act is to choose, and to choose is to offend.

According to this optimistic view, what matters is not what foreign publics think but what their governments do. On that score, the optimists say, the news is good. They point to the Bush administration's tabulations that show that at least fifty countries officially supported the Iraq War, in many cases over the objections of a majority of their population. (Only three other countries, however, contributed combat troops to the war effort, and only one, Great Britain, contributed them in great number.) If foreign governments are going to support U.S. policy even at the risk of offending their own publics, why should Washington care whether their publics are giving the United States thumbs up or the middle finger? Besides, American primacy in world affairs is so great that even if countries oppose what Washington hopes to accomplish, there is little they can do. The inability of France, Germany, and Russia to stop the march to war with Baghdad is a case in point.

Washington—and all Americans—have plenty to worry about, say pessimists. To begin with, seething hatred of the United States in much of the Arab and Islamic world provides willing recruits for terrorist groups like Al Qaeda. Such hatred also makes it easier for terrorists to operate because so many people are sympathetic to their cause. Witness the ability of Osama bin Laden and many of his senior lieutenants to find refuge in Pakistan, whose government is officially America's ally in the war on terrorism.

Pessimists further believe that anger at the United States is not only a problem in the Middle East. They see European resentment of America today as funda-

mentally different than it was in the past. During the Vietnam War and the transatlantic crisis over Pershing II deployments, sizable portions of European publics supported U.S. policy even as protestors marched in the streets to denounce it. Many U.S. foreign policies today have little support anywhere in Europe. Moreover, during the Cold War, the Soviet threat to Western Europe gave Europeans a reason to swallow hard when they disagreed with Washington. That external pressure helping keep the Atlantic Alliance together no longer exists.

For these reasons, pessimists believe that future relations with Europe and other American allies will look much different than past relations. Our traditional allies see us as unwilling to take their interests and views into account. They respond by searching for ways to frustrate and ignore our objectives. That matters because, aside from overthrowing tyrannical regimes, almost everything the United States hopes to accomplish abroad requires the cooperation of others. Pessimists think that Washington could in the future call the world to action and discover that no one follows its lead.

The biggest victims of anger at the United States, according to pessimists, may not be the U.S. government but U.S. companies. Foreign publics can register their displeasure with the United States by ceasing to buy American consumer products. Signs of consumer boycotts of American products already exist in the Middle East. Coca-Cola, for example, estimates that consumer boycotts cost it sales of 50 million cases of soda in Egypt and the Persian Gulf in 2002. Foreign citizens can also decide not to spend their vacation dollars in the United States, a prospect that means little to the people of Akron, Ohio, but a lot to the people of Orlando, Florida.

19-4 What Should Be Done?

What, if anything, should the United States do about its sagging popularity? Pessimists argue that much needs to be done if Americans are to avoid seeing their relations with much of the rest of the world slip into a deep freeze. The nature of their prescription varies with the specific diagnosis they make. Those who believe the problem lies with the hypocrisy of American foreign policy argue that the United States should cease supporting authoritarian governments and devote far more of its resources to combating poverty and injustice around the world. Those who believe the problem lies with the specific style and substance of the Bush administration urge the White House to be less overbearing in the way it treats the rest of the world and more active in addressing problems such as the Middle East peace process and global warming that are priorities to others. Those who believe the problem lies with the deliberate actions by foreign governments and news media to inflame their publics call on Washington to force them to stop. They also argue that Washington should make greater use of the tools of public diplomacy, and especially U.S.-sponsored radio and television programs broadcast in local languages, to win the hearts and minds of people overseas.

But would such steps actually improve the way the United States is viewed overseas? Optimists say no. For them, resentment of the United States is either beyond our control or akin to a summer thunderstorm that will quickly pass on its own. Beyond this, they doubt that the world will repay the pessimists' prescriptions with a surge of gratitude toward America. They argue that if Washington shifts from supporting stable, pro-Western authoritarian regimes to opposing them, the result probably would not be Western-style democracy but either chaos or anti-Western authoritarian governments—and even greater resentment of the United States. Nor will "better" policies necessarily win Washington much credit. A common complaint in the Arab and Islamic worlds is that the United States is waging a war on Muslims. These complaints overlook the fact that the U.S. military interventions in Kuwait in 1991, Bosnia in 1995, Kosovo in 1999, and Afghanistan in 2001 saved the lives of millions of Muslims. The notion that public diplomacy can salvage American popularity is a quaint throwback to a simpler time of few media choices. In a world of 500 cable channels, satellite television, and the Internet, it is unrealistic to believe that American-sponsored programs can break through the clutter.

The debate over the significance of America's declining image and what should be done about it probably will continue for years, as will the deep passions that the debate unleashes. It may only be with time that we discover whether Americans are, in fact, witnessing a quickly passing thunderstorm or the onset of a long, cold winter.

Readings for Further Study

Hertsgaard, Mark. 2002. *The Eagle's Shadow: Why America Fascinates and Infuriates the World.* New York: Farrar, Straus & Giroux.

Rubin, Barry. 2002. "The Real Roots of Arab Anti-Americanism." *Foreign Affairs* 81 (November/December): 73–85.

Zakaria, Fareed. 2003. "The Arrogant Empire." *Newsweek* (March 24): 19–33.

Websites to Check Out

Note: As we went to press, these sites were functional using the URLs provided. Check out the online text for the most up-to-date URLs.

Site name: The Pew Global Attitudes Project

URL: http://people-press.org/pgap/

Provides a compendium of polls being conducted as part of a two-year project to assess the impact of globalization, modernization, rapid technological and cultural change, and September 11 on the values and attitudes of more than 38,000 people in 44 countries worldwide.

Site name: Under Secretary for Public Diplomacy and Public Affairs

URL: http://www.state.gov/r/

The Under Secretary for Public Diplomacy and Public Affairs helps ensure that public diplomacy (engaging, informing, and influencing key international audiences) is practiced in harmony with public affairs (outreach to Americans) and traditional diplomacy to advance U.S. interests and security and to provide the moral basis for U.S. leadership in the world.

Site name: For Mother Earth—Boycott Bush

URL: http://www.motherearth.org/USboycott/

An advocacy website that urges people around the world to boycott U.S. products because of the U.S. government's decision to invade Iraq.

America Unbound:

The Bush Revolution in Foreign Policy

**Ivo H. Daalder and
James M. Lindsay**

When George W. Bush peered out the window of Air Force One as it flew over Baghdad in early June 2003, he had reason to be pleased. He had just completed a successful visit to Europe and the Middle East. The trip began in Warsaw, where he had the opportunity to personally thank Poland for being one of just two European countries to contribute troops to the Iraq War effort. He then traveled to Russia to celebrate the 300th birthday of St. Petersburg. He flew on to Évian, a city in the French Alps, to attend a summit meeting of the heads of the world's major economies. He next stopped in Sharm el Sheik, Egypt, for a meeting with moderate Arab leaders, before heading to Aqaba, Jordan, on the shore of the Red Sea to discuss the prospects for peace with the Israeli and Palestinian prime ministers. He concluded his trip in Doha, Qatar, where troops at U.S. Central Command greeted him with thunderous applause. Now Bush looked down on the city that American troops had seized only weeks before.

Bush's seven-day, six-nation trip was in many ways a victory lap to celebrate America's tri-umph in the Iraq War—a war that many of the leaders Bush met on his trip had opposed. But in a larger sense, he and his advisers saw it as a vindication of his leadership. During his first thirty months in office, the man from Midland had started a foreign-policy revolution. He had discarded many of the constraints that had bound the United States to its allies and redefined key principles that had governed American engagement in the world for more than half a century. Like most revolutions, Bush's had numerous critics. Yet, he now traveled through Europe and the Middle East not as a penitent making amends but as a leader commanding respect. America unbound was remaking the course of international politics. Bush was the rare revolutionary who had succeeded. Or had he?

20-1 The Bush Revolution

What precisely is the Bush revolution in foreign policy? At its broadest level, it rests on two beliefs. The first was that in a dangerous world, the best—if not the only—way to ensure America's security is to shed the constraints imposed by friends, allies, and in-ternational institutions. Maximizing America's freedom to act was essential because the unique position of the United States made it the most likely target for any country or group hostile to the West. Americans could not count on others to protect them; countries inevitably ignored threats that did not involve them. Moreover, formal arrangements would inevitably constrain the ability of the United States to make the most of its unrivaled power. Gulliver must shed the constraints that he helped the Lilliputians weave.

The second belief was that an America unbound should use its strength to change the status quo in the world. Bush did not argue that the United States keep its powder dry while it waited for dangers to gather. Whereas John Quincy Adams—the only other son of a president to occupy the White House—had held that the United States should not go abroad "in search of monsters to destroy," Bush argued that America would be imperiled if it failed to do just that. "Time is not on our side," he declared in his January 2002 State of the Union address as he warned that an "axis of evil" had formed between terrorists and rogue states, such as Iraq, Iran, and North

Korea. "I will not wait on events, while dangers gather. I will not stand by, as peril draws closer and closer. The United States of America will not permit the world's most dangerous regimes to threaten us with the world's most destructive weapons." That logic guided the Iraq War, and it animated Bush's efforts to deal with other rogue states.

These fundamental beliefs had important consequences for the practice of American foreign policy. One was a disdain for the sorts of multinational institutions and arrangements developed by presidents from Truman through Clinton and a decided preference for the unilateral exercise of American power. Unilateralism appealed to Bush and his advisers because it was often easier and more efficient, at least in the short term, than multilateralism. Contrast the war that the Clinton administration had fought with its European allies in Kosovo in 1999, where Bush and his advisers believed that the task of coordinating the views of all NATO members greatly complicated the military effort, with the Afghanistan war, where Pentagon planners did not have to subject any of their decisions to foreign approval. This is not to say that Bush flatly ruled out working with others. Rather, his preferred form of multilateralism—to be indulged when unilateral action was impossible or unwise—involved building ad hoc coalitions of the willing, or what Richard Haass, a former adviser to Colin Powell, called "multilateralism à la carte."

Second, preemption was no longer a last resort of American foreign policy. In a world in which weapons of mass destruction were spreading and terrorists and rogue states were readying to attack in unconventional ways, Bush argued in a report laying out his administration's national security strategy, "the United States can no longer solely rely on a reactive posture as we have in the past. . . . We cannot let our enemies strike first." Indeed, the United States should be prepared to act not just preemptively against imminent threats, but also preventively against potential threats. Vice President Dick Cheney was emphatic on this point in justifying the overthrow of Saddam Hussein on the eve of the Iraq War. "There's no question about who is going to prevail if there is military action. And there's no question but that it is going to be cheaper and less costly to do now than it will be to wait a year or two years or three years until he's developed even more deadly weapons, perhaps nuclear weapons."

Third, the United States should use its unprecedented power to change the regimes in rogue states. The idea of regime change was not new to American foreign policy. The Eisenhower administration engineered the overthrow of Iranian Prime Minister Mohammed Mossadegh in 1953; the CIA trained Cuban exiles in a botched bid at the Bay of Pigs in April 1961 to oust Fidel Castro; Ronald Reagan channeled aid to the Nicaraguan contras in the mid-1980s to overthrow the Sandinistas; and Bill Clinton helped Serb opposition forces in the late 1990s get rid of Slobodan Milosevic. What was different in the Bush presidency was the willingness, even in the absence of a direct attack on the United States, to use U.S. military forces for the express purpose of toppling other governments. This was the gist of both the Afghanistan and the Iraq wars. It rested on the belief that if the United States pushed, nobody could push back.

20-2 September 11

The Bush revolution did not start, as many have suggested, on September 11. The worldview that drove it existed long before jet planes plowed into the Twin Towers and the Pentagon. Bush outlined his philosophy while he was on the campaign trail. Most commentators failed to notice what he was saying because they were more concerned with how much he knew about the world, rather than what he believed. Bush began implementing his ideas as soon as he took the oath of office. His belief in the need for an America unbound was behind his pursuit of missile defense. It was also behind his rejection of the Kyoto Protocol on climate change, the International Criminal Court, and a host of other multilateral agreements he criticized or abandoned during the first eight months of his presidency.

What September 11 provided was the motive to enact the Bush revolution rapidly and without hesitation. Foreign policy went from being a secondary priority of his presidency to being its defining mission. "I'm here for a reason," Bush told his chief political adviser Karl Rove shortly after the attacks, "and this is going to be how we're going to be judged." He told Japanese prime minister Junichiro Koizumi something similar. "History will be the judge, but it won't judge well somebody who doesn't act, somebody who just bides time here." The war on terrorism became an issue that boiled in his blood, and he intended to fight it in his fashion.

September 11 also gave Bush the opportunity to enact his revolution without fear of being challenged at home. Congressional displeasure with Bush's handling of foreign policy had grown throughout the summer of 2001. Some Democrats even thought it could be a winning issue for them in the midterm elections. In the wake of the attacks, however, congressional resistance to Bush's national security policies evaporated. Congress's deference partly reflected the enormity of the attacks and principled belief that lawmakers should defer to strong presidential leadership in times of national crisis. But it also reflected a healthy dose of politics. Rather than blame the president for failing to anticipate the attacks, Americans rallied around him. Bush's newfound popularity translated into political power. Lawmakers may ignore the pleadings of an unpopular president, but they usually heed the demands of a popular one.

20-3 The Neo-conservative Myth

By the end of the Iraq War, most commentators acknowledged that Bush had presided over a revolution in American foreign policy. They doubted, however, that the president was responsible for it. They instead gave the credit (or blame) to "neoconservative" thinkers within the administration, led by Deputy Secretary of Defense Paul Wolfowitz, who they said were determined to use America's great power to transform despotic regimes into liberal democracies. One writer alleged that Bush was "the callow instrument of neoconservative ideologues." Another remarked on the "neoconservative coup" in Washington and wondered if

"George W. fully understands the grand strategy that Wolfowitz and other aides are unfolding." A third thought the neoconservatives' victory was obvious. "Unless you live at the bottom of a well, you've probably noticed that 9/11 and Iraq have a transforming effect on the American Right. The short formulation is that so-called neoconservatism has triumphed."

This conventional wisdom was wrong on at least two counts. First, it fundamentally misunderstood the intellectual currents within the Bush administration and the Republican Party more generally. Neoconservatives were more prominent outside the administration, particularly on the pages of *Commentary* and the *Weekly Standard* and in the television studios of Fox News than they were inside it. The bulk of Bush's advisers, including most notably Dick Cheney and Defense Secretary Don Rumsfeld, were not neocons. They were instead assertive nationalists—traditional hard-line conservatives willing to use American military power to defeat threats to U.S. security but reluctant as a general rule to use American primacy to remake the world in its image. Whereas neoconservatives talked of lengthy and expensive military occupation in Iraq, assertive nationalists spoke of a quick transition and leaving "Iraq for the Iraqis." Lost in all the talk about "neoconservative cabals" was that from the time of the "Axis-of-Evil" speech through Bush's triumphant landing on the *USS Abraham Lincoln* to celebrate "Mission Accomplished," the administration had justified the Iraq War as necessary to prevent Iraq from building weapons of mass destruction and sharing them with terrorists. Democracy became the adminis-

tration's prime rationale only after U.S. troops failed to find the weapons of mass destruction that Bush and his advisers had insisted Iraq possessed.

Although neoconservatives and assertive nationalists differed on whether the United States should actively spread its values abroad, they shared a deep skepticism of the Cold-War consensus on the importance of the rule of law and the relevance of international institutions to American foreign policy. They placed their faith not in diplomacy and treaties, but in power and resolve. Agreement on this key point allowed neoconservatives and assertive nationalists to form a marriage of convenience in overthrowing the Cold-War approach to foreign policy, even as they disagreed about what kind of commitment the United States should make to rebuilding Iraq and remaking the rest of the world.

The second and more important flaw with the neoconservative coup theory was that it grossly underestimated George W. Bush. The man from Midland was not a figurehead in someone else's revolution. He may have entered the Oval Office not knowing which general ran Pakistan, but during his first thirty months in office, he was the puppeteer, not the puppet. He actively solicited the counsel of his seasoned advisers, and he tolerated if not encouraged vigorous disagreement among them. When necessary, he overruled them. George W. Bush led his own revolution.

20-4 Costs and Benefits

Not all revolutions succeed. A year after Air Force One tipped its wings over Baghdad in a gesture of triumph, the benefits of the Bush revolution looked far less obvious than the costs. U.S. troops in Iraq found themselves under attack from a mix of terrorists, local militias, and remnants of Saddam Hussein's regime. Indeed, more American soldiers died occupying Iraq in 2004 than died liberating it twelve months earlier. Anger overseas at what was seen as an arrogant and hypocritical America had swelled. Close allies spoke openly not of how best to work with the United States but how to constrain its ability to act. Many Americans, including some Bush supporters, worried that the president had committed a foreign-policy blunder of epic proportions.

Why had things suddenly turned bleak? Part of the problem with the Bush revolution lay in how Bush and his advisers conducted it. They declined to cloak the iron fist of American power in the velvet glove of diplomacy, preferring instead to express contempt for opinions different from their own. Donald Rumsfeld, as his dismissal of France and Germany as "old Europe" attested, had a particular zeal for insulting friends and allies. They were similarly dismissive of Iraqi complaints that the United States had failed in its responsibility to ensure basic security after ousting Saddam Hussein. "Freedom's untidy," Rumsfeld commented as looters plundered Iraqi cities. Not surprisingly, these attitudes struck many outside the United States—and more than a few within it—as an arrogance born of power, not principle. They resented it profoundly.

The deeper problem, however, was that the fundamental premise of the Bush revolution—that America's security rested on an America unbound—was mistaken. For all the talk at the start of the twenty-first century of the United States being a hyperpower, the world was beyond the ability of any one country to control. Many of the most important challenges America faced overseas could be met only with the active cooperation of others. The question was how best to secure that cooperation.

Bush maintained that if America led, friends and allies would follow. True, they might grumble because they disliked how Washington intended to lead. Some might even decide to wait until they saw the benefits of American action. In the end, however, they would join forces with the United States in combating threats such as terrorism and weapons proliferation because they trusted America's motives and they shared its interests. Countries would not cut off their nose to spite their face.

Iraq exposed the flaw in this thinking. Most countries, including all members of the UN Security Council, shared a major interest in making sure Iraq did not possess weapons of mass destruction, especially nuclear weapons. But that common interest did not automatically translate into active cooperation in a war to oust Saddam Hussein—or even into support for such a war. A few countries actively tried to stop the march to war, and many others simply sat on the sidelines.

Little changed after the toppling of Saddam Hussein's statue in Firdos Square. Although many countries believed that stabilizing postwar Iraq was vitally important—for regional stability, international security, and their own national safety—they did not rush to join the reconstruction effort. In June 2004, American troops constituted more than 80 percent of all foreign forces in Iraq—at an annual cost to the American taxpayer of at least $50 billion. At the same time, more than 90 percent of the foreign casualties in Iraq were American; and more than 95 percent of the reconstruction dollars spent in Iraq were American. Rather than sharing the burden with its allies, the United States was assuming the burden.

The lesson of Iraq, then, was that if America leads badly, few follow. This ultimately is the real danger of the Bush revolution. America's friends and allies seldom can stop Washington from doing as it wishes, no matter how much some commentators opine to the contrary. However, America's friends and allies do not need to resist American policy to make Washington pay a price for its desire to play unbound by any rules. They can simply refuse to come to its aid when their help is most needed or desired. That, in turn, risks not only undermining what America can achieve abroad but also domestic support at home for engaging the world. Americans could rightly ask, if others are unwilling to bear the burdens of meeting tough challenges, why should we? In that respect, an America unbound could ultimately lead to an America that is less secure.

Readings for Further Study

Daalder, Ivo H., and James M. Lindsay. 2003. *America Unbound: The Bush Revolution in Foreign Policy.* Washington, D.C.: Brookings Institution Press.

Woodward, Bob. 2002. *Bush at War.* New York: Simon & Schuster.

Woodward, Bob. 2004. *Plan of Attack.* New York: Simon & Schuster.

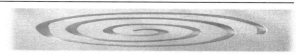

Websites to Check Out

Note: As we went to press, these sites were functional using the URLs provided. Check out the online text for the most up-to-date URLs.

Site name: Brookings Institution

URL: http://www.brookings.edu

One of America's premier think tanks provides comprehensive coverage of American foreign policy and the war on terrorism, including original papers, an extensive list of commentary, and links to major speeches, background documents, and related materials.

Site name: Council on Foreign Relations—Terrorism

URL: http://www.cfr.org/reg_issues.php?id=13|||1

The Council on Foreign Relations, the nation's leading membership organization devoted to world affairs, provides a wide array of writings on the subject of terrorism, as well as an online encyclopedia designed to provide an easy-to-read, authoritative primer on what the experts know and don't know about terrorism.

Site name: The White House—America Responds

URL: http://www.whitehouse.gov/response/

A comprehensive list of presidential actions and speeches on terrorism, background information on the war on terrorism, and links to relevant federal agencies.

Appendix I

President George W. Bush's Address to a Joint Session of Congress, September 20, 2001

Not since President Franklin Delano Roosevelt went to Capitol Hill on December 8, 1941, and gave his famous "a date which will live in infamy" speech had a president had the solemn responsibility of addressing Congress on how to respond to an attack upon the United States. But on September 20, 2001, nine days after the attacks on the World Trade Center and the Pentagon, President George W. Bush appeared before Congress to discuss his strategy for fighting the war on terrorism. President Bush used the speech to publicly identify Osama bin Laden's Al Qaeda organization as the culprit behind the attacks. He also demanded that Afghanistan's Taliban government hand over bin Laden and his lieutenants to the United States. And he announced the creation of a new Cabinet-level Office of Homeland Security to take the lead in making the United States less vulnerable to terrorism. Most important, he laid out what was immediately dubbed the Bush Doctrine—a pledge to fight the war on terrorism until "every terrorist group of global reach has been found, stopped, and defeated." Whether the definition of terrorist groups with "global reach" should be drawn narrowly or broadly immediately became a matter of considerable debate both inside and outside the administration. When Bush subsequently appeared before Congress to give his 2002 State of the Union address, he made it clear that he interpreted his doctrine broadly. What follows is an abridged version of President Bush's September 20 speech.

Mr. Speaker, Mr. President Pro Tempore, members of Congress, and fellow Americans:

...

On September the 11th, enemies of freedom committed an act of war against our country. Americans have known wars—but for the past 136 years, they have been wars on foreign soil, except for one Sunday in 1941. Americans have known the casualties of war—but not at the center of a great city on a peaceful morning. Americans have known surprise attacks—but never before on thousands of civilians. All of this was brought upon us in a single day—and night fell on a different world, a world where freedom itself is under attack.

Americans have many questions tonight. Americans are asking: Who attacked our country? The evidence we have gathered all points to a collection of loosely affiliated terrorist organizations known as Al Qaeda. They are the same murderers indicted for bombing American embassies in Tanzania and Kenya, and responsible for bombing the *USS Cole*.

Al Qaeda is to terror what the mafia is to crime. But its goal is not making money; its goal is remaking the world—and imposing its radical beliefs on people everywhere.

The terrorists practice a fringe form of Islamic extremism that has been rejected by Muslim scholars and the vast majority of Muslim clerics—a fringe movement that perverts the peaceful teachings of Islam. The terrorists' directive commands them to kill Christians and Jews, to kill all Americans, and make no distinction among military and civilians, including women and children.

This group and its leader—a person named Osama bin Laden—are linked to many other organizations in different countries, including the Egyptian Islamic Jihad and the Islamic Movement of Uzbekistan. There are thousands of these terrorists in more than 60 countries. They are recruited from their own nations and neighborhoods and brought to camps in places like Afghanistan, where they are trained in the tactics of terror. They are sent back to their homes or sent to hide in countries around the world to plot evil and destruction.

The leadership of Al Qaeda has great influence in Afghanistan and supports the Taliban regime in controlling most of that country. In Afghanistan, we see Al Qaeda's vision for the world.

Afghanistan's people have been brutalized—many are starving and many have fled. Women are not allowed to attend school. You can be jailed for owning a television. Religion can be practiced only as their leaders dictate. A man can be jailed in Afghanistan if his beard is not long enough.

The United States respects the people of Afghanistan—after all, we are currently its largest source of humanitarian aid—but we condemn the Taliban regime. It is not only repressing its own people, it is threatening people everywhere by sponsoring and sheltering and supplying terrorists. By aiding and abetting murder, the Taliban regime is committing murder.

And tonight, the United States of America makes the following demands on the Taliban: Deliver to United States authorities all the leaders of Al Qaeda who hide in your land. Release all foreign nationals, including American citizens, you have unjustly imprisoned. Protect foreign journalists, diplomats, and aid workers in your country. Close immediately and permanently every terrorist training camp in Afghanistan, and hand over every terrorist, and every person in their support structure, to appropriate authorities. Give the United States full access to terrorist training camps, so we can make sure they are no longer operating.

These demands are not open to negotiation or discussion. The Taliban must act, and act immediately. They will hand over the terrorists, or they will share in their fate.

I also want to speak tonight directly to Muslims throughout the world. We respect your faith. It's practiced freely by many millions of Americans, and by millions more in countries that America counts as friends. Its teachings are good and peaceful, and those who commit evil in the name of Allah blaspheme the name of Allah. The terrorists are traitors to their own faith, trying, in effect, to hijack Islam itself. The enemy of America is not our many Muslim friends; it is not our many Arab friends. Our enemy is a radical network of terrorists, and every government that supports them.

Our war on terror begins with Al Qaeda, but it does not end there. It will not end until every terrorist group of global reach has been found, stopped, and defeated.

Americans are asking, why do they hate us? They hate what we see right here in this chamber—a democratically elected government. Their leaders are self-appointed. They hate our freedoms—our freedom of religion, our freedom of speech, our freedom to vote and assemble and disagree with each other.

They want to overthrow existing governments in many Muslim countries, such as Egypt, Saudi Arabia, and Jordan. They want to drive Israel out of the Middle East. They want to drive Christians and Jews out of vast regions of Asia and Africa.

These terrorists kill not merely to end lives, but to disrupt and end a way of life. With every atrocity, they hope that America grows fearful, retreating from the world and forsaking our friends. They stand against us, because we stand in their way.

We are not deceived by their pretenses to piety. We have seen their kind before. They are the heirs of all the murderous ideologies of the twentieth century. By sacrificing human life to serve their radical visions—by abandoning every value except the will to power—they follow in the path of fascism, and Nazism, and totalitarianism. And they will follow that path all the way, to where it ends: in history's unmarked grave of discarded lies.

Americans are asking: How will we fight and win this war? We will direct every resource at our command—every means of diplomacy, every tool of intelligence, every instrument of law enforcement, every financial influence, and every necessary weapon of war—to the disruption and to the defeat of the global terror network.

This war will not be like the war against Iraq a decade ago, with a decisive liberation of territory and a swift conclusion. It will not look like the air war above Kosovo two years ago, where no ground troops were used and not a single American was lost in combat.

Our response involves far more than instant retaliation and isolated strikes. Americans should not expect one battle, but a lengthy campaign, unlike any other we have ever seen. It may include dramatic strikes, visible on TV, and covert operations, secret even in success. We will starve terrorists of funding, turn them one against another, drive them from place to place, until there is no refuge or no rest. And we will pursue nations that provide aid or safe haven to terrorism. Every nation, in every region, now has a decision to make. Either you are with us, or you are with the terrorists. From this day forward, any nation that continues to harbor or support terrorism will be regarded by the United States as a hostile regime.

Our nation has been put on notice: We are not immune from attack. We will take defensive measures against terrorism to protect Americans. Today, dozens of federal departments and agencies, as well as state and local governments, have responsibilities affecting homeland security. These efforts must be coordinated at the highest level. So tonight I announce the creation of a Cabinet-level position reporting directly to me—the Office of Homeland Security.

And tonight I also announce a distinguished American to lead this effort, to strengthen American security: a military veteran, an effective governor, a true patriot, a trusted friend—Pennsylvania's Tom Ridge. He will lead, oversee, and coordinate a comprehensive national strategy to safeguard our country against terrorism, and respond to any attacks that may come.

These measures are essential. But the only way to defeat terrorism as a threat to our way of life is to stop it, eliminate it, and destroy it where it grows.

Many will be involved in this effort, from FBI agents to intelligence operatives to the reservists we have called to active duty. All deserve our thanks, and all have our prayers. And tonight, a few miles from the damaged Pentagon, I have a message for our military: Be ready. I've called the Armed Forces to alert, and there is a reason. The hour is coming when America will act, and you will make us proud.

This is not, however, just America's fight. And what is at stake is not just America's freedom. This is the world's fight. This is civilization's fight. This is the fight of all who believe in progress and pluralism, tolerance and freedom.

We ask every nation to join us. We will ask, and we will need, the help of police forces, intelligence services, and banking systems around the world. The United States is grateful that many nations and many international organizations have already responded—with sympathy and with support. Nations from Latin America, to Asia, to Africa, to Europe, to the Islamic world. Perhaps the NATO Charter reflects best the attitude of the world: An attack on one is an attack on all.

The civilized world is rallying to America's side. They understand that if this terror goes unpunished, their own cities, their own citizens may be next. Terror, unanswered, cannot only bring down buildings, it can threaten the stability of legitimate governments. And you know what—we're not going to allow it.

Americans are asking: What is expected of us? I ask you to live your lives, and hug your children. I know many citizens have fears tonight, and I ask you to be calm and resolute, even in the face of a continuing threat.

I ask you to uphold the values of America, and remember why so many have come here. We are in a fight for our principles, and our first responsibility is to live by them. No one should be singled out for unfair treatment or unkind words because of their ethnic background or religious faith.

...

After all that has just passed—all the lives taken, and all the possibilities and hopes that died with them—it is natural to wonder if America's future is one of fear. Some speak of an age of terror. I know there are struggles ahead, and dangers to face. But this country will define our times, not be defined by them. As long as the United States of America is determined and strong, this will not be an age of terror; this will be an age of liberty, here and across the world.

Great harm has been done to us. We have suffered great loss. And in our grief and anger, we have found our mission and our moment. Freedom and fear are at war. The advance of human freedom—the great achievement of our time, and the great hope of every time—now depends on us. Our nation—this generation—will lift a dark threat of violence from our people and our future. We will rally the world to this cause by our efforts, by our courage. We will not tire, we will not falter, and we will not fail.

It is my hope that in the months and years ahead, life will return almost to normal. We'll go back to our lives and routines, and that is good. Even grief recedes with time and grace. But our resolve must not pass. Each of us will remember what happened that day, and to whom it happened. . . .

...

The course of this conflict is not known, yet its outcome is certain. Freedom and fear, justice and cruelty, have always been at war, and we know that God is not neutral between them.

Fellow citizens, we'll meet violence with patient justice—assured of the rightness of our cause, and confident of the victories to come. In all that lies before us, may God grant us wisdom, and may He watch over the United States of America.

Thank you.

Appendix 2

President George W. Bush's State of the Union Address, January 29, 2002

Terrorism figured to be a major theme of President Bush's 2002 State of the Union address. Few anticipated, however, that it would dominate the speech, or touch off a row with America's closest allies. He abandoned the traditional approach of using the State of the Union speech as an opportunity to discuss a laundry list of administration initiatives—most of them dealing with domestic issues. Instead, he spoke at great length about the threats to U.S. security and pledged his administration to protecting Americans against them.

President Bush's speech had two notable elements. First, he made clear that his war on terrorism would target terrorist groups besides Osama bin Laden's Al Qaeda. He explicitly named the Palestinian groups Hamas, Hezbollah, and Islamic Jihad, all of which had launched terrorist attacks against Israel. He also named the Pakistani group Jaish-i-Mohammed, which had conducted terrorist attacks against India.

Second, in many ways more significantly, President Bush expanded the war on terrorism beyond terrorist groups. It would now also target Iran, Iraq, and North Korea, three states that in his view formed an "axis of evil." He accused all three countries of sponsoring terrorism, though he offered no evidence nor made any allegations that they were linked to September 11. But the thrust of his remarks was that these countries posed an unacceptably grave danger because they were ag-

gressively seeking to develop weapons of mass destruction, weapons that might some day be used against the United States.

President Bush did not say, however, what steps he would, or wouldn't take, to stop the Iranian, Iraqi, and North Korean programs. Immediately following the speech, administration officials sought to dampen speculation that war with these countries was likely. The White House insisted that the president was "not sending a signal that military action is imminent." Pentagon officials said that they were focused on defeating terrorist groups in the Philippines and Somalia, not modern armies in Iran, Iraq, and North Korea. State Department officials noted that Ronald Reagan negotiated with the Soviets even as he denounced them as evil, and they suggested that engagement remained an option with Pyongyang and Teheran, if not Baghdad.

These efforts to soften the president's speech did not reassure American allies, many of which thought his remarks were belligerent and counterproductive. The anger was especially great in Europe, where many recoiled at the idea of expanding the war on terrorism to include Iran, Iraq, and North Korea. The French Foreign Minister complained, "Today we are threatened by a new simplistic approach that reduces all the problems in the world to the struggle against terrorism." The German Foreign Minister warned, "The international coalition against

terror is not the basis to take action against someone—least of all unilaterally." And the British Foreign Minister argued, "The president's State of the Union speech is best understood in the context of the midterm elections in November." In the months that followed, what to do about the axis of evil nations, and especially Iraq, became a dominant issue in U.S. alliance relations.

Excerpts from President Bush's 2002 State of the Union address follow.

Mr. Speaker, Vice President Cheney, members of Congress, distinguished guests, fellow citizens: As we gather tonight, our nation is at war, our economy is in recession, and the civilized world faces unprecedented dangers. Yet the state of our Union has never been stronger.

We last met in an hour of shock and suffering. In four short months, our nation has comforted the victims, begun to rebuild New York and the Pentagon, rallied a great coalition, captured, arrested, and rid the world of thousands of terrorists, destroyed Afghanistan's terrorist training camps, saved a people from starvation, and freed a country from brutal oppression.

The American flag flies again over our embassy in Kabul. Terrorists who once occupied Afghanistan now occupy cells at Guantanamo Bay. And terrorist leaders who urged followers to sacrifice their lives are running for their own.

…

Our progress is a tribute to the spirit of the Afghan people, to the resolve of our coalition, and to the might of the United States military. When I called our troops into action, I did so with complete confidence in their courage and skill. And tonight, thanks to them, we are winning the war on terror. The men and women of our Armed Forces have delivered a message now clear to every enemy of the United States: Even 7,000 miles away, across oceans and continents, on mountaintops and in caves—you will not escape the justice of this nation.

…

Our cause is just, and it continues. Our discoveries in Afghanistan confirmed our worst fears, and showed us the true scope of the task ahead. We have seen the depth of our enemies' hatred in videos, where they laugh about the loss of innocent life. And the depth of their hatred is equaled by the madness of the destruction they design. We have found diagrams of American nuclear power plants and public water facilities, detailed instructions for making chemical weapons, surveillance maps of American cities, and thorough descriptions of landmarks in America and throughout the world.

What we have found in Afghanistan confirms that, far from ending there, our war against terror is only beginning. Most of the 19 men who hijacked planes on September the 11th were trained in Afghanistan's camps, and so were tens of thousands of others. Thousands of dangerous killers, schooled in the methods of murder, often sup-

ported by outlaw regimes, are now spread throughout the world like ticking time bombs, set to go off without warning.

Thanks to the work of our law enforcement officials and coalition partners, hundreds of terrorists have been arrested. Yet, tens of thousands of trained terrorists are still at large. These enemies view the entire world as a battlefield, and we must pursue them wherever they are. So long as training camps operate, so long as nations harbor terrorists, freedom is at risk. And America and our allies must not, and will not, allow it.

Our nation will continue to be steadfast and patient and persistent in the pursuit of two great objectives. First, we will shut down terrorist camps, disrupt terrorist plans, and bring terrorists to justice. And, second, we must prevent the terrorists and regimes who seek chemical, biological, or nuclear weapons from threatening the United States and the world.

Our military has put the terror training camps of Afghanistan out of business, yet camps still exist in at least a dozen countries. A terrorist underworld—including groups like Hamas, Hezbollah, Islamic Jihad, Jaish-i-Mohammed—operates in remote jungles and deserts, and hides in the centers of large cities.

While the most visible military action is in Afghanistan, America is acting elsewhere. We now have troops in the Philippines, helping to train that country's armed forces to go after terrorist cells that have executed an American, and still hold hostages. Our soldiers, working with the Bosnian government, seized terrorists who were plotting to bomb our embassy. Our Navy is patrolling the coast of

Africa to block the shipment of weapons and the establishment of terrorist camps in Somalia.

My hope is that all nations will heed our call, and eliminate the terrorist parasites who threaten their countries and our own. Many nations are acting forcefully. Pakistan is now cracking down on terror, and I admire the strong leadership of President Musharraf.

But some governments will be timid in the face of terror. And make no mistake about it: If they do not act, America will.

Our second goal is to prevent regimes that sponsor terror from threatening America or our friends and allies with weapons of mass destruction. Some of these regimes have been pretty quiet since September the 11th. But we know their true nature. North Korea is a regime arming with missiles and weapons of mass destruction, while starving its citizens.

Iran aggressively pursues these weapons and exports terror, while an unelected few repress the Iranian people's hope for freedom.

Iraq continues to flaunt its hostility toward America and to support terror. The Iraqi regime has plotted to develop anthrax, and nerve gas, and nuclear weapons for over a decade. This is a regime that has already used poison gas to murder thousands of its own citizens— leaving the bodies of mothers huddled over their dead children. This is a regime that agreed to international inspections—then kicked out the inspectors. This is a regime that has something to hide from the civilized world.

States like these, and their terrorist allies, constitute an axis of evil, arming to threaten the peace of the world. By seeking weapons of mass destruction, these regimes pose a grave and growing danger. They could provide these arms to terrorists, giving them the means to match their hatred. They could attack our allies or attempt to blackmail the United States. In any of these cases, the price of indifference would be catastrophic.

We will work closely with our coalition to deny terrorists and their state sponsors the materials, technology, and expertise to make and deliver weapons of mass destruction. We will develop and deploy effective missile defenses to protect America and our allies from sudden attack. And all nations should know: America will do what is necessary to ensure our nation's security.

We'll be deliberate, yet time is not on our side. I will not wait on events, while dangers gather. I will not stand by, as peril draws closer and closer. The United States of America will not permit the world's most dangerous regimes to threaten us with the world's most destructive weapons.

Our war on terror is well begun, but it is only begun. This campaign may not be finished on our watch—yet it must be and it will be waged on our watch.

We can't stop short. If we stop now—leaving terror camps intact and terror states unchecked—our sense of security would be false and temporary. History has called America and our allies to action, and it is both our responsibility and our privilege to fight freedom's fight.

Our first priority must always be the security of our nation, and that will be reflected in the budget I send to Congress. My budget supports three great goals for America: We will win this war; we'll protect our homeland; and we will revive our economy.

September the 11th brought out the best in America, and the best in this Congress. And I join the American people in applauding your unity and resolve. Now Americans deserve to have this same spirit directed toward addressing problems here at home. I'm a proud member of my party—yet as we act to win the war, protect our people, and create jobs in America, we must act, first and foremost, not as Republicans, not as Democrats, but as Americans.

It costs a lot to fight this war. We have spent more than a billion dollars a month—over $30 million a day—and we must be prepared for future operations. Afghanistan proved that expensive precision weapons defeat the enemy and spare innocent lives, and we need more of them. We need to replace aging aircraft and make our military more agile, to put our troops anywhere in the world quickly and safely. Our men and women in uniform deserve the best weapons, the best equipment, the best training—and they also deserve another pay raise.

My budget includes the largest increase in defense spending in two decades—because while the price of freedom and security is high, it is never too high. Whatever it costs to defend our country, we will pay.

The next priority of my budget is to do everything possible to protect our citizens and strengthen our nation against the ongoing threat of another attack. Time and distance from the events of September the 11th will not make us safer unless we act on its lessons. America is no longer protected by vast oceans. We are protected from attack only by vigorous action abroad, and increased vigilance at home.

My budget nearly doubles funding for a sustained strategy of homeland security, focused on four key areas: bioterrorism, emergency response, airport and border security, and improved intelligence. We will develop vaccines to fight anthrax and other deadly diseases. We'll increase funding to help states and communities train and equip our heroic police and firefighters. We will improve intelligence collection and sharing, expand patrols at our borders, strengthen the security of air travel, and use technology to track the arrivals and departures of visitors to the United States.

...

And America needs citizens to extend the compassion of our country to every part of the world. So we will renew the promise of the Peace Corps, double its volunteers over the next five years—and ask it to join a new effort to encourage development and education and opportunity in the Islamic world.

This time of adversity offers a unique moment of opportunity—a moment we must seize to change our culture. Through the gathering momentum of millions of acts of service and decency and kindness, I know we can overcome evil with greater good. And we have a great opportunity during this time of war to lead the world toward the values that will bring lasting peace.

All fathers and mothers, in all societies, want their children to be educated, and live free from poverty and violence. No people on Earth yearn to be oppressed, or aspire to servitude, or eagerly await the midnight knock of the secret police.

If anyone doubts this, let them look to Afghanistan, where the Islamic "street" greeted the fall of tyranny with song and celebration. Let the skeptics look to Islam's own rich history, with its centuries of learning, and tolerance and progress. America will lead by defending liberty and justice because they are right and true and unchanging for all people everywhere.

No nation owns these aspirations, and no nation is exempt from them. We have no intention of imposing our culture. But America will always stand firm for the non-negotiable demands of human dignity: the rule of law; limits on the power of the state; respect for women; private property; free speech; equal justice; and religious tolerance.

America will take the side of brave men and women who advocate these values around the world, including the Islamic world, because we have a greater objective than eliminating threats and containing resentment. We seek a just and peaceful world beyond the war on terror.

In this moment of opportunity, a common danger is erasing old rivalries. America is working with Russia and China and India, in ways we have never before, to achieve peace and prosperity. In every region, free markets and free trade and free societies are proving their power to lift lives. Together with friends and allies from Europe to Asia, and Africa to Latin America, we will demonstrate that the forces of terror cannot stop the momentum of freedom.

The last time I spoke here, I expressed the hope that life would return to normal. In some ways, it has. In others, it never will. Those of us who have lived through these challenging times have been changed by them. We've come to know truths that we will never question: Evil is real, and it must be opposed. Beyond all differences of race or creed, we are one country, mourning together and facing danger together. Deep in the American character, there is honor, and it is stronger than cynicism. And many have discovered again that even in tragedy—especially in tragedy—God is near.

In a single instant, we realized that this will be a decisive decade in the history of liberty, that we've been called to a unique role in human events. Rarely has the world faced a choice more clear or consequential.

Our enemies send other people's children on missions of suicide and murder. They embrace tyranny and death as a cause and a creed. We stand for a different choice, made long ago, on the day of our founding. We affirm it again today. We choose freedom and the dignity of every life.

Steadfast in our purpose, we now press on. We have known freedom's price. We have shown freedom's power. And in this great conflict, my fellow Americans, we will see freedom's victory.

Thank you all. May God bless.

Appendix 3

President George W. Bush's Address to the United Nations, September 12, 2002

President George W. Bush used his 2002 State of the Union address to put the "axis of evil"—Iran, Iraq, and North Korea—at the forefront of U.S. national security policy. By early spring 2002, the president had made clear he had no intention of going to war with either Iran or North Korea. Iraq was another matter entirely. But if the United States did go to war to remove Saddam Hussein from power, how would it get there?

That question was hotly debated within the Bush administration during the spring and summer of 2002. Hard-liners—who predominated in the vice president's office and the Pentagon—argued that the president should not go to the United Nations as his father had before the 1991 Gulf War. They argued that the UN Security Council would likely resist military action against Iraq. Instead, it would call for reinstating the weapons inspections process in Iraq that had been suspended back in 1998. After inspections began, the other members of the Security Council would argue, regardless of what the inspectors found, that war was unnecessary. If the inspectors found nothing, the argument would be that there was no cause for war. If the inspectors found anything, the argument would be that this proved the inspections process was working. Rather than working through the UN, hard-liners urged the president to assemble an ad hoc group of like-minded countries—a so-called coalition of the willing—to invade Iraq.

The hard-liners' opponents in the administration—primarily Secretary of State Colin Powell and his advisers—responded that it would be disastrous for U.S. interests if the president ignored the United Nations. They argued that the United States could not fight and win a war in Iraq without the help of others, and that few others would be willing to join Washington's coalition if the president did not first try to gain UN authorization. Moreover, they told the president that he could get the support of the UN Security Council—if he put his mind to it. The benefits he would garner from taking the time to assemble a broad international coalition would more than make up for the time and trouble it would take.

By late August 2002, the hard-liners looked to have won the argument within the administration. Throughout the summer, the president and his senior advisers had talked repeatedly about a new doctrine of preemption. This doctrine essentially asserted that the United States would not wait until it perceived an attack was imminent before responding. It instead reserved the right to attack other countries before they could threaten the United States. This view of preemption—which equated it with preventive war—held out no role for seeking UN authorization. Then on August 26, Vice President Dick Cheney publicly dismissed the idea of restarting the weapons inspections process. He warned that "a return of inspectors would provide no assurance whatsoever of [Saddam's] compliance with U.N. resolutions. On the contrary, there is a great danger that it would provide false comfort that Saddam was somehow 'back in his box.'" Most observers assumed that Cheney was speaking on behalf of the president.

These observers were surprised, then, when President Bush ultimately sided with Secretary Powell. On September 12, 2002, the president spoke before the UN General Assembly. Instead of trumpeting his doctrine of preemption or talking about coalitions of the willing, he told the UN member states that he was prepared to work with them to see that the UN resolutions on Iraq were enforced.

President Bush's speech to the United Nations marked a major turning point in international diplomacy on Iraq. In November 2002, the UN Security Council unanimously adopted a new resolution restarting the weapons inspections process and giving Iraq one final chance to disarm. In the end, however, Bush failed to persuade the Security Council to explicitly authorize the use of force against Iraq. In March 2003, the United States, aided by a coalition of the willing that consisted of Britain, Australia, and Poland, invaded Iraq without the UN's blessing.

President Bush's address to the United Nations follows.

Mr. Secretary General, Mr. President, distinguished delegates, and ladies and gentlemen: We meet one year and one day after a terrorist attack brought grief to my country, and brought grief to many citizens of our world. Yesterday, we remembered the innocent lives taken that terrible morning. Today, we turn to the urgent duty of protecting other lives, without illusion and without fear.

We've accomplished much in the last year—in Afghanistan and beyond. We have much yet to do—in Afghanistan and beyond. Many nations represented here have joined in the fight against global terror, and the people of the United States are grateful.

The United Nations was born in the hope that survived a world war—the hope of a world moving toward justice, escaping old patterns of conflict and fear. The founding members resolved that the peace of the world must never again be destroyed by the will and wickedness of any man. We created the United Nations Security Council, so that, unlike the League of Nations, our deliberations would be more than talk, our resolutions would be more than wishes. After generations of deceitful dictators and broken treaties and squandered lives, we dedicated ourselves to standards of human dignity shared by all, and to a system of security defended by all.

Today, these standards, and this security, are challenged. Our commitment to human dignity is challenged by persistent poverty and raging disease. The suffering is great, and our responsibilities are clear. The United States is joining with the world to supply aid where it reaches people and lifts up lives, to extend trade and the prosperity it brings, and to bring medical care where it is desperately needed.

As a symbol of our commitment to human dignity, the United States will return to UNESCO. (Applause.) This organization has been reformed and America will participate fully in its mission to advance human rights and tolerance and learning.

Our common security is challenged by regional conflicts—ethnic and religious strife that is ancient, but not inevitable. In the Middle East, there can be no peace for either side without freedom for both sides. America stands committed to an independent and democratic Palestine, living side by side with Israel in peace and security. Like all other people, Palestinians deserve a government that serves their interests and listens to their voices. My nation will continue to encourage all parties to step up to their responsibilities as we seek a just and comprehensive settlement to the conflict.

Above all, our principles and our security are challenged today by outlaw groups and regimes that accept no law of morality and have no limit to their violent ambitions. In the attacks on America a year ago, we saw the destructive intentions of our enemies. This threat hides within many nations, including my own. In cells and camps, terrorists are plotting further destruction, and building new bases for their war against civilization. And our greatest fear is that terrorists will find a shortcut to their mad ambitions when an outlaw regime supplies them with the technologies to kill on a massive scale.

In one place—in one regime—we find all these dangers, in their most lethal and aggressive forms, exactly the kind of aggressive threat the United Nations was born to confront.

Twelve years ago, Iraq invaded Kuwait without provocation. And the regime's forces were poised to continue their march to seize other countries and their resources. Had Saddam Hussein been appeased instead of stopped, he would have endangered the peace and stability of the world. Yet this aggression was stopped—by the might of coalition forces and the will of the United Nations.

To suspend hostilities, to spare himself, Iraq's dictator accepted a series of commitments. The terms were clear, to him and to all. And he agreed to prove he is complying with every one of those obligations.

He has proven instead only his contempt for the United Nations, and for all his pledges. By breaking every pledge—by his deceptions, and by his cruelties—Saddam Hussein has made the case against himself.

In 1991, Security Council Resolution 688 demanded that the Iraqi regime cease at once the repression of its own people, including the systematic repression of minorities—which the Council said, threatened international peace and security in the region. This demand goes ignored.

Last year, the U.N. Commission on Human Rights found that Iraq continues to commit extremely grave violations of human rights, and that the regime's repression is all pervasive. Tens of thousands of political opponents and ordinary citizens have been subjected to arbitrary arrest and imprisonment, summary execution, and torture by beating and burning, electric shock, starvation, mutilation, and rape. Wives are tortured in front of their husbands, children in the presence of their parents—and all of these horrors concealed from the world by the apparatus of a totalitarian state.

In 1991, the U.N. Security Council, through Resolutions 686 and 687, demanded that Iraq return all prisoners from Kuwait and other lands. Iraq's regime agreed. It broke its promise. Last year the Secretary General's high-level coordinator for this issue reported that Kuwait, Saudi, Indian, Syrian, Lebanese, Iranian, Egyptian, Bahraini, and Omani nationals remain unaccounted for—more than 600 people. One American pilot is among them.

In 1991, the U.N. Security Council, through Resolution 687, demanded that Iraq renounce all involvement with terrorism, and permit no terrorist organizations to operate in Iraq. Iraq's regime agreed. It broke this promise. In violation of Security Council Resolution 1373, Iraq continues to shelter and support terrorist organizations that direct violence against Iran, Israel, and Western governments. Iraqi dissidents abroad are targeted for murder. In 1993, Iraq attempted to assassinate the Emir of Kuwait and a former American President. Iraq's government openly praised the attacks of September the 11th. And Al Qaeda terrorists escaped from Afghanistan and are known to be in Iraq.

In 1991, the Iraqi regime agreed to destroy and stop developing all weapons of mass destruction and long-range missiles, and to prove to the world it has done so by complying with rigorous inspections. Iraq has broken every aspect of this fundamental pledge.

From 1991 to 1995, the Iraqi regime said it had no biological weapons. After a senior official in its weapons program defected and exposed this lie, the regime admitted to producing tens of

thousands of liters of anthrax and other deadly biological agents for use with Scud warheads, aerial bombs, and aircraft spray tanks. U.N. inspectors believe Iraq has produced two to four times the amount of biological agents it declared, and has failed to account for more than three metric tons of material that could be used to produce biological weapons. Right now, Iraq is expanding and improving facilities that were used for the production of biological weapons.

United Nations' inspections also revealed that Iraq likely maintains stockpiles of VX, mustard and other chemical agents, and that the regime is rebuilding and expanding facilities capable of producing chemical weapons.

And in 1995, after four years of deception, Iraq finally admitted it had a crash nuclear weapons program prior to the Gulf War. We know now, were it not for that war, the regime in Iraq would likely have possessed a nuclear weapon no later than 1993.

Today, Iraq continues to withhold important information about its nuclear program—weapons design, procurement logs, experiment data, an accounting of nuclear materials and documentation of foreign assistance. Iraq employs capable nuclear scientists and technicians. It retains physical infrastructure needed to build a nuclear weapon. Iraq has made several attempts to buy high-strength aluminum tubes used to enrich uranium for a nuclear weapon. Should Iraq acquire fissile material, it would be able to build a nuclear weapon within a year. And Iraq's state-controlled media has reported numerous meetings between Saddam Hussein and his nuclear scientists, leaving little doubt

about his continued appetite for these weapons.

Iraq also possesses a force of Scud-type missiles with ranges beyond the 150 kilometers permitted by the U.N. Work at testing and production facilities shows that Iraq is building more long-range missiles that it can inflict mass death throughout the region.

In 1990, after Iraq's invasion of Kuwait, the world imposed economic sanctions on Iraq. Those sanctions were maintained after the war to compel the regime's compliance with Security Council resolutions. In time, Iraq was allowed to use oil revenues to buy food. Saddam Hussein has subverted this program, working around the sanctions to buy missile technology and military materials. He blames the suffering of Iraq's people on the United Nations, even as he uses his oil wealth to build lavish palaces for himself, and to buy arms for his country. By refusing to comply with his own agreements, he bears full guilt for the hunger and misery of innocent Iraqi citizens.

In 1991, Iraq promised U.N. inspectors immediate and unrestricted access to verify Iraq's commitment to rid itself of weapons of mass destruction and long-range missiles. Iraq broke this promise, spending seven years deceiving, evading, and harassing U.N. inspectors before ceasing cooperation entirely. Just months after the 1991 cease-fire, the Security Council twice renewed its demand that the Iraqi regime cooperate fully with inspectors, condemning Iraq's serious violations of its obligations. The Security Council again renewed that demand in 1994, and twice more in 1996, deploring Iraq's clear violations of its obligations. The Security Council renewed its demand three more times in 1997, citing flagrant violations; and three more times in 1998, calling Iraq's behavior totally unacceptable. And in 1999, the demand was renewed yet again.

As we meet today, it's been almost four years since the last U.N. inspectors set foot in Iraq, four years for the Iraqi regime to plan, and to build, and to test behind the cloak of secrecy.

We know that Saddam Hussein pursued weapons of mass murder even when inspectors were in his country. Are we to assume that he stopped when they left? The history, the logic, and the facts lead to one conclusion: Saddam Hussein's regime is a grave and gathering danger. To suggest otherwise is to hope against the evidence. To assume this regime's good faith is to bet the lives of millions and the peace of the world in a reckless gamble. And this is a risk we must not take.

Delegates to the General Assembly, we have been more than patient. We've tried sanctions. We've tried the carrot of oil for food, and the stick of coalition military strikes. But Saddam Hussein has defied all these efforts and continues to develop weapons of mass destruction. The first time we may be completely certain he has nuclear weapons is when, God forbid, he uses one. We owe it to all our citizens to do everything in our power to prevent that day from coming.

The conduct of the Iraqi regime is a threat to the authority of the United Nations, and a threat to peace. Iraq has answered a decade of U.N. demands with a decade of defiance. All the world now faces a test, and the United

Nations a difficult and defining moment. Are Security Council resolutions to be honored and enforced, or cast aside without consequence? Will the United Nations serve the purpose of its founding, or will it be irrelevant?

The United States helped found the United Nations. We want the United Nations to be effective, and respectful, and successful. We want the resolutions of the world's most important multilateral body to be enforced. And right now, those resolutions are being unilaterally subverted by the Iraqi regime. Our partnership of nations can meet the test before us, by making clear what we now expect of the Iraqi regime.

If the Iraqi regime wishes peace, it will immediately and unconditionally forswear, disclose, and remove or destroy all weapons of mass destruction, long-range missiles, and all related material.

If the Iraqi regime wishes peace, it will immediately end all support for terrorism and act to suppress it, as all states are required to do by U.N. Security Council resolutions.

If the Iraqi regime wishes peace, it will cease persecution of its civilian population, including Shi'a, Sunnis, Kurds, Turkomans, and others, again as required by Security Council resolutions.

If the Iraqi regime wishes peace, it will release or account for all Gulf War personnel whose fate is still unknown. It will return the remains of any who are deceased, return stolen property, accept liability for losses resulting from the invasion of Kuwait, and fully cooperate with international efforts to resolve these issues, as required by Security Council resolutions.

If the Iraqi regime wishes peace, it will immediately end all illicit trade outside the oil-for-food program. It will accept U.N. administration of funds from that program, to ensure that the money is used fairly and promptly for the benefit of the Iraqi people.

If all these steps are taken, it will signal a new openness and accountability in Iraq. And it could open the prospect of the United Nations helping to build a government that represents all Iraqis—a government based on respect for human rights, economic liberty, and internationally supervised elections.

The United States has no quarrel with the Iraqi people; they've suffered too long in silent captivity. Liberty for the Iraqi people is a great moral cause, and a great strategic goal. The people of Iraq deserve it; the security of all nations requires it. Free societies do not intimidate through cruelty and conquest, and open societies do not threaten the world with mass murder. The United States supports political and economic liberty in a unified Iraq.

We can harbor no illusions—and that's important today to remember. Saddam Hussein attacked Iran in 1980 and Kuwait in 1990. He's fired ballistic missiles at Iran and Saudi Arabia, Bahrain, and Israel. His regime once ordered the killing of every person between the ages of 15 and 70 in certain Kurdish villages in northern Iraq. He has gassed many Iranians, and 40 Iraqi villages.

My nation will work with the U.N. Security Council to meet our common challenge. If Iraq's regime defies us again, the world must move deliberately, decisively to hold Iraq to account. We will work with the U.N. Security Council for the necessary resolutions. But the purposes of the United States should not be doubted. The Security Council resolutions will be enforced—the just demands of peace and security will be met—or action will be unavoidable. And a regime that has lost its legitimacy will also lose its power.

Events can turn in one of two ways: If we fail to act in the face of danger, the people of Iraq will continue to live in brutal submission. The regime will have new power to bully and dominate and conquer its neighbors, condemning the Middle East to more years of bloodshed and fear. The regime will remain unstable—the region will remain unstable, with little hope of freedom, and iso-lated from the progress of our times. With every step the Iraqi regime takes toward gaining and deploying the most terrible weapons, our own options to confront that regime will narrow. And if an emboldened regime were to supply these weapons to terrorist allies, then the attacks of September the 11th would be a prelude to far greater horrors.

If we meet our responsibilities, if we overcome this danger, we can arrive at a very different future. The people of Iraq can shake off their captivity. They can one day join a democratic Afghanistan and a democratic Palestine, inspiring reforms throughout the Muslim world. These nations can show by their example that honest government, and respect for women, and the great Islamic tradition of learning can triumph in the Middle East and beyond. And we will show that the promise of the United Nations can be fulfilled in our time.

Neither of these outcomes is certain. Both have been set before us. We must choose between a world of fear and a world of progress. We cannot stand by and do nothing while dangers gather. We must stand up for our security, and for the permanent rights and the hopes of mankind. By heritage and by choice, the United States of America will make that stand. And, delegates to the United Nations, you have the power to make that stand, as well.

Thank you very much.

Appendix 4

President George W. Bush's State of the Union Address, January 28, 2003

Domestic policy and the war on terrorism figured to be major themes of President Bush's 2003 State of the Union address. The president did not disappoint. Perhaps mindful that his father lost his reelection bid in part because of the widespread perception that he spent too much time on foreign policy, the younger Bush devoted the first third of the speech to laying out his four main domestic priorities: tax cuts, health care reform, energy independence, and compassion for those in need. With Republicans having taken control of both houses of Congress in the 2002 midterm elections, the president had a better chance to translate his policy preferences into law.

Before tackling the topic of terrorism, President Bush surprised many people by proposing a major new initiative to tackle the scourge of AIDS in Africa and the Caribbean. On the topic of terrorism, he recounted his administration's successes in disrupting Al Qaeda's operations and reaffirmed his commitment to winning the war on terror.

It was not until the final third of the speech that President Bush addressed the issue on most people's minds—his policy toward Iraq. He repeated the argument he had made time and again since his "axis of evil" speech a year earlier—that the "the gravest danger facing America" comes from "outlaw regimes that seek and possess nuclear, chemical, and biological weapons." He recounted how Saddam Hussein had agreed to give up weapons of mass destruction in the wake of the Gulf War in 1991, only to systematically violate that agreement. He noted that the UN Security Council had voted in November 2002 to give Iraq a final chance to disarm, and Hussein had still not complied. He rejected the claim that the Iraqi threat could be contained and that the United States should not act until the threat was imminent. He warned the United Nations that if it did not vote to enforce its resolutions on Iraq, he was prepared to lead a coalition of states that would. But he gave no hint as to when war might begin.

Reactions to the 2003 State of the Union address were predictable. The president's supporters applauded his calls for tax cuts as the right antidote for a weak economy. They also hailed his vision and courage for being willing to stand up to Saddam Hussein, with or without the blessing of the United Nations.

The president's critics argued that further tax cuts would be reckless fiscal policy that would endanger the long-term health of the economy. Critics also complained that America's progress in the war on terrorism had been less impressive than the president claimed and that the United States remained dangerously vulnerable to new attacks. And critics argued that even if the president had made the case that war with Iraq could be justified, he hadn't even attempted to make the case that it would be wise.

Excerpts from President Bush's 2003 State of the Union address follow.

Mr. Speaker, Vice President Cheney, members of Congress, distinguished citizens and fellow citizens: Every year, by law and by custom, we meet here to consider the state of the union. This year, we gather in this chamber deeply aware of decisive days that lie ahead.

You and I serve our country in a time of great consequence. During this session of Congress, we have the duty to reform domestic programs vital to our country; we have the opportunity to save millions of lives abroad from a terrible disease. We will work for a prosperity that is broadly shared, and we will answer every danger and every enemy that threatens the American people.

In all these days of promise and days of reckoning, we can be confident. In a whirlwind of change and hope and peril, our faith is sure, our resolve is firm, and our union is strong.

This country has many challenges. We will not deny, we will not ignore, we will not pass along our problems to other Congresses, to other presidents, and other generations. We will confront them with focus and clarity and courage.

...

Our first goal is clear: We must have an economy that grows fast enough to employ every man and woman who seeks a job. After recession, terrorist attacks, corporate scandals, and stock market declines, our economy is recovering—yet it's not growing fast enough, or strongly enough. With unemployment rising, our nation needs more small businesses to open, more companies to invest and expand, more employers to put up the sign that says, "Help Wanted."

Jobs are created when the economy grows; the economy grows when Americans have more money to spend and invest; and the best and fairest way to make sure Americans have that money is not to tax it away in the first place.

I am proposing that all the income tax reductions set for 2004 and 2006 be made permanent and effective this year. And under my plan, as soon as I sign the bill, this extra money will start showing up in workers' paychecks. Instead of gradually reducing the marriage penalty, we should do it now. Instead of slowly raising the child credit to $1,000, we should send the checks to American families now.

The tax relief is for everyone who pays income taxes—and it will help our economy immediately: 92 million Americans will keep, this year, an average of almost $1,000 more of their own money. A family of four with an income of $40,000 would see their federal income taxes fall from $1,178 to $45 per year. Our plan will improve the bottom line for more than 23 million small businesses.

You, the Congress, have already passed all these reductions, and promised them for future years. If this tax relief is good for Americans three, or five, or seven years from now, it is even better for Americans today.

We should also strengthen the economy by treating investors equally in our tax laws. It's fair to tax a company's profits. It is not fair to again tax the shareholder on the same profits. To boost investor confidence, and to help the nearly 10 million seniors who receive dividend income, I ask you to end the unfair double taxation of dividends.

...

Our second goal is high quality, affordable health care for all Americans. The American system of medicine is a model of skill and innovation, with a pace of discovery that is adding good years to our lives. Yet for many people, medical care costs too much—and many have no coverage at all. These problems will not be solved with a nationalized health care system that dictates coverage and rations care.

Instead, we must work toward a system in which all Americans have a good insurance policy, choose their own doctors, and seniors and low-income Americans receive the help they need. Instead of bureaucrats and trial lawyers and HMOs, we must put doctors and nurses and patients back in charge of American medicine.

...

Our third goal is to promote energy independence for our country, while dramatically improving the environment. I have sent you a comprehensive energy plan to promote energy efficiency and conservation, to develop cleaner technology, and to produce more energy at home. I have sent you Clear Skies legislation that mandates a 70-percent cut in air pollution from power plants over the next 15 years. I have sent you a Healthy Forests Initiative, to help prevent the catastrophic fires that devastate communities, kill wildlife, and burn away millions of acres of treasured forest.

I urge you to pass these measures, for the good of both our environment and our economy. Even more, I ask you to take a crucial step and protect our environment in ways that generations before us could not have imagined.

In this century, the greatest environmental progress will come about not through endless lawsuits or command-and-control regulations, but through technology and innovation. Tonight I'm proposing $1.2 billion in research funding so that America can lead the world in developing clean, hydrogen-powered automobiles.

...

Our fourth goal is to apply the compassion of America to the deepest problems of America. For so many in our country—the homeless and the fatherless, the addicted—the need is great. Yet there's power, wonder-working power, in the goodness and idealism and faith of the American people.

Americans are doing the work of compassion every day—visiting prisoners, providing shelter for battered women, bringing companionship to lonely seniors. These good works deserve our praise; they deserve our personal support; and when appropriate, they deserve the assistance of the federal government.

I urge you to pass both my faith-based initiative and the Citizen Service Act, to encourage acts of compassion that can transform America, one heart and one soul at a time.

...

We have confronted, and will continue to confront, HIV/AIDS in our own country. And to meet a severe and urgent crisis abroad, tonight I propose the Emergency Plan for AIDS Relief—a work of mercy beyond all current international efforts to help the people of Africa. This comprehensive plan will prevent 7 million new AIDS infections, treat at least 2 million people with life-extending drugs, and provide humane care for millions of people suffering from AIDS, and for children orphaned by AIDS.

I ask the Congress to commit $15 billion over the next five years, including nearly $10 billion in new money, to turn the tide against AIDS in the most afflicted nations of Africa and the Caribbean.

This nation can lead the world in sparing innocent people from a plague of nature. And this nation is leading the world in confronting and defeating the man-made evil of international terrorism.

There are days when our fellow citizens do not hear news about the war on terror. There's never a day when I do not learn of another threat, or receive reports of operations in progress, or give an order in this global war against a scattered network of killers. The war goes on, and we are winning.

To date, we've arrested or otherwise dealt with many key commanders of Al Qaeda. They include a man who directed logistics and funding for the September the 11th attacks; the chief of Al Qaeda operations in the Persian Gulf, who planned the bombings of our embassies in East Africa and the *USS Cole;* an Al Qaeda operations chief from Southeast Asia; a former director of Al Qaeda's training camps in Afghanistan; a key Al Qaeda operative in Europe; a major Al Qaeda leader in Yemen. All told,

more than 3,000 suspected terrorists have been arrested in many countries. Many others have met a different fate. Let's put it this way—they are no longer a problem to the United States and our friends and allies.

...

Today, the gravest danger in the war on terror, the gravest danger facing America and the world, is outlaw regimes that seek and possess nuclear, chemical, and biological weapons. These regimes could use such weapons for blackmail, terror, and mass murder. They could also give or sell those weapons to terrorist allies, who would use them without the least hesitation.

This threat is new; America's duty is familiar. Throughout the 20th century, small groups of men seized control of great nations, built armies and arsenals, and set out to dominate the weak and intimidate the world. In each case, their ambitions of cruelty and murder had no limit. In each case, the ambitions of Hitlerism, militarism, and communism were defeated by the will of free peoples, by the strength of great alliances, and by the might of the United States of America.

Now, in this century, the ideology of power and domination has appeared again, and seeks to gain the ultimate weapons of terror. Once again, this nation and all our friends are all that stand between a world at peace, and a world of chaos and constant alarm. Once again, we are called to defend the safety of our people, and the hopes of all mankind. And we accept this responsibility.

America is making a broad and determined effort to confront these dangers. We have called on the United Nations to fulfill its charter and stand by its demand

that Iraq disarm. We're strongly supporting the International Atomic Energy Agency in its mission to track and control nuclear materials around the world. We're working with other governments to secure nuclear materials in the former Soviet Union, and to strengthen global treaties banning the production and shipment of missile technologies and weapons of mass destruction.

In all these efforts, however, America's purpose is more than to follow a process—it is to achieve a result: the end of terrible threats to the civilized world. All free nations have a stake in preventing sudden and catastrophic attacks. And we're asking them to join us, and many are doing so. Yet the course of this nation does not depend on the decisions of others. Whatever action is required, whenever action is necessary, I will defend the freedom and security of the American people.

...

Twelve years ago, Saddam Hussein faced the prospect of being the last casualty in a war he had started and lost. To spare himself, he agreed to disarm of all weapons of mass destruction. For the next 12 years, he systematically violated that agreement. He pursued chemical, biological, and nuclear weapons, even while inspectors were in his country. Nothing to date has restrained him from his pursuit of these weapons—not economic sanctions, not isolation from the civilized world, not even cruise missile strikes on his military facilities.

Almost three months ago, the United Nations Security Council gave Saddam Hussein his final chance to disarm. He has shown instead utter contempt for the

United Nations, and for the opinion of the world. The 108 U.N. inspectors were sent to conduct—were not sent to conduct a scavenger hunt for hidden materials across a country the size of California. The job of the inspectors is to verify that Iraq's regime is disarming. It is up to Iraq to show exactly where it is hiding its banned weapons, lay those weapons out for the world to see, and destroy them as directed. Nothing like this has happened.

...

With nuclear arms or a full arsenal of chemical and biological weapons, Saddam Hussein could resume his ambitions of conquest in the Middle East and create deadly havoc in that region. And this Congress and the American people must recognize another threat. Evidence from intelligence sources, secret communications, and statements by people now in custody reveal that Saddam Hussein aids and protects terrorists, including members of Al Qaeda. Secretly, and without fingerprints, he could provide one of his hidden weapons to terrorists, or help them develop their own.

Before September the 11th, many in the world believed that Saddam Hussein could be contained. But chemical agents, lethal viruses, and shadowy terrorist networks are not easily contained. Imagine those 19 hijackers with other weapons and other plans—this time armed by Saddam Hussein. It would take one vial, one canister, one crate slipped into this country to bring a day of horror like none we have ever known. We will do everything in our power to make sure that that day never comes.

Some have said we must not act until the threat is imminent. Since when have terrorists and tyrants announced their intentions, politely putting us on notice before they strike? If this threat is permitted to fully and suddenly emerge, all actions, all words, and all recriminations would come too late. Trusting in the sanity and restraint of Saddam Hussein is not a strategy, and it is not an option.

...

Many challenges, abroad and at home, have arrived in a single season. In two years, America has gone from a sense of invulnerability to an awareness of peril; from bitter division in small matters to calm unity in great causes. And we go forward with confidence, because this call of history has come to the right country.

Americans are a resolute people who have risen to every test of our time. Adversity has revealed the character of our country, to the world and to ourselves. America is a strong nation, and honorable in the use of our strength. We exercise power without conquest, and we sacrifice for the liberty of strangers.

Americans are a free people, who know that freedom is the right of every person and the future of every nation. The liberty we prize is not America's gift to the world; it is God's gift to humanity.

We Americans have faith in ourselves, but not in ourselves alone. We do not know—we do not claim to know all the ways of Providence, yet we can trust in them, placing our confidence in the loving God behind all of life, and all of history.

May He guide us now. And may God continue to bless the United States of America.

Appendix 5

Congress Authorizes the Use of Military Force after September 11

Whether and under what circumstances the president can order U.S. troops into combat on his own authority has been disputed since the mid-1960s, when debate erupted over whether the Vietnam War was properly authorized under the Constitution. On the issue of the war power, unlike many other areas of constitutional law, the Supreme Court has never spoken definitively. It is widely agreed that presidents have the authority to order U.S. troops to defend the United States if it is attacked. Beyond that point, however, the consensus breaks down.

Those who believe the president has wide latitude to initiate the use of force argue that the Constitution names the president the commander in chief and gives him the executive power. They say that past practice has further legitimated this presidential power. Successive administrations have sent troops into combat without requesting congressional authorization, most notably when President Harry Truman decided on his own to commit the United States to defending South Korea from attack in 1950. Those who believe Congress controls the war power note that the Constitution explicitly gives Congress the power to declare war; that the framers of the Constitution explicitly rejected (indeed, ridiculed) a motion to give the president authority to declare war; that early practice and court decisions support a restrictive view of presidential power; and that it was not until World War II that presidents began *to speak of the commander-in-chief clause as conveying authority to wage war rather than giving the president a title as the civilian commander of the military.*

These disputes did not surface in the immediate aftermath of September 11. Whatever powers President Bush had to act on his own authority, Congress passed a resolution on September 14, 2001, adding to them by authorizing him "to use all necessary and appropriate force against those" responsible for the attacks. Because both political branches endorsed the war on Al Qaeda, anyone seeking to challenge the legality of the war in court—say, because they did not want to be shipped off to fight or have their tax dollars pay for the war—would find it very difficult to prove their case.

The full text of Congress's September 14, 2001, resolution follows. The resolution passed by a vote of 98–0 in the Senate and 420–1 in the House. The lone dissenting vote was cast by Barbara Lee, a Democrat who represented California's Ninth Congressional District, which encompassed the cities of Oakland, Alameda, and Berkeley.

S.J.Res.23
One Hundred Seventh Congress
of the
United States of America

AT THE FIRST SESSION

Begun and held at the City of Washington on Wednesday, the third day of January, two thousand and one

Joint Resolution

To authorize the use of United States Armed Forces against those responsible for the recent attacks launched against the United States.

Whereas, on September 11, 2001, acts of treacherous violence were committed against the United States and its citizens; and

Whereas, such acts render it both necessary and appropriate that the United States exercise its rights to self-defense and to protect United States citizens both at home and abroad; and

Whereas, in light of the threat to the national security and foreign policy of the United States posed by these grave acts of violence; and

Whereas, such acts continue to pose an unusual and extraordinary threat to the national security and foreign policy of the United States; and

Whereas, the President has authority under the Constitution to take action to deter and prevent acts of international terrorism against the United States: Now, therefore, be it

Resolved by the Senate and House of Representatives of the United States of America in Congress assembled,

SECTION 1. SHORT TITLE.

This joint resolution may be cited as the "Authorization for Use of Military Force."

SECTION 2. AUTHORIZATION FOR USE OF UNITED STATES ARMED FORCES.

(a) IN GENERAL—That the President is authorized to use all necessary and appropriate force against those nations, organizations, or persons he determines planned, authorized, committed, or aided the terrorist attacks that occurred on September 11, 2001, or harbored such organizations or persons, in order to prevent any future acts of international terrorism against the United States by such nations, organizations or persons.

(b) War Powers Resolution Requirements—

(1) SPECIFIC STATUTORY AUTHORIZATION—Consistent with section 8(a)(1) of the War Powers Resolution, the Congress declares that this section is intended to constitute specific statutory authorization within the meaning of section 5(b) of the War Powers Resolution.

(2) APPLICABILITY OF OTHER REQUIREMENTS—Nothing in this resolution supercedes any requirement of the War Powers Resolution.

Speaker of the House of Representatives.

Appendix 6

Congress Authorizes the Use of Military Force against Iraq

The Bush administration's bellicose talk in the spring and summer of 2002 about overthrowing Saddam Hussein raised the question of whether President George W. Bush had the authority to launch a war against Iraq without specific congressional approval. At first, his advisers insisted he did. They pointed to his powers as commander in chief. They also argued that he derived authority from the 1991 law Congress passed authorizing his father to liberate Kuwait. They noted that that law specifically authorized the president to enforce UN Security Council resolutions on Iraq. Because Saddam Hussein had not complied with the Security Council's demands, the authority Congress delegated to the White House in 1991 was still in effect.

The White House decided in September 2002, however, to seek specific congressional authorization. The administration did not say its legal analysis was wrong. Instead, it concluded that seeking congressional authorization was both good policy and good politics. Getting congressional approval would strengthen the administration's hand as it sought a new UN Security Council resolution demanding Iraq's disarmament. And with midterm elections looming in November and Democrats fearful of being labeled unpatriotic, the White House was certain it would get its way.

The draft legislation the White House sent to Capitol Hill was remarkably broad. It would have authorized the president "to use all

means that he determines to be appropriate" not only to "defend the national security interests of the United States against the threat posed by Iraq" and to bring Iraq into compliance with United Nations Security Council resolutions, but also to "restore international peace and security in the region." Many lawmakers in both political parties argued that this latter wording was so broad that it empowered the president to wage war against any country between Morocco and Afghanistan for any reason he chose. The phrase was dropped from the final version of the authorization resolution.

This and other changes did not satisfy the president's critics. They argued that authorizing war was premature. They noted that the president was asking Congress to do something virtually without precedent in American history—authorize a war before the White House had decided to wage it. The critics warned that Congress's war power is a use-it-and-lose-it authority—once it is delegated, it is difficult to reclaim. To authorize the president to use force before knowing the precise circumstances under which he might act would give the White House a blank check to begin a war the nation might not support.

President Bush countered his critics by arguing that it was essential Congress back his policy of confronting Iraq. Only by speaking clearly with one voice could the United States force Iraq to come clean about its weapons of mass de-

struction. "If you want to keep the peace," the president told the nation, "you've got to have the authorization to use force."

President Bush eventually prevailed. On October 10, 2002, the House of Representatives voted 296 to 133 to approve the Iraqi war resolution. The following day the Senate gave its approval on a 77 to 23 vote. The full text of the resolution follows.

H.J.Res.114
One Hundred Seventh
Congress of the
United States of America

AT THE SECOND SESSION

Begun and held at the City of Washington on Wednesday, the third day of January, two thousand and two

Joint Resolution

To authorize the use of United States Armed Forces against Iraq.

Whereas in 1990 in response to Iraq's war of aggression against and illegal occupation of Kuwait, the United States forged a coalition of nations to liberate Kuwait and its people in order to defend the national security of the United States and enforce United Nations Security Council resolutions relating to Iraq;

Whereas after the liberation of Kuwait in 1991, Iraq entered into a United Nations sponsored cease-fire agreement pursuant to which Iraq unequivocally agreed, among other things, to eliminate its nuclear, biological, and chemical weapons programs and the means to deliver and develop them, and to end its support for international terrorism;

Whereas the efforts of international weapons inspectors, United States intelligence agencies, and Iraqi defectors led to the discovery that Iraq had large stockpiles of chemical weapons and a large-scale biological weapons program, and that Iraq had an advanced nuclear weapons development program that was much closer to producing a nuclear weapon than intelligence reporting had previously indicated;

Whereas Iraq, in direct and flagrant violation of the cease-fire, attempted to thwart the efforts of weapons inspectors to identify and destroy Iraq's weapons of mass destruction stockpiles and development capabilities, which finally resulted in the withdrawal of inspectors from Iraq on October 31, 1998;

Whereas in Public Law 105-235 (August 14, 1998), Congress concluded that Iraq's continuing weapons of mass destruction programs threatened vital United States interests and international peace and security, declared Iraq to be in 'material and unacceptable breach of its international obligations' and urged the President 'to take appropriate action, in accordance with the Constitution and relevant laws of the United States, to bring Iraq into compliance with its international obligations';

Whereas Iraq both poses a continuing threat to the national security of the United States and international peace and security in the Persian Gulf region and remains in material and unaccept-

able breach of its international obligations by, among other things, continuing to possess and develop a significant chemical and biological weapons capability, actively seeking a nuclear weapons capability, and supporting and harboring terrorist organizations;

Whereas Iraq persists in violating resolution of the United Nations Security Council by continuing to engage in brutal repression of its civilian population thereby threatening international peace and security in the region, by refusing to release, repatriate, or account for non-Iraqi citizens wrongfully detained by Iraq, including an American serviceman, and by failing to return property wrongfully seized by Iraq from Kuwait;

Whereas the current Iraqi regime has demonstrated its capability and willingness to use weapons of mass destruction against other nations and its own people;

Whereas the current Iraqi regime has demonstrated its continuing hostility toward, and willingness to attack, the United States, including by attempting in 1993 to assassinate former President Bush and by firing on many thousands of occasions on United States and Coalition Armed Forces engaged in enforcing the resolutions of the United Nations Security Council;

Whereas members of al Qaida, an organization bearing responsibility for attacks on the United States, its citizens, and interests, including the attacks that occurred on September 11, 2001, are known to be in Iraq;

Whereas Iraq continues to aid and harbor other international terrorist organizations, including organizations that threaten the

lives and safety of United States citizens;

Whereas the attacks on the United States of September 11, 2001, underscored the gravity of the threat posed by the acquisition of weapons of mass destruction by international terrorist organizations;

Whereas Iraq's demonstrated capability and willingness to use weapons of mass destruction, the risk that the current Iraqi regime will either employ those weapons to launch a surprise attack against the United States or its Armed Forces or provide them to international terrorists who would do so, and the extreme magnitude of harm that would result to the United States and its citizens from such an attack, combine to justify action by the United States to defend itself;

Whereas United Nations Security Council Resolution 678 (1990) authorizes the use of all necessary means to enforce United Nations Security Council Resolution 660 (1990) and subsequent relevant resolutions and to compel Iraq to cease certain activities that threaten international peace and security, including the development of weapons of mass destruction and refusal or obstruction of United Nations weapons inspections in violation of United Nations Security Council Resolution 687 (1991), repression of its civilian population in violation of United Nations Security Council Resolution 688 (1991), and threatening its neighbors or United Nations operations in Iraq in violation of United Nations Security Council Resolution 949 (1994);

Whereas in the Authorization for Use of Military Force Against Iraq Resolution (Public Law 102-1), Congress has authorized the

President 'to use United States Armed Forces pursuant to United Nations Security Council Resolution 678 (1990) in order to achieve implementation of Security Council Resolution 660, 661, 662, 664, 665, 666, 667, 669, 670, 674, and 677';

Whereas in December 1991, Congress expressed its sense that it 'supports the use of all necessary means to achieve the goals of United Nations Security Council Resolution 687 as being consistent with the Authorization of Use of Military Force Against Iraq Resolution (Public Law 102-1),' that Iraq's repression of its civilian population violates United Nations Security Council Resolution 688 and 'constitutes a continuing threat to the peace, security, and stability of the Persian Gulf region,' and that Congress, 'supports the use of all necessary means to achieve the goals of United Nations Security Council Resolution 688';

Whereas the Iraq Liberation Act of 1998 (Public Law 105-338) expressed the sense of Congress that it should be the policy of the United States to support efforts to remove from power the current Iraqi regime and promote the emergence of a democratic government to replace that regime;

Whereas on September 12, 2002, President Bush committed the United States to 'work with the United Nations Security Council to meet our common challenge' posed by Iraq and to 'work for the necessary resolutions,' while also making clear that 'the Security Council resolutions will be enforced, and the just demands of peace and security will be met, or action will be unavoidable';

Whereas the United States is determined to prosecute the war on terrorism and Iraq's ongoing support for international terrorist groups combined with its development of weapons of mass destruction in direct violation of its obligations under the 1991 ceasefire and other United Nations Security Council resolutions make clear that it is in the national security interests of the United States and in furtherance of the war on terrorism that all relevant United Nations Security Council resolutions be enforced, including through the use of force if necessary;

Whereas Congress has taken steps to pursue vigorously the war on terrorism through the provision of authorities and funding requested by the President to take the necessary actions against international terrorists and terrorist organizations, including those nations, organizations, or persons who planned, authorized, committed, or aided the terrorist attacks that occurred on September 11, 2001, or harbored such persons or organizations;

Whereas the President and Congress are determined to continue to take all appropriate actions against international terrorists and terrorist organizations, including those nations, organizations, or persons who planned, authorized, committed, or aided the terrorist attacks that occurred on September 11, 2001, or harbored such persons or organizations;

Whereas the President has authority under the Constitution to take action in order to deter and prevent acts of international terrorism against the United States, as Congress recognized in the joint resolution on Authorization for Use of Military Force (Public Law 107-40); and

Whereas it is in the national security interests of the United States to restore international peace and security to the Persian Gulf region: Now, therefore, be it

Resolved by the Senate and House of Representatives of the United States of America in Congress assembled,

SECTION 1. SHORT TITLE.

This joint resolution may be cited as the 'Authorization for Use of Military Force Against Iraq Resolution of 2002'.

SECTION 2. SUPPORT FOR UNITED STATES DIPLOMATIC EFFORTS.

The Congress of the United States supports the efforts by the President to—

(1) strictly enforce through the United Nations Security Council all relevant Security Council resolutions regarding Iraq and encourages him in those efforts; and

(2) obtain prompt and decisive action by the Security Council to ensure that Iraq abandons its strategy of delay, evasion and noncompliance and promptly and strictly complies with all relevant Security Council resolutions regarding Iraq.

SECTION 3. AUTHORIZATION FOR USE OF UNITED STATES ARMED FORCES.

(a) AUTHORIZATION—The President is authorized to use the Armed Forces of the United States as he determines to be necessary and appropriate in order to—

(1) defend the national security of the United States against the continuing threat posed by Iraq; and
(2) enforce all relevant United

Nations Security Council resolutions regarding Iraq.

(b) PRESIDENTIAL DETERMINATION—In connection with the exercise of the authority granted in subsection (a) to use force the President shall, prior to such exercise or as soon thereafter as may be feasible, but no later than 48 hours after exercising such authority, make available to the Speaker of the House of Representatives and the President pro tempore of the Senate his determination that—

(1) reliance by the United States on further diplomatic or other peaceful means alone either (A) will not adequately protect the national security of the United States against the continuing threat posed by Iraq or (B) is not likely to lead to enforcement of all relevant United Nations Security Council resolutions regarding Iraq; and

(2) acting pursuant to this joint resolution is consistent with the United States and other countries continuing to take the necessary actions against international terrorist and terrorist organizations, including those nations, organizations, or persons who planned, authorized, committed or aided the terrorist attacks that occurred on September 11, 2001.

(c) WAR POWERS RESOLUTION REQUIREMENTS—

(1) SPECIFIC STATUTORY AUTHORIZATION—Consistent with section 8(a)(1) of the War Powers Resolution, the Congress declares that this section is intended to constitute specific statutory authorization within the meaning of section 5(b) of the War Powers Resolution.

(2) APPLICABILITY OF OTHER REQUIREMENTS—Nothing in this joint resolution supersedes any requirement of the War Powers Resolution.

SECTION 4. REPORTS TO CONGRESS.

(a) REPORTS—The President shall, at least once every 60 days, submit to the Congress a report on matters relevant to this joint resolution, including actions taken pursuant to the exercise of authority granted in section 3 and the status of planning for efforts that are expected to be required after such actions are completed, including those actions described in section 7 of the Iraq Liberation Act of 1998 (Public Law 105-338).

(b) SINGLE CONSOLIDATED REPORT—To the extent that the submission of any report described in subsection (a) coincides with the submission of any other report on matters relevant to this joint resolution otherwise required to be submitted to Congress pursuant to the reporting requirements of the War Powers Resolution (Public Law 93-148), all such reports may be submitted as a single consolidated report to the Congress.

(c) RULE OF CONSTRUCTION—To the extent that the information required by section 3 of the Authorization for Use of Military Force Against Iraq Resolution (Public Law 102-1) is included in the report required by this section, such report shall be considered as meeting the requirements of section 3 of such resolution.

Appendix 7

Profile of the 108th Congress

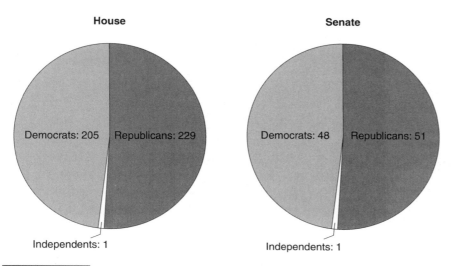

House

Democrats: 205   Republicans: 229

Independents: 1

Senate

Democrats: 48   Republicans: 51

Independents: 1

Figure A7-1 Partisan balance. The 108th Congress is narrowly divided between Democrats and Republicans, with the Republicans controlling both the House and Senate. Both independents come from Vermont.

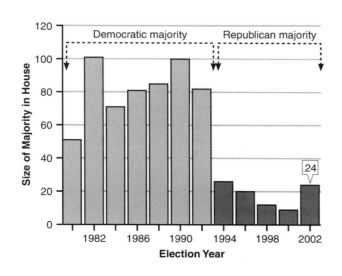

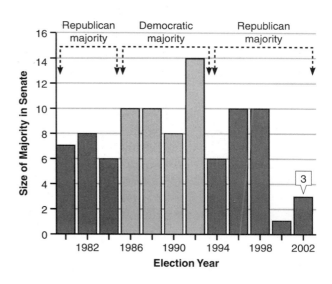

Figure A7-2 The size of the majority. The size of the majority's lead is smaller today than it has been in the past, especially in the House. **Note:** Republicans had a one-vote margin when the 107th Congress began. A senator later switched parties, giving control of the Senate to the Democrats.

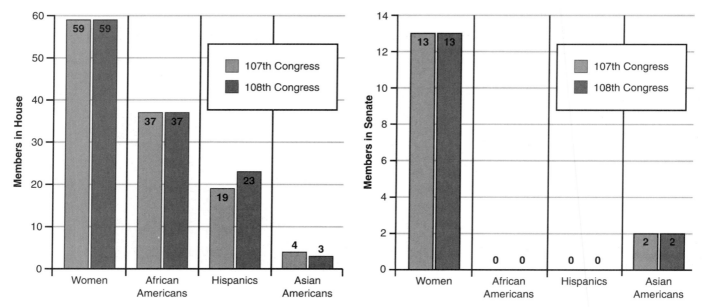

Figure A7-3 Women and minorities in Congress. Women, African Americans, Hispanics, and Asian Americans remain distinct minorities in Congress, though the House is significantly more diverse than the Senate.

Table A7-1 The 2004 Senate Races

Thirty-four Senate seats are up for election in 2004. Democrats have 19 incumbents whose terms are expiring, five of whom have decided against running for reelection. The Republicans have 15 incumbents whose terms are expiring, three of whom have decided against running for reelection. With more Democratic seats at risk and more Democratic incumbents deciding to retire, Republicans are in a good position to increase the size of their majority in the Senate.

Republican Seats Up for Election		Democratic Seats Up for Election	
Alabama • Richard Shelby	*Kentucky* • Jim Bunning	*Arkansas* • Blanche Lincoln	*New York* • Charles Schumer
Alaska • Lisa Murkowski	*Missouri* • Christopher Bond	*California* • Barbara Boxer	*North Carolina* • John Edwards (retiring)
Arizona • John McCain	*New Hampshire* • Judd Gregg	*Connecticut* • Christopher Dodd	*North Dakota* • Byron Dorgan
Colorado • Ben Nighthorse Campbell (retiring)	*Ohio* • George Voinovich	*Florida* • Bob Graham (retiring)	*Oregon* • Ron Wyden
Idaho • Mike Crapo	*Oklahoma* • Don Nickles (retiring)	*Georgia* • Zell Miller (retiring)	*South Carolina* • Ernest Hollings (retiring)
Illinois • Peter Fitzgerald (retiring)	*Pennsylvania* • Arlen Specter	*Hawaii* • Daniel Inouye	*South Dakota* • Tom Daschle
Iowa • Chuck Grassley	*Utah* • Robert Bennett	*Indiana* • Evan Bayh	*Vermont* • Patrick Leahy
Kansas • Sam Brownback		*Louisiana* • John Breaux (retiring)	*Washington* • Patty Murray
		Maryland • Barbara Mikulski	*Wisconsin* • Russ Feingold
		Nevada • Harry Reid	

Appendix 8

Afghanistan and Iraq

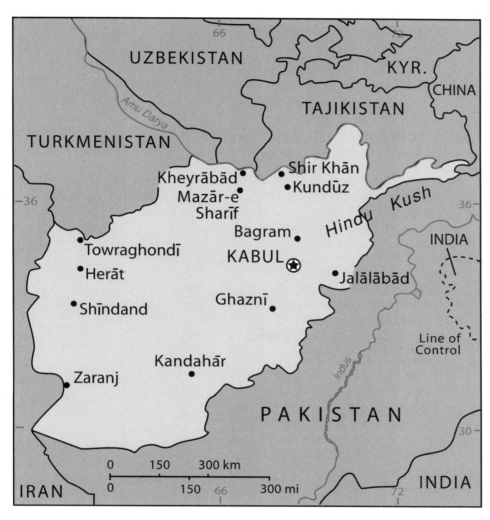

Afghanistan

Capital: Kabul

Population: 26,813,057 (July 2001 est.)

Ethnic groups: Pashtun 38%, Tajik 25%, Hazara 19%, minor ethnic groups (Aimaks, Turkmen, Baloch, and others) 12%, Uzbek 6%

Religions: Sunni Muslim 84%, Shi'a Muslim 15%, other 1%

Languages: Pashtu 35%, Afghan Persian (Dari) 50%, Turkic languages (primarily Uzbek and Turkmen) 11%, 30 minor languages (primarily Balochi and Pashai) 4%, much bilingualism

Area: *total:* 647,500 sq km
land: 647,500 sq km
water: 0 sq km

Land boundaries: *total:* 5,529 km

Border countries:
China 76 km, Iran 936 km, Pakistan 2,430 km, Tajikistan 1,206 km, Turkmenistan 744 km, Uzbekistan 137 km

Source: CIA World Fact Book 2001. Available at http://www.cia.gov/cia/publications/factbook/index.html

Iraq

Capital: Baghdad

Population: 24,001,816
(July 2002 est.)

Ethnic groups: Arab 75%–80%;
Kurdish 15%–20%; Turkoman,
Assyrian, or other 5%

Religions: Muslim 97%
(Shi'a 60%–65%, Sunni 32%–37%),
Christian or other 3%

Languages: Arabic, Kurdish
(official in Kurdish regions),
Assyrian, Armenian

Area: *total:* 437,072 sq km
          land: 432,162 sq km
          water: 4,910 sq km

Land boundaries: *total:* 3,650 km

Border countries: Iran 1,458 km,
Jordan 181 km, Kuwait 240 km,
Saudi Arabia 814 km, Syria
605 km, Turkey 352 km

Source: CIA World Fact Book 2001. Available at
http://www.cia.gov/cia/publications/
factbook/index.html

Index

Note: Page numbers in *italics* identify information that appears in illustrations. An italic *t* next to a page number (e.g., 177*t*) indicates information that appears in a table.

Defense Advanced Research
    Projects Agency, 38
Defense contractors, 74
Defense Department, relations
    with news media, 58–61
Defense spending
    as cause of budget surplus
        disappearance, 117, 118, 119
    war on terrorism impact, 146
Deficits in federal budget, 115–19
Democrats
    108th Congress, *163*
    2002 election results, 15–20
    2004 election strategy, 70
    2004 presidential nomination,
        5–13
    bipartisanship after Sept. 11, 80
    caution in criticizing Bush, 81
    effect of Sept. 11 attacks on
        public approval, 66–67
    position on homeland security
        agency, 95–96
    public views of on selected
        issues, *70t*
    racial profiling views, 47
    senators up for reelection
        in 2004, *164t*
Department of Defense,
    Information Awareness
    Office website, 41
Department of Energy, 95
Department of Health and Human
    Services, 112–13
Department of Homeland Security
    (DHS), 93–99, 100
Detailed Defense Counsel
    (DDC), 105
Discrimination, racial/ethnic, 31–33
District Court for the Eastern
    District of Virginia, 25, 107
Dividend tax cut, 154
Dodd, Christopher, 7
Do-everything approach, to anti-
    terrorism regulations for
    private sector, 122
Domestic issues
    decline in importance following
        Sept. 11, 79–80, 86–87
    as early Bush priority, 85
    resurgence, 82–83, 154–55
Domestic spending, impact on
    budget surplus, 117–19
Domestic spying, 37
Domestic terrorism, 37
Do-nothing approach, to anti-
    terrorism regulations for
    private sector, 121–22
Double jeopardy, 103
Driver's license laws, 112
"Driving While Black," 43

E

Economic conditions
    as 2004 election issue, 70
    budget surplus disappearance,
        115–19
    effect on states' ability to fund
        anti-terrorism measures, 111
    impact on president's domestic
        agenda, 154–55
    public optimism following
        Sept. 11, 67–68
Edwards, John, 5–12

Egypt, criticisms of United
    States, 129
Electoral College, changes in
    apportionment of votes, 1–2
Electronic surveillance, 37–38
Embedded journalists, 60–61
Emergency Management
    Association Compact, 112
Emergency medical technicians, 109
Emergency Plan for AIDS Relief, 155
Emergency Preparedness
    and Response directorate
    (DHS), 98
Environmental Liberation Front, 37
Envy, as cause of
    anti-Americanism, 129
Errors in news coverage, 59–60
Espionage Act, 36
EthnicMajority.com—Racial
    Profiling website, 48
Evidence rules, in military
    commissions, *104t*, 105–106
Executive orders, 88, 91
Ex parte Quirin, 102–3

F

Faith-based initiative, 154
False positives, in racial profiling,
    45, 47
Favorability ratings of America,
    128–29
Federal Bureau of Investigation
    (FBI), 38
Federal courts, potential role in
    military commissions, 107
Federal Election Commission
    website, 14
Federal Emergency Management
    Agency (FEMA), 98
Federal government
    budget surplus disappearance,
        115–19
    Department of Homeland
        Security creation, 93–99
    effect of Sept. 11 attacks on
        public approval, 67
    potential effects of terrorist
        attacks on, 83
    private-sector antiterrorism
        regulation options, 121–25
Federal grants, for anti-terrorism
    measures, 112–13
Federalizing private property, 122
Federal Register—Orders
    website, 91
Feingold, Russ, 6
Fifth Amendment protections, 103
FindLaw's Tribunal Forum
    website, 108
Firefighters, 109
FirstGov website, 100
Florida, anti-terrorism measures,
    110, 112
"Flying While Arab," 45
Foreign policy
    as 2004 election issue, 69–70
    Bush revolution in, 135–38
    as cause of anti-Americanism,
        130–31
    Cold-War approach to, 137
    overview of Sept. 11 influence
        on, 49–54
Foreign students, 75

For Mother Earth website, 133
Fourteenth Amendment, racial
    profiling and, 44
Fourth Court of Appeals, 25–26
Fox, Vincente, 73
Freedoms, restrictions on, 35–40
Free trade, 50

G

Gallup Organization website, 71
Georgia, 18, 112
Gephardt, Richard, 5, 6, 7, 8, 10,
    11, 95
Gerrymandering, 16
Globalization, as cause
    of anti-Americanism, 130
Gore, Al, 2, 3, 6–7, 44
Gore Commission, 45
Greenpeace, 37
Gubernatorial elections, 16, 17, 18
Gulf War, 64, 69

H

Habeas corpus, 36, 107
Hamas, 144
Hard news, 57–58, 60
Hate crimes, 32, 33
Hawaii, impact of Sept. 11
    attacks on, 111
Health care goals, 154
Healthy Forests Initiative, 154
Hearsay, 105
Help America Vote Act, 3
Hezbollah, 144
Higher education, effect of Sept. 11
    attacks on, 75
Hispanics
    as victims of racial profiling, 44
    growth in population of, 2
Homeland security
    as 2002 election issue, 17
    creation of department, 93–99
    state and local government role,
        109–13
    websites, 100
Homeland Security Council (HSC),
    93–94
Homeland Security Institute
    website, 100
House of Representatives
    2002 election results, 16, 17,
        88–89
    as potential terrorism target, 83
Hussein, Saddam, 136, 138, 149–52,
    155–56

I

Idaho, anti-terrorism measures, 111
Immigration, 29–30, 73–74
Immigration and Naturalization
    Service (INS), 99
Impartiality of military
    commissions, 104
Income tax cuts, 85, 117, 118.
    See also Taxes
Incumbents, effect of crises on
    support for, 63–64
Independent civilian review, 107
Information Analysis and
    Infrastructure Protection
    directorate (DHS), 96–98

Insurance (anti-terrorism), 123–24
Interest groups, 52, 73–77
International Criminal Court,
    50, 136
Internationalism, public support
    for, 50–51
Internment, 36
Interstate Compact on Adult
    Offender Supervision, 112
Intimidation, in domestic
    terrorism, 37
Iowa
    anti-terrorism measures,
        110, 111
    caucuses, 7, 10, 11
    redistricting in, 16
Iran as rogue state, 145
Iranian revolution, 64
Iraq
    Bush's opposition to leadership,
        145, 149–52, 155–56
    map and key statistics, 166
Iraq invasion
    Bush's case to UN for, 149–52
    Congressional support, 53,
        159–62
    debates over, 90, 148
    effect on president's popularity,
        65, 69
    effects on public support
        for leadership, 69
    impact on Congress, 89–90
    overseas opposition to, 130–31
Iraq Liberation Act of 1998, 161
Isaac, Teresa, 33
Islam. *See* Muslims
Islamic Jihad, 144
Isolationism, public support for,
    49–50
Israel, renewed U.S. support, 75–76
Israeli-Palestinian conflict, 149
IWS—The Information Warfare
    Site, 41

J

Jackson, Jesse, 44
Jaish-i-Mohammed, 144
Japanese Americans, World War II
    relocations, 36
Jeffords, Jim, 15
Johnson, Tim, 17–18
Journalism.org website, 62
Jurist: Legal Intelligence website, 27
Jury trials, 104
Justice Department investigation
    of Arab residents, 38

K

Kaptur, Marcy, 6
Kawakita, Tomoya, 24
Kerry, John, 5–13
Kucinich, Dennis, 6, 7, 8
Kuwait liberation, effect on Bush
    popularity, 64
Kyoto Protocol, 136

L

Latino interest groups, 73
League of Women Voters
    website, 21
Lebanese immigrants to U.S., 30